The Curry School of Education at the University of Virginia 1905–2005

PREPARING MEN AND WOMEN FOR LEADERSHIP IN SCIENTIFIC EDUCATIONAL WORK

Eleanor Vernon Wilson

To all whose lives have been touched
by the Curry School in the past one hundred years:
students and faculty, staff and alumni,
and the pupils, teachers, and administrators
of the schools of the Commonwealth and the nation.

Table of Contents

1. Does you read the story

Preface

The University of Virginia was only one of several elements in Thomas Jefferson's comprehensive plan for public education in the state of Virginia. For the University's founder, education was the key to human fulfillment and social harmony. In an 1822 letter to Cornelius Blatchly, he wrote, "I look to the diffusion of light and education as the resource most to be relied on for ameliorating the conditions, promoting the virtue and advancing the happiness of man." Mr. Jefferson worked through much of his adult life to mobilize support for publicly funded, accessible schools for Virginians of all backgrounds and all levels of wealth.

With the establishment of the Curry School of Education in 1905, the University took a major step toward building the vigorous system of public education in Virginia that Mr. Jefferson imagined. Today, the teacher programs and scores of research projects under way in the Curry School advance Mr. Jefferson's visionary idea.

The University's commitment to public education has always been apparent, but never more so than in 1905, when the University appointed as its first president the former superintendent of the Goldsboro, North Carolina, public school system (not to mention the former president of the University of North Carolina and Tulane University). Edwin Anderson Alderman, in his dedication to the public good, has served as the model for his successors in office. We have seen him as the embodiment of the right kind of rectitude—not a stodgy obedience to the status quo, but a right-minded and visionary commitment to the promise and future of the American republic.

Mr. Alderman entered office with the aim of developing educational opportunity and access. His role in the founding of the Curry School earned him a place in the history of the University and in the history of American public education, and his vision laid the groundwork for the development of the Curry School over the past hundred years. At the University,

as we improve access to higher education, we also work to kindle interest in the teaching profession and to build excellence in teacher training by developing the curriculum, faculty, infrastructure, and educational resources in the Curry School.

Many unrealized goals remain. Mr. Alderman wanted teaching to be as thoroughly professional in practice and reputation, as socially elevated, and as well rewarded as the work done by the graduates of schools of law, business, and medicine. We still have a long way to go in that regard.

The Curry School has many loyal alumni and friends who, along with grateful graduates of public schools, have been generous in sharing their hopes for their children and their country, and in sharing their wealth to help achieve these aspirations. At this moment in time we are redefining what it means to be a public university; but I believe that Mr. Jefferson's original idea about the purposes of public education—that education is meant to better the ills and advance the pleasures and decencies of the human condition—will always prevail. For one hundred years, the Curry School has served a noble purpose, advancing education for the people of Virginia and the world beyond our state's borders.

John T. Casteen III
President of the University of Virginia

FOREWORD

I arrived at the Curry School as dean in July 1995, a full ten years before the school would celebrate its centennial anniversary, but one of my early memories was a conversation with faculty member Ellie Wilson regarding the writing of the school's history as part of our centennial observation. Although our hundredth anniversary seemed distant to me at the time, it clearly made sense to begin the work on the project.

The school did not have well-organized and detailed archives, meaning that Professor Wilson would be required to dig through endless boxes of materials, much of it in the University's Special Collections, as well as search extensively for the photographs that could make the story come alive. The results of nearly a decade's work is before you, and all of us affiliated with Curry are deeply in debt to Professor Wilson for her boundless enthusiasm and energy for a project that at times she must surely have regretted undertaking.

The book charts the ebb and flow of the Curry School of Education over the years. It describes the school's periods of remarkable expansion as well as its times of limited growth, even contraction. In many ways, this history has tracked the movement of public education in this country.

The demographic patterns of changing birth rates and family size have translated into periods of sharp expansion in public schooling, followed by times of limited growth or contraction, with resulting impacts on the demand for teachers and other education professionals. Social challenges and concerns across the state and the nation have influenced changes in departmental configurations, research centers, investigative projects, and alliances with businesses, schools, and agencies. Support for educational research has also varied over the past century, a factor of considerable importance to Curry as it has become primarily a graduate school, producing hundreds of graduates with doctorates and master's degrees.

Curry graduates are to be found throughout the commonwealth and the nation, serving in leadership roles in classrooms, research settings, clinics, government agencies, foundations, and private companies. Many graduates have moved on to careers outside formal education, the work they did at Curry serving them well no matter what their occupations.

As we look forward to the next century of service, the school has never been stronger intellectually, financially, or professionally. A new building is on the drawing boards, planned so that it will allow all faculty to gather together in a common site; educational research support from federal, state, and private agencies is at an all-time high; and the quality and diversity of faculty and students are a source of pride to all.

Unlike some research universities, the University of Virginia and the Curry School remain deeply committed to teacher education, and we are nationally recognized for our commitment to that vital activity. Our faculty are leaders in the use of innovative educational technology and its applications in teaching and learning; they are also focused on improving the educational experiences of young people at risk for educational failure.

In short, we believe that in our first hundred years we have met the hopes and aspirations of Edwin A. Alderman and John D. Rockefeller, who combined their efforts to create the Curry School of Education at the University of Virginia. We likewise believe that the Curry School will continue to prosper in its service to society, fulfilling those hopes and more, for years to come.

David W. Breneman
University Professor and Dean
Newton and Rita Meyers Professor,
Economics of Education

The Curry School of Education at the University of Virginia 1905–2005

University of Virginia

The Curry Memorial School of Education

The Curry Memorial School of Education.

FACULTY

Edwin A. Alderman, D. C. L., LL.D., - - *President*
W. H. Heck, M. A., - - - *Professor of Education*
Albert Lefevre, A. B. Ph.D., LL.D., *Professor of Philosophy*
Bruce R. Payne, M. A., Ph.D., - - - - - - - - *Professor of Secondary Education*

The purposes of the Curry School may be defined as follows: (1) To include in a college curriculum courses in education as the most important phase of sociology and civics; (2) to prepare departmental teachers for secondary schools, and principals and supervisors for both elementary and secondary schools; (3) to be a center for the advanced study of educational principles, with special regard to conditions in Virginia and the South.

The courses will be open to third and fourth year men, and to Graduates, except for individual reasons of weight. Courses 1 and 2 will be included in Group IV of the catalogue electives for the B. A. degree. A special library on education will offer opportunity for extensive parallel reading and special reports. In addition to books and articles for required reading, bibliographies will be given for further study. Schools in Charlottesville, Albemarle County, and elsewhere will be reported on after personal observation by the students.

The courses offered for the session 1905–6 are as follows:

1. **The Principles of Education.** A review of the principles of educational psychology, sociology, and philosophy, and of school administration, school hygiene, general method, and special methods in secondary schools. (Three periods a week.)

2. **History of Education.** A study of educational ideals and methods as conditioned by the development of national life and as interpreted by great educators. (Three periods a week.)

3. **Seminar in Southern Education.** Course 1, or its equivalent, prerequisite. A detailed investigation of Southern schools of all grades in comparison with those of other States and of other countries. (Two periods a week.)

For courses in psychology, philosophy, ethics, and logic, see announcement of the School of Philosophy. Through the cooperation of the General Education Board of New York, a professor of secondary education has been elected for the next session to carry on a campaign for the investigation and promotion of public high schools in Virginia. He will give also one or two courses in education at the University during the Spring term.

First brochure, announcing anticipated course offerings, 1905

Introduction

The story of the Curry School of Education's first hundred years is told through its students, faculty, and staff as well as through the many projects and programs that have evolved under its umbrella. This book attempts, in words and pictures, to tell that story.

The title of this history comes from University of Virginia President Edwin A. Alderman's 1917 report prepared for the General Education Board, "Functions and Needs of Schools of Education in Universities and Colleges." Words from the man responsible for founding an education school at the University of Virginia best reflect its initial, central, and ongoing themes during these hundred years: a commitment to prepare teachers and administrators and to provide service to the education profession, together with the intent to further the scholarly research on which to base effective educational practices. Over time, the Curry School has remained remarkably consistent to these themes and to the aspirations of the man who first articulated them here.

This history is organized chronologically. Many programs span several decades, but they are most often discussed during the period in which they originated. The history concludes with a summary of a meeting of the five living deans that took place in Ruffner Hall in December 2001. Their conversations reflected more than fifty years of activities in the Curry School. The meeting provided a vivid picture of the key issues each dean had faced. All generously shared personal views on their deanships and their aspirations for Curry School in the twenty-first century.

On the day of his inauguration as the first president of the University of Virginia, April 13, 1905, Edwin Anderson Alderman secured a gift of $100,000 from oil magnate John D. Rockefeller, Sr., to establish a school of education. Rockefeller and Alderman intended the school to provide training for future secondary teachers in the state, to help develop administrators in the public schools, to partner actively with state educational organizations, and to generate and support educational research. In the spirit of the school and the name that he gave it, President Alderman wished to honor the memory of the recently deceased J. L. M. Curry, a distinguished educator and proponent of improved public education in the South.

The school was known initially as the Curry Memorial School of Education. From 1920 to 1950 it was the Curry Memorial Department of Education. After 1950, in accordance with a University-wide reorganization, it became the Curry Memorial School of Education. In the mid-1980s, the name was shortened to the Curry School of Education. Over time the growth, development, and challenges faced by the education faculty have mirrored trends in the national educational establishment. The school opened in 1905 with two faculty members and granted its first two degrees—a B.S.Ed. and an M.S.Ed.—in 1920. Today more than 130 full-time and part-time faculty members are associated with the school. In 2004–2005 more than seven hundred degrees were granted, 99 percent of them at the graduate level. More than 1,200 students enrolled in the Fall 2005 semester.

From its inception, the School of Education has been responsive to local, state, and national needs and trends in education. The school has long valued programs that improve the educational practices of those in leadership and teaching roles. It has offered resident and nonresident classes, advanced standards for professional certification, and provided expertise gained through research for the furtherance of policy. The school's first course catalog announced courses on educational theory, courses designed to prepare teachers for secondary schools, courses especially for principals and supervisors of elementary and secondary schools, and activities supporting the "advanced study" of educational principles. This three-pronged mission—preparing professionals, supporting professional organizations, and furthering research—has continued over the past hundred years.

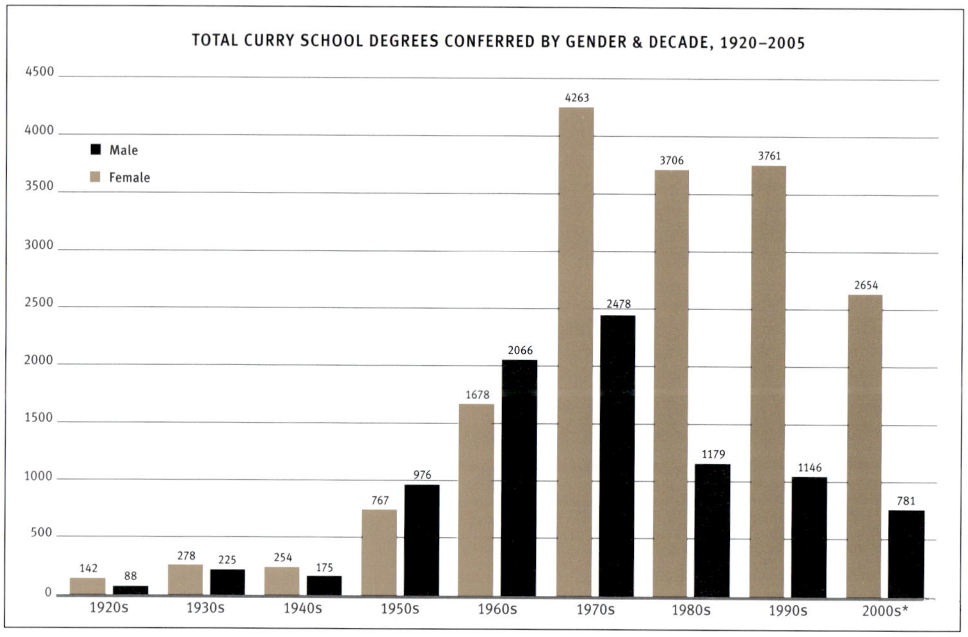

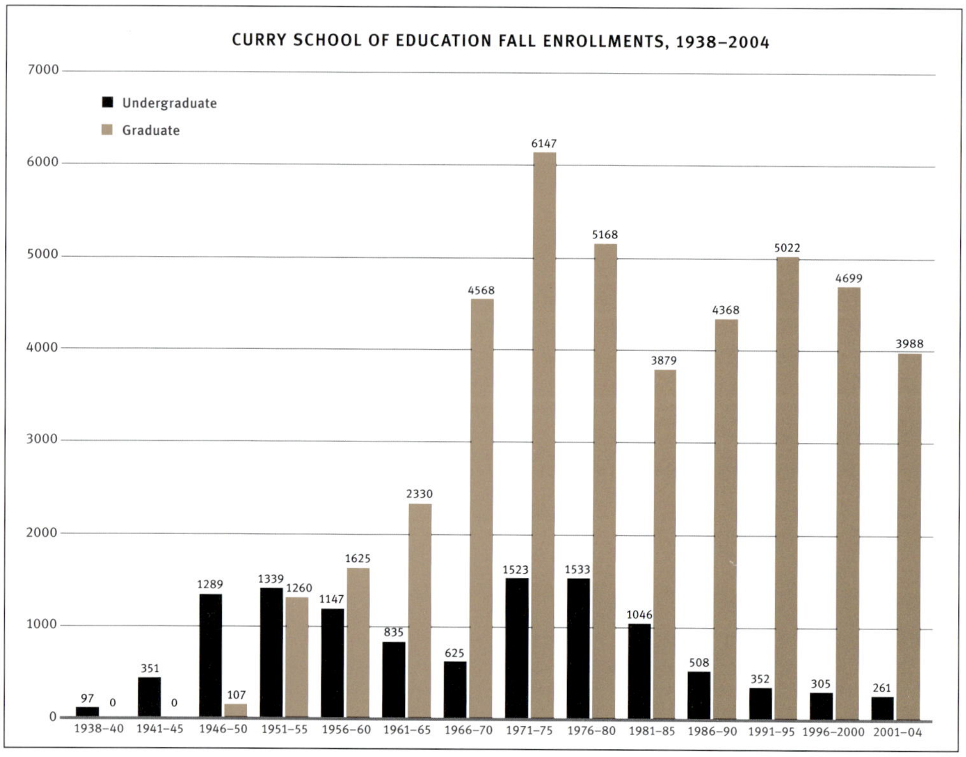

Some facts are better known than others about the Curry School. In 1953 the School of Education became the first university division in the South to award a doctorate to an African American. In 1968, one of the first women to be appointed full professor from within University ranks was a member of the education faculty. In 1968, education professor Nathan Johnson was the first African American appointed to the University of Virginia faculty.

Women were admitted to the Department of Education as undergraduates (and as graduate students, as in other schools of the University) at times when male enrollments faltered. Beginning in 1920, third-year women were admitted to the school for preparation to become teachers. Between 1921 (when it first became possible for women to earn professional degrees at the University of Virginia) and 1970 (when women were formally admitted to the University on an equal basis), close to half the degrees awarded to women throughout the University went to women in education.

For many years, faculty holding joint appointments in the Curry School headed the Summer School and the Extension Division. The School of Education had a close relationship with statewide professional organizations from its earliest days. Perhaps most importantly, President Alderman's commitment to preparing educated teachers and administrators for the public schools—combined with his view that teachers should have a strong background in liberal arts as well as in methods of instruction—provided the framework for ongoing relationships between the school and the larger educational community at the University and beyond.

The education school's continuing sense of a threefold mission enhanced its survival at times when other universities were discontinuing their teacher education programs and becoming graduate schools specializing in educational policy, research, or other areas. The Curry School's undergraduate programs for teacher education were seriously questioned several times, and in each instance reorganization efforts helped those programs not only survive but flourish. At the start of the twenty-first century, three vanguard areas—dubbed "spires of excellence"—were identified to provide future direction for the school: teacher education, technology, and program development for at-risk students. Upon reflection, the spires of excellence turn out to be modern iterations of the school's earliest emphases, combining service and research with the preparation of leaders for the educational community.

One strength of the Curry School of Education has been longevity of leadership. The first dean, John Levi Manahan, held the position for almost thirty years. Manahan was followed by deans in office on average of ten years, a period long enough for program changes and new directions to settle into stable patterns. The consistency of leadership in the Curry School was paralleled by similarly long terms held by many of the presidents of the University.

The first president of the University of Virginia established the School of Education as one of his top priorities. From that point on, the professional background of each dean and each one's relationship to the University president has been critical to the character and success of the Curry School. John L. Manahan, an educational administrator, was appointed by President Alderman, who had an all-inclusive vision of the possibilities for an education department. John L. Newcomb, an engineer, succeeded Alderman as president, and most departmental operations proceeded routinely through the aftermath of the Depression and then World War II. When Colgate Darden became president of the University, his political strengths evoked new enthusiasm for public service and school outreach. Darden appointed Lindley Stiles to be dean on Manahan's retirement. Stiles came from a background in English education and led the school in new directions of professional outreach. Darden also hired Ralph Cherry, another leader with expertise in educational administration, who led the school to departmentalize its varied programs.

Edgar Shannon, staunch advocate for educational equity and opportunity, succeeded Colgate Darden as president and appointed Frederick Cyphert as dean. With a background in curriculum and teacher education and a commitment to developing educational research, Cyphert sought a balance between those two important efforts of the school, more than doubling its size and developing its research potential as well. The fifth president of the University, Frank Hereford, oversaw a comprehensive plan for private giving to the University. At the same time Richard Brandt, the fifth dean of the Curry School, shared Hereford's recognition of the importance of developing a financial base of support for the University and the School of Education.

James Cooper, the sixth Curry School dean, came to the position with a nationally recognized background in teacher education. He moved teacher education into graduate status, a move enthusiastically supported by President Robert O'Neill, a professor and researcher of the law. Seventh University President John T. Casteen III—a former professor of English at Virginia who was Secretary of Education for the Commonwealth—championed efforts to build the school's reputation for educational excellence. The current dean, David Breneman, came to the Curry School with an academic background as an economist and experience in higher education administration. He has both strengthened and solidified programs and generated private financial support for new facilities in a way that ensures the school's continued economic health and stature.

From the earliest days, faculty members fostered communication with Curry graduates as well as other educational professionals in the state and nation, a tradition of reciprocity that has enhanced the vitality of the school over time. Early faculty members such as Bruce Payne and Harry Heck shared President Alderman's desire to provide research-based services to public schools in Virginia and beyond, a practice that continued with William Smithey's twenty-year-long publication of *Secondary Education in Virginia*, Richard Meade's influence in the field of English education, and Frank Lankford's work in mathematics education. George Zehmer and Charles Maphis established the University of Virginia's Extension Division and Summer School, putting education courses within reach of thousands more Virginians. The School of Education consistently initiated and supported research, and for more than thirty years during the latter part of the twentieth century, its Bureau of Educational Research provided information influential for state and national practices, policies, and decisions.

SCHOOL OF EDUCATION DEGREES CONFERRED, 1920–2005

YEAR	BSEd	BSNEd	BS Phys Ed	MSEd	MT	MA*	MAT*	MEd	EdS	PhD*	EdD
1920s	185	0	0	14	0	31	0	0	0	0	0
1930s	338	29	0	38	0	88	0	0	0	10	0
1940s	230	69	7	0	0	119	0	0	0	4	0
1950s	504	55	40	0	0	36	0	1054	0	7	47
1960s	491	0	0	0	0	0	92	2953	0	8	200
1970s	1085	0	0	0	0	14	77	4937	69	97	462
1980s	929	0	0	0	14	10	59	3082	135	337	319
1990s	319	0	0	0	1040	0	29	2715	68	501	235
2000s	155	0	0	0	499	0	0	2083	195	406	97

Note: These numbers reflect degrees conferred in the Summer Session as well as during the academic year.
* MA, MAT, and PhD degrees conferred by the College of Arts and Sciences through August 1996.

Many projects still essential to the Curry School have significantly influenced current educational theory and practice. The work of the McGuffey Reading Center, the programs in kinesiology, advances in communications disorders, the clinical preparation of school psychologists, new approaches in gifted education—these are just a few. For many years two residential summer programs, the Young Writer's Program and the Summer Enrichment Program, have attracted students from across the country, and each spring a Saturday Enrichment Program draws nearby students to supplement their regular school curriculum. Numerous faculty members have had significant impact on educational practices. They have traveled the state, nation, and world, providing consultations in the schools and organizing conferences for teachers. They take seriously the commitment to participate in and provide leadership for state and national professional organizations. It is also fair to say that the Curry School has had its share of colorful faculty members, the memory of whom often brings a chuckle.

As in any institution, there have been years of growth and years of stagnation. Yet the school has remained attentive to current educational trends and continues to work toward developing programs reflecting these. While responding to the calls of policy makers to improve educational practices (especially the training of teachers), the school did not succumb to pressures to change its course offerings completely. Buffeted by various trends, the school has continued to provide graduate and undergraduate degree programs throughout its hundred-year history, becoming by the present day primarily a graduate institution.

This introduction is by no means an exhaustive account of all the details of the Curry School's history, nor is the book it introduces. Both are attempts to provide a broad sweep of the school's history, told against the backdrop of history at the University of Virginia and the educational systems across the United States. Deans and faculty members have left their marks in the institutional records of the Curry School, and many stories of educational contributions throughout the school's first hundred years remain untold.

The contributions of staff members over time are critical to the Curry School's survival. Mary Rush, departmental secretary for more than thirty years, is one of many unsung heroines, for example. Consistently praised for her work by deans, faculty, and students, her steady presence guided the progress of the school through many crises and triumphs. Similarly Helen Clark, Linda Berry, and Rebecca Burbach (now executive assistant for Dean David Breneman) have each served the Curry School for more than thirty years in key administrative positions. Another figure important to Curry School history—his name comes up over and over through a critical thirty-year period—is Vincent Shea, provost and vice president of the University, whose willingness to give education school deans access to his office facilitated their accomplishments in significant ways.

In 2005 the Curry School of Education begins its second century, ranked solidly among the nation's outstanding schools of education and emboldened with a generous pledge of support for a new building. The future of the professional school of education envisioned by Edwin Anderson Alderman in 1905 seems assured.

Students and teachers, Midway School, Charlottesville, 1901

CHAPTER 1

The Study of Education in the Nineteenth Century

Education . . . engrafts a new man of the native stock, and improves what in his nature was vicious and perverse into qualities of virtue and social worth. . . . Each generation succeeding to the knowledge acquired by all those who preceded it, adding to it their own acquisitions and discoveries, and handing the mass down for successive and constant accumulation, must advance the knowledge and well-being of mankind, not infinitely *but* indefinitely, *and to a term which no one can fix and foresee.*[1]

— Thomas Jefferson, 1818

While the Curry Memorial School of Education was officially established in 1905, the origins of a school of education lay in the founding of the University of Virginia. Central to the ethos of the University's founder, Thomas Jefferson, was his conviction that education was essential to creating an enlightened and responsible citizenry. At a time when most colleges were training scholars for the clergy and academia, Jefferson founded a university to educate leaders in practical affairs and public service. Jefferson outlined the institution's purpose, designed its buildings, garnered legislative support, supervised its construction, planned its curriculum, and directed the recruitment of faculty. He designed the University to be completely public and secular. He wished to establish, he wrote, "a University on a plan so broad and liberal and modern as to be worth patronizing with the public support."[2]

When the University of Virginia opened its doors in March 1825, it was composed of eight schools, each offering an area of study taught by a single professor: ancient languages, modern languages, mathematics, natural philosophy (physics), natural history (botany and zoology), anatomy and medicine, moral philosophy, and law. By year's end, 116 students had enrolled.[3] Initially, the course of study offered was at a graduate level only, intended for students who had completed college. The only degree offered was in medicine; other students received a document verifying graduation from the University of Virginia. In 1832 this practice changed to reflect policy changes at other universities, and for the first time a master's degree was awarded. Many students did not stay long enough to earn a degree, however. Enrollment remained at about two hundred for the next two decades; then, in the 1850s, it expanded to more than five hundred. From its founding through the nineteenth century, the University was run by a Board of Visitors,

University of Virginia Lawn, 1824

William Henry Ruffner

and the faculty governed itself, a practice that continued until Edwin Anderson Alderman was installed as the first president of the University of Virginia in 1905.[4]

Responding to the Public Need for Education

From its first year, the University produced teachers and headmasters to staff the private academies and preparatory schools of Virginia. Graduates of these schools in turn entered the University, some to become teachers and headmasters themselves. With the adoption of a new constitution in 1869, Virginia's system of public education formally began, although it would take almost forty more years before plans were fully authorized by the state. University faculty members understood how important it was to envision a full-scale state education system. In an 1871 report to the Board of Visitors, the faculty noted, "now that the state has recognized the importance of generally educating the masses of the people, it must admit the necessity of a regular system and gradation of instruction, beginning at the common school and culminating in the University."[5]

In the 1870s William Henry Ruffner, Virginia's first superintendent of public instruction, undertook a campaign for universal public schools.

Within that mission, he noted the need to improve the training of schoolteachers. Ruffner proposed state normal schools and institutes to provide higher education for Virginia's schoolteachers, most of whom were women. In 1879 Ruffner received funds to support summer normal institutes, one in Lynchburg for African American teachers and one at the University of Virginia for white teachers. The University's Board of Visitors held that since the summer normal institute was not part of the regular academic program, its students could not receive university credit. In spite of this, five hundred students attended the first institute at the University, 312 of them women.[6]

Efforts to link the University with the fledgling public school system were unsuccessful in the 1870s. In 1880 the faculty complained of the isolation between the two and requested that "in the regular sphere of action" provision be made for teacher preparation and training, noting that as more University graduates were entering public school teaching, the occupation should be elevated to a professional status. The faculty report suggested establishing new professorships, one in Pedagogy and one in English, to give the University more influence over content in teacher preparation.[7] Their plan, they argued, would save the expense of establishing normal schools. Further, stated the report, "We favor the admission to this new department of women who are already teachers or who may desire to be teachers."[8]

The proposal was not approved by the Board of Visitors, but six years later the University catalog announced: "White male teachers and superintendents of the Free Schools of Virginia will be admitted during the last three months of the session to the Academic Department of the University without payment of fees." The faculty initiated special courses for public school administrators and teachers, including two in natural philosophy (electricity and practical laboratory physics), three in pedagogy (psychology and theory of education, history of education, and methods of teaching history), and additional courses in Latin, Greek, French, German, English, mathematics, geography, chemistry, and botany.[9] Courses varied over the following years as the faculty attempted to provide a curriculum that would best benefit these first "education" students at the University of Virginia.

Nineteenth-century readers

Summer School of Methods

In 1894 the state superintendent of education lobbied the General Assembly to provide special funding to support summer institutes for teachers. By 1898 a School of Methods, hosted by the University of Virginia, received not only additional University funding but also aid from the City of Charlottesville, the Peabody Fund, and the General Education Board.[10]

The School of Methods attracted more than one thousand students in 1902 and again in 1903. Attendees included more than sixty black teachers, who were taught separately by white instructors in a public school building. The University's October 1903 *Alumni Bulletin* told its readers that they would be "astonished" if they returned to their alma mater during the month of July and saw the "boarding-houses and dormitories filled, and lawns and arcades crowded with earnest-faced men and women." Institute attendees represented "almost all ages," the article continued:

> There is the bright-eyed miss just out of high school, armed with pad and pencil, on her way to the model school to gather ideas from the pedagogical experts, and the gray-haired woman, whose life has perhaps been spent in teaching first grade tots, and who now at the evening has come to take the longed-for deeper draught at the Pierian font. But wherever one sees them, whether on the lawn, in the lecture rooms, or at the concerts or evening lectures, there is something inspiring in their energy and enthusiasm in the hot vacation month.[11]

According to Philip Bruce, an early historian of the University of Virginia, the summer institutes became "the most important agency in the Commonwealth for increasing the knowledge, and improving the skill, of the public school teachers."[12]

The School of Methods continued as an independent teachers' institute in cooperation with the University until 1907. Enrollments gradually declined, in part because of competition with other schools for teachers such as the State Female Normal School at Farmville and the State Normal School for Women at Madison. Eventually the School of Methods was incorporated into the broader University Summer School sessions.[13] The early efforts to provide training for young men to become teachers, combined with the considerable impact of the School of Methods, which broadened its student base to include women and African Americans, established a legacy of teacher training and service to state education. This foundation provided the strong base from which Edwin Alderman could propose to create a school of education in the early twentieth century—one of his most important initiatives as the newly appointed president of the University of Virginia.

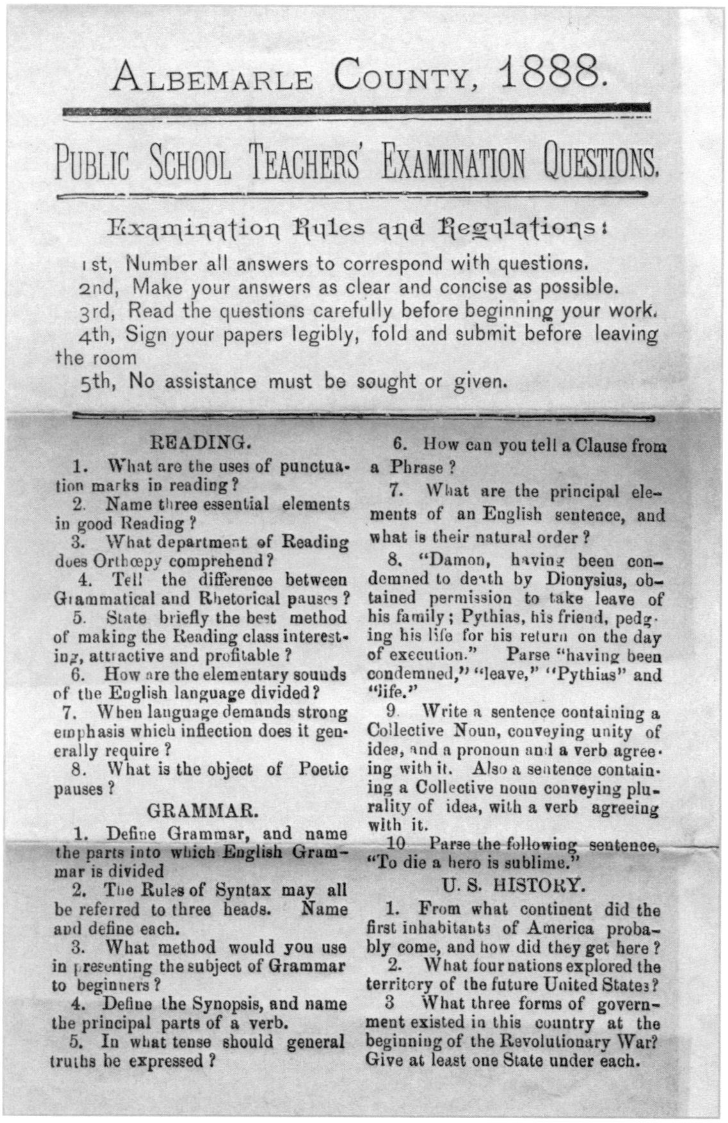
ALBEMARLE COUNTY, 1888.

PUBLIC SCHOOL TEACHERS' EXAMINATION QUESTIONS.

Examination Rules and Regulations:

1st, Number all answers to correspond with questions.
2nd, Make your answers as clear and concise as possible.
3rd, Read the questions carefully before beginning your work.
4th, Sign your papers legibly, fold and submit before leaving the room
5th, No assistance must be sought or given.

READING.

1. What are the uses of punctuation marks in reading?
2. Name three essential elements in good Reading?
3. What department of Reading does Orthœpy comprehend?
4. Tell the difference between Grammatical and Rhetorical pauses?
5. State briefly the best method of making the Reading class interesting, attractive and profitable?
6. How are the elementary sounds of the English language divided?
7. When language demands strong emphasis which inflection does it generally require?
8. What is the object of Poetic pauses?

GRAMMAR.

1. Define Grammar, and name the parts into which English Grammar is divided
2. The Rules of Syntax may all be referred to three heads. Name and define each.
3. What method would you use in presenting the subject of Grammar to beginners?
4. Define the Synopsis, and name the principal parts of a verb.
5. In what tense should general truths be expressed?
6. How can you tell a Clause from a Phrase?
7. What are the principal elements of an English sentence, and what is their natural order?
8. "Damon, having been condemned to death by Dionysius, obtained permission to take leave of his family; Pythias, his friend, pedging his life for his return on the day of execution." Parse "having been condemned," "leave," "Pythias" and "life."
9. Write a sentence containing a Collective Noun, conveying unity of idea, and a pronoun and a verb agreeing with it. Also a sentence containing a Collective noun conveying plurality of idea, with a verb agreeing with it.
10. Parse the following sentence, "To die a hero is sublime."

U. S. HISTORY.

1. From what continent did the first inhabitants of America probably come, and how did they get here?
2. What four nations explored the territory of the future United States?
3. What three forms of government existed in this country at the beginning of the Revolutionary War? Give at least one State under each.

Summer school maypole, ca. 1905

Alderman's inaugural banquet in the Rotunda, 1905

CHAPTER 2

Founding the Curry Memorial School of Education

The Vision of Edwin A. Alderman, 1905–1920

The first forward step would be the establishment here of a school of education of such power that its teachers could approach . . . problems of educational statesmanship with insight and authority. This school should comprise the philosopher, but also the sociologist, the organizer, and the sympathetic publicist.[1]

— Edwin Anderson Alderman, *Inaugural Address,* 1905

The appointment of Edwin Anderson Alderman as the first president of the University of Virginia marked a new era in the institution's history. Alderman came into the position with a longstanding commitment to public education. In 1904, the year he was selected to lead the University, he remarked that his "first day's work in this world was for the public schools and I have never known a day unconnected with service of some sort for them."[2] One of his first actions as president was to solicit funds to establish a school of education.

Alderman the Educator

Alderman, a North Carolinian, was a lifelong educator. Graduating from the University of North Carolina in 1882, he became a teacher and then superintendent of the Goldsboro schools. He served as president of the North Carolina teachers' assembly, and in 1889 the State Board of Education elected him a State Institute Instructor. In this capacity he gave teacher workshops around the state. Together with Charles D. McIver, Alderman is credited with establishing the Normal and Industrial School for Women in Greensboro (now the University of North Carolina–Greensboro), which opened in 1891 with McIver as president and Alderman as head of the faculty.

Appointed the first professor of history and philosophy of education at the University of North Carolina, in 1893, Alderman firmly believed that "the teaching profession would be established on terms of equality with law and medicine."[3] In Chapel Hill, he directed the University of North Carolina's summer school for teachers. In 1896, at the age of thirty-five, Alderman became president of the University of North Carolina. Four years later, he was named president of Tulane

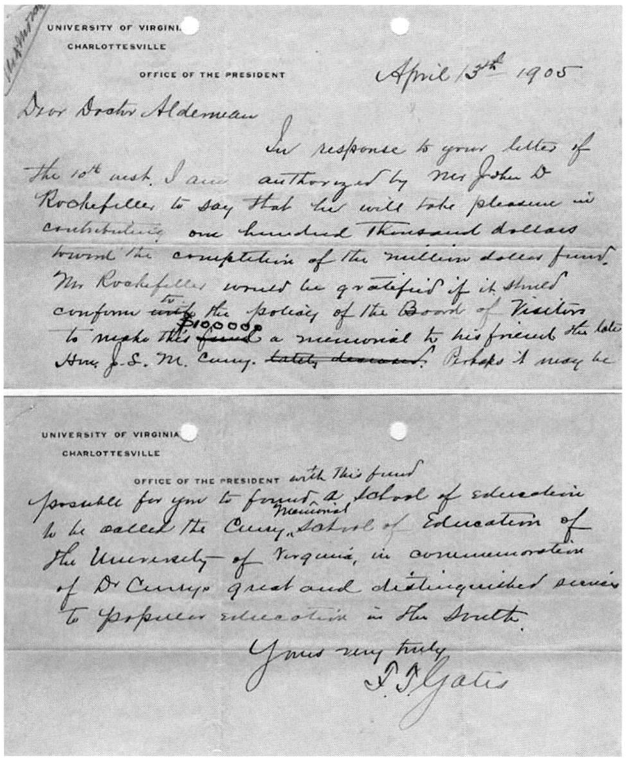
UNIVERSITY OF VIRGINIA
CHARLOTTESVILLE
OFFICE OF THE PRESIDENT

April 13th 1905

Dear Doctor Alderman

In response to your letter of the 10th inst. I am authorized by Mr John D Rockefeller to say that he will take pleasure in contributing one hundred Thousand dollars toward the completion of the million dollar fund. Mr. Rockefeller would be gratified if it should conform to the policy of the Board of Visitors to make this $100,000 a memorial to his friend the late Hon. J. L. M. Curry. Perhaps it may be

UNIVERSITY OF VIRGINIA
CHARLOTTESVILLE
OFFICE OF THE PRESIDENT

possible for you to found with this fund a School of education to be called the Curry Memorial School of Education of the University of Virginia, in commemoration of Dr Curry's great and distinguished service to popular education in the South.

Yours very truly,
F. T. Gates

Gates conveys Rockefeller gift, using Alderman's stationery

University.[4] In 1904, when offered the newly established presidency of the University of Virginia, Alderman clearly came with an already articulated educational mission. In his first address to teachers at the School of Methods in June 1904, reported the Charlottesville *Daily Progress*, "He referred pointedly to the inadequate pay of our school teachers and to the great need for better school houses in many sections."[5]

Alderman immediately turned his attention to establishing a school of education at the University. Normal schools were being established in Virginia, compulsory secondary education was a key issue, and educational leaders were increasingly interested in the quality of teacher preparation. Influenced by his experiences in North Carolina and as a founding member of the Southern Educational Board, Alderman's view was that education should be considered a science in the University curriculum. He was concerned about its reputation in the broader academic world, as he stated here:

> The trouble with most normal schools as such, detached from universities, has been that they made a type of man who stood strongly upon technique and method but somehow lacked the quality of scholarship which gave him equality and contact with the real scholars, and differentiated him, so to speak, as a mere master of method. This worked harm to the scholars by giving them the conceit of scholarship and contempt of method, and it has worked harm to the normal school man by isolating him.[6]

During the winter of 1904–1905, Alderman drafted a budget for the proposed education school, envisioning three faculty positions, several "recitation rooms," and a library. "I have not included expenses for a model school," he noted, although he clearly did anticipate one.[7]

Alderman secured a $100,000 donation from John D. Rockefeller, Sr., for the new school. Rockefeller's agent, Frederick T. Gates, signed a pledge on Alderman's letterhead, dated April 13, 1905, Founder's Day and the day of Alderman's inauguration as president of the University.[8] The pledge stipulated that the money would fund a school of education as a memorial to J. L. M. Curry, a well-known Southern advocate of public education.

Born in Georgia in 1825, Jabez Lamar Monroe Curry received an elementary education in an "old field school" in his home community. He graduated from Franklin College in 1843 and began a long career as an educator. President of Howard College in Alabama from 1865 to 1868, Curry traveled extensively in the South, urging the education of both black and white children. He served as general agent of the Peabody Fund, one of the nation's earliest philanthropic foundations, founded in 1867 to ensure educational opportunities for newly freed slaves.[9] Curry also served as an executive officer of the Slater Fund, established in 1882 to improve Negro education in the South; as a member of the General Education Board, a philanthropic organization dedicated to educating Americans irrespective of race, sex, or creed; as a trustee of the State Female Normal

School in Farmville, today's Longwood University; and as professor of English at Richmond College in Virginia, where he inaugurated one of the nation's first systematic college courses in English.

Alderman had worked closely with Curry to develop a comprehensive plan for education in the South. He expressed his admiration in a biography of Curry that he coauthored in 1911. Speaking at the Conference for Education in the South on April 26, 1903, just after Curry had died, Alderman said:

> I once heard him declare to an audience that it was the proudest duty of the South to accomplish the education of every child in its borders—high or low, bond or free, black or white. The only response to his appeal was silence. He shouted, "I will make you applaud that sentiment."[10]

By naming the University of Virginia's new education school in honor of J. L. M. Curry, Alderman did more than applaud—he institutionalized that dedication to equal, high-quality education for all citizens.

J. L. M. Curry

The Curry Memorial School of Education

The 1905–1906 *University of Virginia Record* listed the first course offerings of the new Curry Memorial School of Education. President Alderman appointed two distinguished faculty members, Bruce Rayburn Payne and William Henry Heck, to teach at the University and work with the public schools. Coming from William and Mary College, Payne was appointed professor of secondary education. Funding for his position came from the General Education Board. The hiring of Heck—a protégé of leading educator Nicholas Murray Butler, president of Columbia University—was equally significant.[11] In 1902, Heck had become assistant secretary of the General Education Board, for which he investigated the condition of public education in Southern states.[12] At the University of Virginia, Heck was appointed the Curry Memorial Professor of Education. He traveled the state working with parents, teachers, and public school students, especially emphasizing health and hygiene, urging schools to make up for parental deficiencies in these lessons and practices.

That first year, five courses were offered in the Curry School, as listed in the *Record*. Designed for undergraduates, they included History of Education, Psychology and Philosophy of Education (investigating principles involved in a "scientific theory of education"), and Secondary Education. Two courses were open to graduate students as well: Principles of Education and School Administration. The graduate course in Principles was designed to help students "learn to express original opinions upon matters psychological and sociological" and to study education "in its relation to the practical affairs of life." Its curriculum included a review of "the Principles of Educational Psychology, Sociology, and Philosophy and of Administration, School Hygiene, General Methods, and specific methods in secondary schools."

Bruce Rayburn Payne (top)

William Henry Heck

Seven undergraduates and four graduate students enrolled in the Curry School that first year: 11 students out of an entire University student body of 297 undergraduates and 35 graduates. Although after the first year Payne transferred to the School of Philosophy, becoming professor of secondary education, logic, and psychology, he continued to push the cause of public education. Heck remained as the only full-time professor in the School of Education. He added a new undergraduate course, Sociological Basis of Education, whose curriculum remained essentially the same until 1911 and focused on the individual's development in society.[13]

In 1906 Alderman was able to proudly cite the University of Virginia as one of the first institutions of the South to offer a course for secondary teachers in training. "The progressive high school teacher of today who hopes for any degree of success must become acquainted with the fundamental principles of controlling influence in the educative process," he stated. "These are either of a sociological or a psychological character," fields of study now available to prospective teachers at the Curry Memorial School of Education.[14]

The State of Education in the Commonwealth

Bruce Payne immediately began a study of public high schools in the state of Virginia, noting in an October 15, 1905, report to President Alderman that "practically never has been any high school legislation in Virginia" and that existing lists of high schools are "largely worthless," since "many of the so-called schools could not meet the required standard as it is understood over the country as a whole."[15] Payne hosted a November 1906 conference in Charlottesville on public school education, bringing together many state and national leaders in education at a time when few American locales had public-supported secondary school systems. The conference received national attention and praise for its attempt to "reach down to the secondary schools and aid in relating them properly to the schools below and the schools above."[16] Proudly calling it the largest educational gathering ever held in Virginia, Payne also believed the 1906 conference to be "the most far-reaching in its concrete results of any similar meeting ever held in America."[17]

Even more significantly, Payne campaigned statewide to ensure passage of a 1906 bill creating a unified system of high schools throughout Virginia.[18] Payne sought a new law mandating that each local community provide a high school building and raise half the cost of teacher salaries. In 1910 he stated that "the time must not be far distant when there shall exist as good a four-year high school in each county of Virginia as is to be found in the average county of another state."[19] In 1905, there were only forty-four secondary schools in the state, ten of them offering four-year programs.[20] "Six years ago there was no system of high schools in this State," Payne reported to Alderman in 1911. "There is today a well-organized system with about 100 four-year high schools . . . There were not 5,000 students in the public and private high schools of Virginia in 1905. There are over 15,000 now."[21]

In 1908 a statewide commission was created to determine qualifications for those aspiring to teach, a move that would have consequences for the new school of education. President

Alderman chaired the commission; Charles Maphis, then University of Virginia registrar, served as secretary. The General Assembly charged the commission to "devise a stable, systematic method for the maintenance, management, and expansion of the higher educational institutions of the state" according to the needs of each and "with reference to a definite and harmonious system." As a result of the commission report, in 1911 the General Assembly issued resolutions stating that all educational institutions chartered by the state should be under the supervision of the Board of Education, and that "no person shall teach in the state without having secured from the Board of Education license so to do, under such regulations as may be prescribed by the legislature."[22] That same year the University was placed on the Carnegie Foundation list of approved colleges, in part as a result of "the work that has been done by the University in the development of the secondary schools of the state." The citation acknowledged the eminence of the faculty and its achievements, the school's advanced standards of admission, and especially its successful efforts to develop and improve secondary schools.[23]

In 1911 Payne resigned from the University to become president of Peabody College for Teachers, and Charles Maphis was appointed to replace him as professor of secondary education.[24] Five years later, the improvement in public high schools showed up in University admissions figures. In 1916 President Alderman could report that thanks "in large measure to the zealous energy" of his faculty in education, "the number of young men from public schools steadily augmented the registration lists of the University . . . between 1910 and 1916." The numbers of public school students entering the University of Virginia gradually increased, with ninety-five

School in Earlysville, Virginia, ca. 1910

public school graduates admitted for the academic year 1915–1916, compared to eight in classes prior to 1906. "This means," Alderman announced triumphantly, "we have tied the University by logical ties to the real democratic life of the State."[25]

Summer School

Along with his commitment to a school of education, President Alderman wished to strengthen a summer school at the University. The School of Law first offered summer courses in 1869 as an extension of the academic year. Summer courses in medicine were offered in 1871.[26] The School of Methods, held on Grounds but with no official University connection, emphasized "methods of teaching" and presented lectures in cultural fields. Operating under the direction of E. C. Glass, superintendent of schools in Lynchburg, its attendance peaked at 1,200, but slipped to less than 500 by its later years.[27]

In 1906 Bruce Payne, newly appointed professor of education, took on leadership of the University of Virginia Summer Session. In 1907, the first Summer Session catalog appeared. Called upon to organize Summer School classes for teachers, Payne focused on the "solid and substantial training of high school teachers."[28] Courses increased in quality, and by 1911 President Alderman proposed that the summer school become a University department.[29] Enrollment grew from 700 in 1907 to 1,350 by 1912; at the same time, the number of courses offered increased from 63 to 101.[30] Pageants on the University Lawn were graced with the presence of female students, nearly invisible from the scene during the academic year. When 1,263 students enrolled in 1911 summer courses, their numbers topped those of full-year students at the University and brought the year-round enrollment total to 2,000.[31] In 1919 the summer school formally became an integral part of the university year with full course offerings. In 1920 summer course offerings expanded to fill a full academic quarter with two terms, one five and one six weeks long.

Charles Maphis

Summer school was not meant to replace existing curricula for those wanting to become teachers. Rather it was intended to expand the background of those already teaching by broadening the array of courses available to both female and male teachers and making it possible for public school teachers to meet certification requirements.[32] In 1907 the state superintendent of public instruction, Joseph D. Eggleston, provided the program with $4,000, increased to $10,500 in 1914, on the condition that every registered teacher from Virginia be admitted without paying tuition.[33] Thus "an industrious and ambitious young man" could attend three sessions during his four university years, thereby shortening the time spent earning a B.A. by at least a year. Women were not eligible to earn degrees until 1920.[34]

The developing School of Education linked comfortably with another new arm of the University, the Bureau of Extension, formally organized in 1915. Education professor Charles Maphis served as director of the summer school from 1912 to 1920, at which time his title changed to dean of the summer quarter. He also served as director of the Bureau of Extension through 1925. Maphis announced that the 1913 Summer School would be the largest in its history. Students from three dozen or more states studied under a faculty numbering more than one hundred, "practically all of whom were full professors or heads of some special department of work in a standard institution," reported Maphis, citing among their home institutions Peabody College, Harvard University, Randolph-Macon College, and Wake Forest College. "No instructors and assistants are employed. The grade and quality of work therefore is of the highest rank." That summer, thirty-three courses in education were offered in an effort to "meet the needs of teachers of all grades."[35]

The 1913–1914 Summer School course list included School Management and Methods, School Administration, Matter and Method in the high school, and several courses in elementary education. The catalog identified those courses that satisfied requirements for teacher certification and announced that a weeklong series of lectures on "The Montessori Method," given by a collaborator of Dr. Maria Montessori, "will be the most authoritative presentation of this subject made in any summer school in this country and should attract many persons who are interested in this work."[36]

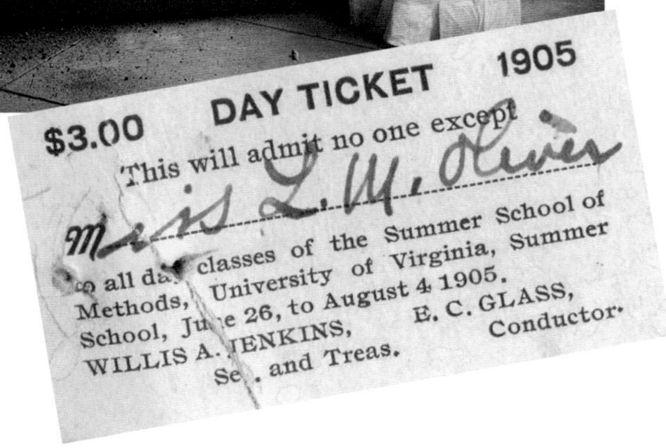

Montessori students in sandbox on University Grounds, ca. 1913 (top)

Summer school admission ticket, 1905

Heck, Health, and Hygiene

William Henry "Harry" Heck proved to be as influential as Bruce Payne at the University of Virginia. He toured the state, delivering his message about the importance of health and hygiene as part of a public school education. A September 1905 article in *College Topics*, the University of Virginia student newspaper, described Heck's ideal of education not as "a succession of facts gathered in the lecture room" but rather "the development of ideas which brings about the power of original thinking and research." Heck wanted a health and hygiene program at the University "not only for those students who planned to become teachers" but also for "those men . . . who, after their university careers, will enter into civic affairs where questions of education are becoming more pressing and insistent every day."[37]

Harry Heck became an advisor to the State Board of Education and reviewed plans for school buildings submitted for the Board's approval. A colleague later wrote that to the people of Virginia he represented "the most modern principles of hygiene of school life and the sanitation of school buildings."[38] His untimely death at the age of 39 during the influenza epidemic of 1919 was

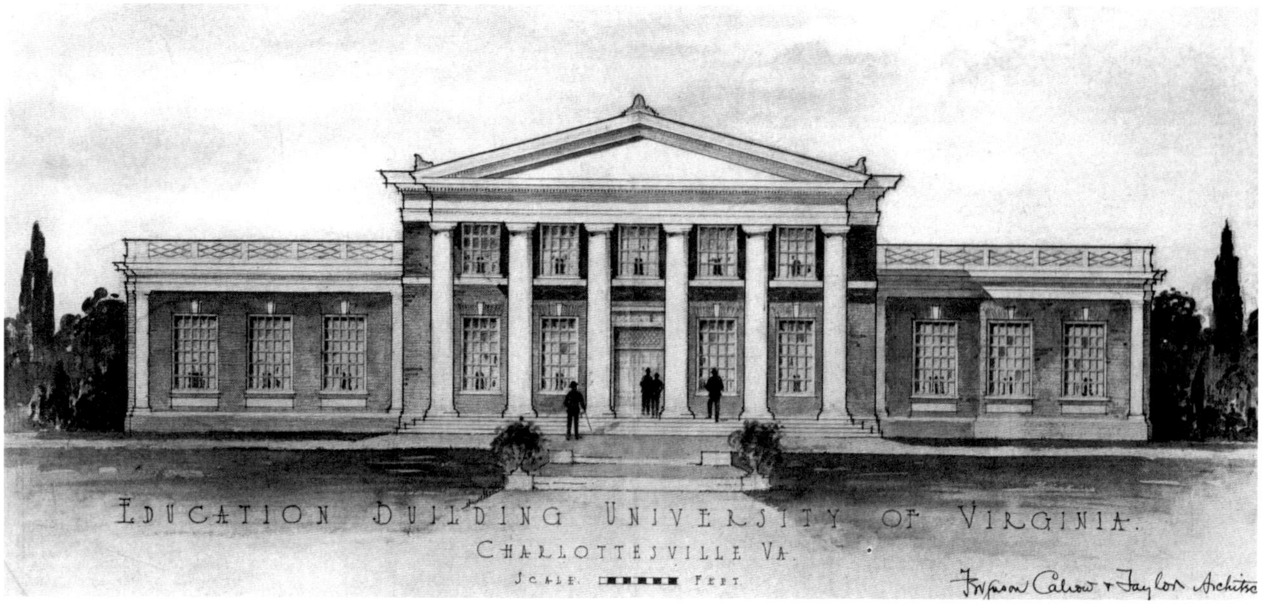

Architect's drawing of Peabody Hall, ca. 1911

a blow for the Curry Memorial School of Education. Undoubtedly, the work of Payne and Heck laid the course for the School of Education with their concern that graduates should study the "practical conditions entering into modern school administration" while acquiring a "solid basis of knowledge of such vital themes as psychology, sociology, biology, hygiene and physiology."[39]

Enrollment in the new Curry Memorial School of Education was small. Heck wrote President Alderman in 1907, saying that he had been offered a deanship at the University of Missouri and questioning Alderman's offer to his colleague Payne that he become dean of a department of education at Virginia. "I do not think the University of Virginia is ready for a department of education," wrote Heck. "With the few students so far enrolled in education here there is no sign of an increase sufficient to demand a department and there seems little opportunity to get by 'drumming' a sufficient number for some years to come." He told Alderman that he believed "the normal schools, with lower standards, meet the needs of most Southern men desiring complete normal courses."[40]

Heck's concerns were countered by C. Ormond Stone, then director of the summer school. Stone wrote Alderman that he observed an entrenched "heresy" at the University of Virginia in the prevailing belief teachers needed no training other than knowledge of the subject matter to be taught. "Only through an organized school of education can ultimate success be expected," argued Stone.[41] His view ultimately prevailed, and Alderman continued organizing a department of education, planning a new building, and contacting colleagues about a "good man" to head it. That search finally ended in 1920 with the appointment of John L. Manahan as the first dean of the Curry Memorial School of Education.[42]

The First Extension Program

"Universities must . . . draw nearer to the people, young and old, in helpfulness and service," Alderman unswervingly believed. "University extension is the name given to [the] great connecting link between every part of a University and the actual conditions of life in the state."[43] Since 1891 the University had offered a loose form of extension services, but not until 1912, under the directorship of education professor Harry Heck, was the extension lecture system formalized.[44] This first informal link between the School of Education and extension programs laid the groundwork for the relationship that continues to the present between the Curry School and what developed into the School of Continuing and Professional Studies. Charles Maphis, professor of secondary education, managed extension efforts for a decade, directing the Bureau of Extension from 1915 to 1922 and the Division of Extension from 1922 to 1925. His leadership formed useful connections between the education school, extension programs, and the summer school.

Heck initiated a school hygiene campaign during the first years of extension activity; by 1915 that work expanded into the University and around the state. He inspected and advised on school hygiene in many communities, organized local conferences for teachers, and gave public addresses in many communities, with titles such as "Clean Schools," "The Out-of-School Life of Schoolchildren," and "Health and Character in Education." He also carried out studies of "mental fatigue" in grammar schools in Lynchburg and Roanoke; in 1915–1916 he conducted a study of school recesses. Together with University of Virginia medical faculty, Heck gave demonstrations on the value and methods of school medical inspections in Manassas, Orange, and Prince William counties.[45]

Peabody Hall

Alderman campaigned vigorously for funds for a new building in which to house the education school, dedicated, in Alderman's words, to the purpose of training "men capable of carrying forward this work of education in this State and in the South." He continued, "while scholarship is the precious stuff out of which a teacher must be made, technical training in administration, in the history and principles of education, and in the whole problem of adjusting education to the needs of a free people, will be necessary for the equipment of a highly trained expert in educational work."[46] In his 1911–1912 annual report, Alderman proudly cited accomplishments of the year, including growing University enrollments and a $40,000 gift from the Peabody Education Fund—money that was put toward building Peabody Hall.[47]

Architects Ferguson, Calrow, and Taylor met with the University's building committee to select the location of the building, set to be called Peabody Hall, in 1912. Alderman emphasized the importance of placing it west of the Lawn and designing a building with a large temple portico, echoing Jefferson's original academical village designs. "It is almost a necessity," he wrote, "to make an architectural assertion that the [education] department is of equal rank and dignity with any other department of the University and that we do and should of right give it a situation which proclaims this fact."[48] As an indication of his commitment to the school of education, Alderman moved his presidential offices into the new building, finished in 1914.[49] So proud was Alderman of the legacy of this building, he wrote Bruce Payne in 1926, answering a question about the usefulness of the Peabody Education Fund to the University of Virginia:

> In my opinion, the gift of $40,000.00 from the Peabody Education Fund made possible our present Education Building [and] has enabled the University to render a larger

Summer School address
to students, 1917

Summer School

Building on the School of Methods, which had first operated in 1898 and had developed into a full-fledged summer arm of the Curry School, the University of Virginia formally established a summer school in 1919. From this juncture, the summer student population expanded from just school administrators and teachers seeking certification to include students from other schools in the University.[1] Virginia was the first school in the South to dovetail a summer quarter into its official academic year and to offer Arts and Sciences summer courses equivalent in credit to those offered during the normal academic year. Among summer students enrolled in 1920, every county in the state was represented, approximately a third enrolled in courses leading to teacher certification or renewal.[2] Enrollments grew fast in the 1920s, often exceeding 2,500, mostly public school teachers working toward a bachelor's degree.[3]

By the summer of 1923, according to one scholar, the school ranked seventh in enrollment among U.S. summer schools. An outside observer reported that "the majority of students are teachers equipping themselves for more efficient and higher service in their schools and communities" and predicted that Summer School would prove to represent "untold value in the elevation of standards of content and efficiency in the elementary schools and colleges of Virginia and the nation."[4] An expanded Summer School also made it possible to "confer degrees upon women students of the summer session who meet the entrance requirements of the University and complete satisfactorily the requirements for such a degree."[5]

Charles Maphis directed the Summer School until his death in 1937; George Zehmer held the position from 1938 until 1951. World War II brought Summer School to a temporary close, but University faculty took their courses on the road to Mary Washington College, where summer classes were still offered.[6] Lindley Stiles, dean of the School of Education, assumed the role of Summer Session director in 1952, a move to gain more education faculty influence over the courses taught. To make Summer School more accessible to teachers, Stiles shortened the term to six weeks. He maintained a separate Summer School budget and reported directly to the president of the university.[7]

In 1956, when Ralph Cherry assumed the Curry School's deanship, he also took on leadership of the Summer School, continuing in that post until his retirement in 1974. From the onset, the Summer School was to be self-supporting in its instructional costs, but by 1972, Cherry had to limit course offerings to those that produced income.[8] While historically the position of Summer School director was held by Curry School faculty, including Alton Taylor—who became director in 1974—now each school in the university appoints a summer chair, responsible for courses, budget, and teaching staff.

Under Taylor's twenty-nine-year leadership, the Summer School expanded its offerings and increased its enrollments, especially in the College of Arts and Sciences. By 2002, 4,453 students from all schools in the university were enrolled in summer courses, and 480 students received undergraduate degrees that August.[9]

Today the Summer School's missions include supplementing academic-year course offerings, allowing fulfillment of degree requirements, and "extending access to the resources of the University to students enrolled in other colleges or universities, rising high school juniors and seniors, and lifelong learners."[10] Ninety percent of those enrolled in Summer Session programs are matriculated students at the University. In the winter of 2005, a new J[anuary]-term was added under the auspices of the Summer Session office, offering students a two-week term as yet another way to expedite their academic progress.[11]

Outdoor lecture during Summer School, ca. 1915

> service than the gift of any similar amount received. . . . Without this building or a similar one it would never have been possible to organize and develop and Department of Education. . . . It has served as an object lesson in school architecture to thousands of teachers and administrators who come to us from year to year.[50]

Alderman noted as well that the Summer School could not have developed further without Peabody Hall.

In April 1914 *College Topics* described the new education building, rapidly nearing completion on its site opposite the West Range, as a "model building, as far as construction, furnishings and hygienic comport." The article described four large classrooms with private offices attached to each for "the use of 4 professors who will constitute the Educational Faculty next year." An "interesting feature" reported of the ground floor assembly was a built-in fireproof space where a "lantern for showing stereopticon views and moving pictures will be permanently installed. A permanent screen will also be kept on readiness for all illustrated lectures in recognition of the fact that moving pictures have a great educational as well as amusement value."[51]

Charles Maphis stated, "The erection of this new building shows the continually growing recognition of teaching as a profession as distinct and separate as law, engineering, or medicine." He believed that "the Department of Education in the University [would] be a thoroughly professional school when it moves into the new building next year," presenting a model for all teachers passing through it.[52] Once in use, though, the building's one flaw was discovered. A newly designed ventilation system worked so well that aromas wafted in from the nineteenth-century anatomical laboratory to the west, known as "Stiff Hall" for the cadavers used for medical school dissections. Occupants of Peabody breathed a sigh of relief when the building, by then a storeroom, was demolished in the 1950s to make way for Newcomb Hall.[53]

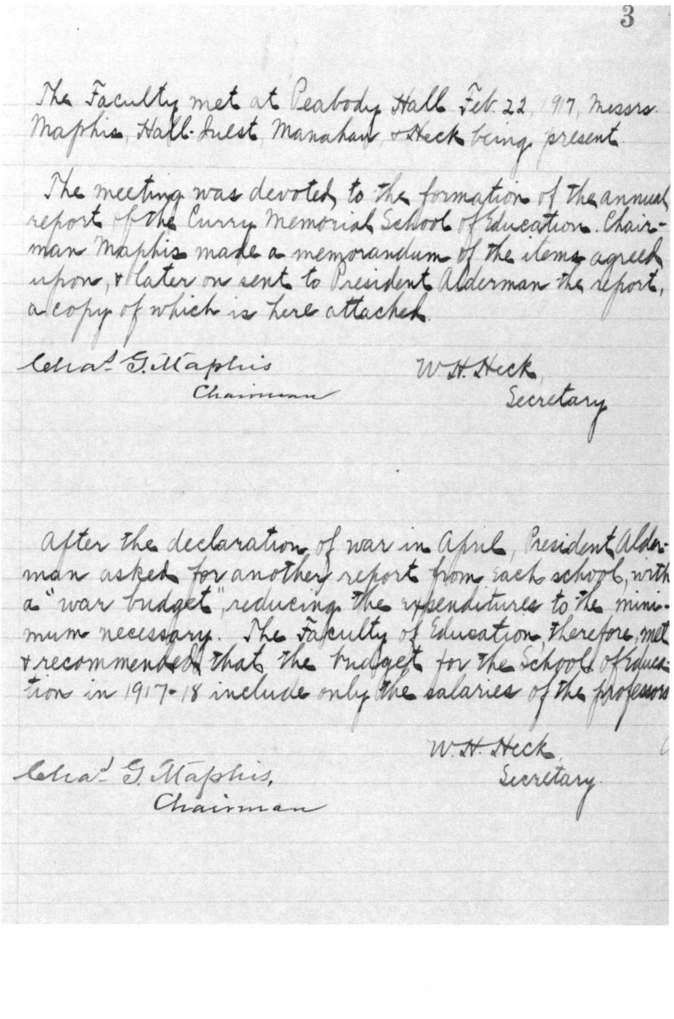
3

The Faculty met at Peabody Hall Feb. 22, '17, Messrs. Maphis, Hall-Quest, Manahan & Heck being present.

The meeting was devoted to the formation of the annual report of the Curry Memorial School of Education. Chairman Maphis made a memorandum of the items agreed upon, & later on sent to President Alderman the report, a copy of which is here attached.

Chas. G. Maphis, Chairman — W. H. Heck, Secretary

After the declaration of war in April, President Alderman asked for another report from each school, with a "war budget," reducing the expenditures to the minimum necessary. The Faculty of Education, therefore, met & recommended that the budget for the School of Education in 1917-18 include only the salaries of the professors.

W. H. Heck, Secretary — Chas. G. Maphis, Chairman

Curry faculty minutes, 1917

To honor the opening of Peabody Hall, the Curry Memorial School of Education published a catalog announcing course offerings illustrated by photographs of the new education building.[54] The introduction cited the progress of the last nine years, saying that the "activities of the school have been in five directions: class instruction, inspection of high schools, management of the summer school, a school of hygiene campaign, and organization of a University Extension Lecture Series." The catalog advertised eight courses related to high school teaching and educational administration, announced the availability of a "general academic degree," and described the Bureau of Appointments, a service open to all members of the University community.

"The use of the splendid Education building for the first time this year greatly facilitated the work of administration and relieved the congestion in the classrooms and enabled the work to be done with greater ease than ever before," wrote Charles Maphis in his 1914 annual report to the president. More teachers were pursuing advanced courses, and the Summer School was bringing high school teachers from Virginia and the rest of the South into closer personal contact with University faculty members. "These high school teachers, who are largely responsible for directing their students to the higher institutions," commented Maphis, "go away from here feeling a sense of loyalty and devotion which causes them to recommend it to their students."[55]

Clarifying the Curriculum

In 1916 the faculty numbered four, each holding a "chair" that represented a division of the school's offerings: Charles Maphis in secondary education, Harry Heck in education, Alfred Hall-Quest in psychology and principles of teaching, and a newly appointed faculty member, John Levi Manahan, in educational administration. The entrance requirement for the School of Education was the successful completion of one year of college. The course offerings changed little over the first nine years—four or five courses for graduates and undergraduates, including Heck's in school hygiene and Maphis's in secondary education and educational administration. The faculty also focused much attention on developing extension and summer school programs.[56] In 1913 Heck changed his Principles of Education course to Evolution, Heredity and Education.[57] When Alfred Hall-Quest joined the faculty in 1914, he introduced not only a course on teaching techniques but also one on Psychology of Biography, which included an analysis of "the qualities of greatness" and met "either in Peabody Hall or at his home."[58]

In the 1916 catalog, the opening "Purpose of the School of Education" reiterated the goals of providing both professional training for teachers and others in public education as well as more general "cultural background" courses:

> In the rapid development of educational science and the resulting attention given to the improvement of the several phases of public education, it is important that all who are interested in the growth of this great agency of democracy, generally or professionally, be given ample opportunity to study its underlying principles, organization, and most practical applications.[59]

Classes met in "handsome Peabody Hall, designed and equipped for the growing needs of the School of Education," while "observation and practice teaching will be provided for in city and county schools." A "wide range of courses" for the professional training of teachers and public school administration composed "one curriculum leading to the degree of B.S. in Education and one curriculum leading to a teacher's certificate only." Additionally, "Saturday courses in any subject offered in the School of Education will be arranged for teachers in service, if requested by at least three teachers." The eleven courses described included Methods of Teaching and Study and a course in Elementary School Organization introduced by Manahan that year.[60]

At a meeting on January 18, 1917, the faculty recommended the "formation of a department of Education to go into effect the session of 1918–19"[61] with Maphis as chair and Heck as secretary. Although faculty members wrote an annual report in February 1917, America's entry into World War I in April meant that it had to be modified for publication, so the report just listed

The Bureau of Appointments

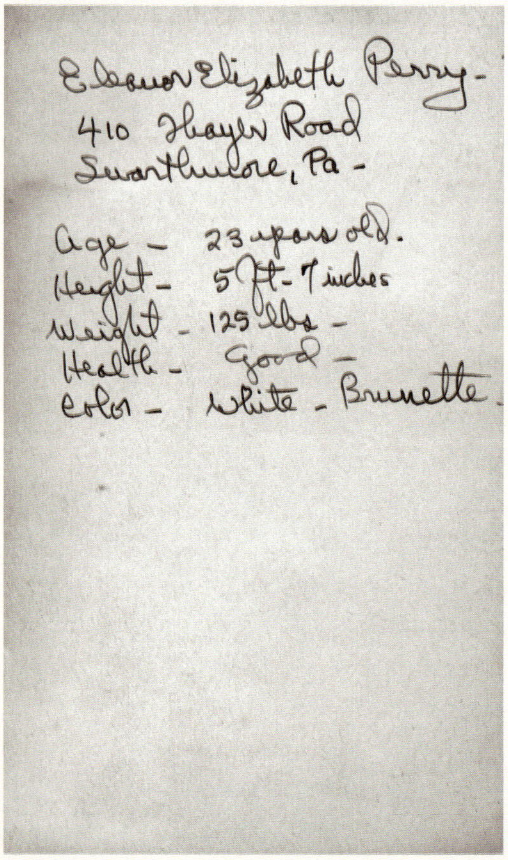

Photograph, front and back, enclosed with an application sent to Bureau of Appointments

Once founded, the school of education established the Bureau of Appointments as a way to help students find employment: an office "through which positions are secured, not only for students of the School of Education but for students in other departments where they are known to be fitted to fill the vacancies reported."[1] The Bureau expanded its mission quickly, as the demand for teachers was greater than the supply. During the 1920s and 1930s, the Bureau placed candidates for teaching and administrative positions, helping on average sixty people out of two hundred secure positions listed yearly, most secondary school teaching positions.[2]

George Zehmer headed the Bureau for many years, with Arthur Jarman serving as secretary. By 1945 the name of the office changed to Teacher Placement. Beginning in 1946, Frank Lankford directed the Teacher Placement Office and in his six-year tenure expanded its services throughout the University. In 1960, under Dean Ralph Cherry's leadership, a Division of Teacher Placement and Field Services was created under the auspices of the executive office for the Virginia School Boards Association, directed by George Holmes and then James Bash through the late 1960s. The division incorporated a variety of activities including advising the superintendents' study groups and coordinating the activities of the Curry School's newly formed alumni association, in addition to arranging teaching and administrative job placements.

By 1976, the services of this office became part of the University-wide Office of Career Services and Planning, with the needs of Curry School students coordinated by an education placement officer. The University Career Services office today continues to provide many services for Curry students, including information about writing resumes, programs on interviewing, and access to job postings in Virginia and beyond. A key service provided by this office, in coordination with the Curry School, is the Educators Expo, a two-day event held every winter for teachers, administrators, school counselors, and other education-related job seekers. In 2005, 117 districts from thirteen states and other organizations with national and overseas placement opportunities attended the fair.[3]

faculty salaries. Students completing the B.S. degree would receive the Professional Collegiate Certificate. Those who did not could take a two-year course leading to a Teacher's Diploma and Certificate. Courses elected in education could count toward a "cultural degree" awarded in the College of Arts and Sciences.

The faculty met intermittently during the years of World War I, and in May 1919 restated their resolution that the Curry Memorial School of Education be reorganized as a Department of Education and that an "announcement be prepared at once in order that plans may be perfected for effective work during the next semester." The faculty decreased during the academic year 1918–1919 with Manahan's leave for service in the military and Harry Heck's untimely death from influenza on January 4, 1919. William Smithey joined the department that year, starting a long and fruitful career as a professor of secondary education.

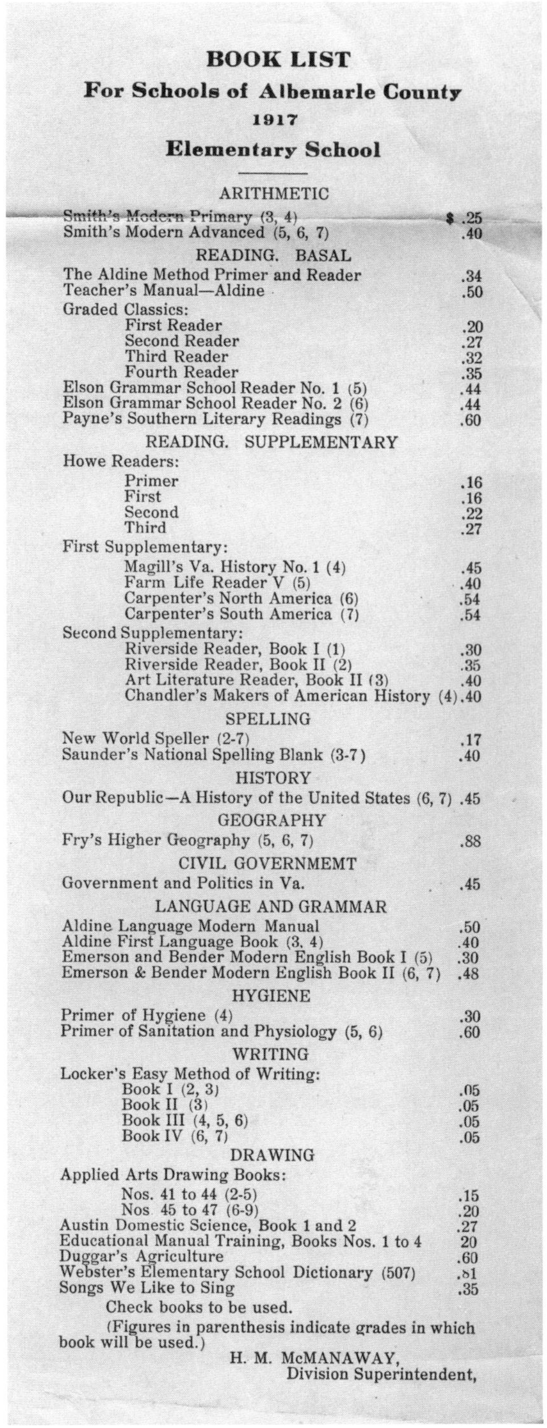

BOOK LIST

For Schools of Albemarle County

1917

Elementary School

ARITHMETIC

Smith's Modern Primary (3, 4)	$ .25
Smith's Modern Advanced (5, 6, 7)	.40
READING. BASAL	
The Aldine Method Primer and Reader	.34
Teacher's Manual—Aldine	.50
Graded Classics:	
First Reader	.20
Second Reader	.27
Third Reader	.32
Fourth Reader	.35
Elson Grammar School Reader No. 1 (5)	.44
Elson Grammar School Reader No. 2 (6)	.44
Payne's Southern Literary Readings (7)	.60
READING. SUPPLEMENTARY	
Howe Readers:	
Primer	.16
First	.16
Second	.22
Third	.27
First Supplementary:	
Magill's Va. History No. 1 (4)	.45
Farm Life Reader V (5)	.40
Carpenter's North America (6)	.54
Carpenter's South America (7)	.54
Second Supplementary:	
Riverside Reader, Book I (1)	.30
Riverside Reader, Book II (2)	.35
Art Literature Reader, Book II (3)	.40
Chandler's Makers of American History (4)	.40
SPELLING	
New World Speller (2-7)	.17
Saunder's National Spelling Blank (3-7)	.40
HISTORY	
Our Republic—A History of the United States (6, 7)	.45
GEOGRAPHY	
Fry's Higher Geography (5, 6, 7)	.88
CIVIL GOVERNMEMT	
Government and Politics in Va.	.45
LANGUAGE AND GRAMMAR	
Aldine Language Modern Manual	.50
Aldine First Language Book (3, 4)	.40
Emerson and Bender Modern English Book I (5)	.30
Emerson & Bender Modern English Book II (6, 7)	.48
HYGIENE	
Primer of Hygiene (4)	.30
Primer of Sanitation and Physiology (5, 6)	.60
WRITING	
Locker's Easy Method of Writing:	
Book I (2, 3)	.05
Book II (3)	.05
Book III (4, 5, 6)	.05
Book IV (6, 7)	.05
DRAWING	
Applied Arts Drawing Books:	
Nos. 41 to 44 (2-5)	.15
Nos 45 to 47 (6-9)	.20
Austin Domestic Science, Book 1 and 2	.27
Educational Manual Training, Books Nos. 1 to 4	20
Duggar's Agriculture	.60
Webster's Elementary School Dictionary (507)	.81
Songs We Like to Sing	.35

Check books to be used.

(Figures in parenthesis indicate grades in which book will be used.)

H. M. McMANAWAY,
Division Superintendent,

A Degree-Granting Department

President Alderman's search for someone to head the School of Education continued through the construction of Peabody Hall. In 1916 he offered the position of professor of educational administration to John Levi Manahan, a young Harvard University graduate on the faculty of Miami University of Ohio.[62] In a letter of recommendation, Paul Hanus at Harvard called Manahan "a man of excellent personal qualities and of unusual ability and industry" who "also possesses marked ability as an executive" and is "a promising research man."[63]

In 1919, five thousand copies of an announcement of the Curry Memorial Department of Education were prepared by Professors Manahan and Maphis and distributed. It included passages on the department's history and purpose, on Peabody Hall ("a model of excellence [and] one of the best-equipped buildings"), on the newly founded Heck Memorial Library, and on "Observation and Directed Teaching." Nineteen course offerings were listed. The announcement also stated that "arrangements have been made whereby students in Education will do observation work and directed teaching in the City Schools under close supervision by the City Superintendent of Schools and the Education faculty."[64]

The General Assembly enacted a bill in 1918 authorizing the University of Virginia to offer 119 scholarships to Virginia residents, providing "tuition in the college, room rent, light, heat and attendance free of charge." The University's Board of Visitors amended the scholarship requirements, specifying that recipients would be expected to work as administrative officers or teachers in Virginia's public school system two out of the four years following graduation.[65] Initially, the scholarships were awarded to all those who applied. Scholarships were awarded into the 1930s, when the initiative ended.[66]

Student presentation, McGuffey School, Charlottesville, 1917

On January 12, 1920, the Board of Visitors moved "that the request of the Curry Memorial School of Education for authority to organize said school into a Department, coordinate with the other professional departments of the University, with power to confer appropriate professional degrees be granted."[67] The Curry School had achieved the level of professionalism already enjoyed by other schools at the University. In 1920 two students received the first degrees granted in education: one a bachelor of science, the other a master of science.[68]

The State of Education Nationwide

In the same spirit with which he founded Virginia's Curry Memorial School of Education, Edwin A. Alderman played a significant role in university schools of education nationwide. For the General Education Board—a foundation formed to aid education "without distinction of race, sex, or creed"—Alderman surveyed seventy-eight teachers, scholars, and administrators in 1917 and found that the "prevailing conception of liberal education needs to include no small amount of the large heritage of knowledge now technically termed education."[69] The report emphasized the importance of research in education schools, exposing students to "experiments in education and how to adapt these results to the problems of the classroom." Professors of education ought to provide advice on all matters relating to school buildings, school administration, school management, and classroom management. A department of education should be able to bridge the gap between practice and theory, maintaining a "bureau of information" or an educational clearinghouse to promote sound educational legislation and advance the wisest educational practice along administrative and managerial lines.[70] In Alderman's opinion, "the school or college of education in a university should be a professional school like the schools of medicine, engineering, and law" and "should aim to prepare young men and women of liberal culture for leadership in scientific educational work." Alderman granted, however, that "what is deemed scientific or valid in education may, of course, change with time."[71]

Alderman's report emphasized the importance of "observation and practical work in Departments of Education," noting that all his respondents considered on-site experience and research necessary to teacher training: "Practical work or practice teaching as it is sometimes untactfully called, and experimentation are necessary adjuncts of a professional school for the training of teachers." He recommended cooperative arrangements among schools of education and public schools, suggesting that a university department of education should possess "a school of its own, not necessarily a model school, but simply one in which it may define and exemplify its ideals, and wherein opportunity for minute studies of educational processes may be immediately at hand." This General Education Board report represented the views of leading educators of the day and laid the groundwork for further definition of education schools within universities in the 1920s. In spite of chronic health problems, Alderman continued to play an active role in developing the Curry Memorial Department of Education's curriculum, programs, and faculty recruitment of faculty until his death in 1931.[72]

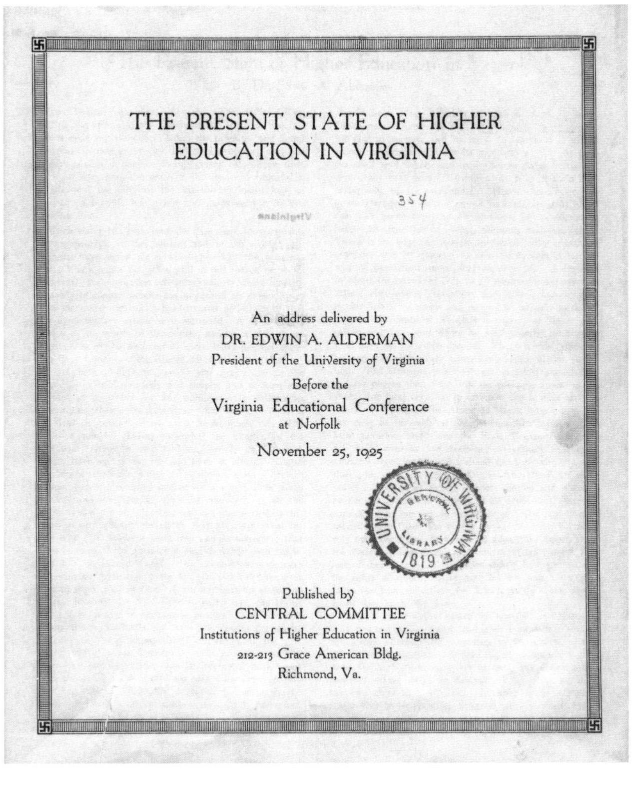
THE PRESENT STATE OF HIGHER EDUCATION IN VIRGINIA

354

An address delivered by
DR. EDWIN A. ALDERMAN
President of the University of Virginia
Before the
Virginia Educational Conference
at Norfolk
November 25, 1925

Published by
CENTRAL COMMITTEE
Institutions of Higher Education in Virginia
212-213 Grace American Bldg.
Richmond, Va.

Charlottesville public school faculty, 1916, with Superintendent James Johnson, center, in front of Midway School

CHAPTER 3

Establishing the Curry Memorial Department of Education

John L. Manahan, 1920–1930

I fully appreciate the opportunities and responsibilities of election to the position of Professor of Education at the University of Virginia and know that the welcome and cooperation accorded to me by the faculty and visitors will be of much service in making a complete success of my work. I assure you I shall do all in my power to render the highest service to the University and State.[1]

— John L. Manahan, 1916

Edwin Alderman's vision guided the early mission of the Curry Memorial School of Education. With Peabody Hall completed, education faculty and students shared their own home, and Extension and Summer School programs had space as well. President Alderman's national search for a leader of the school ended early in 1920 when John Levi Manahan, hired as professor of educational administration in 1916, was named the first dean of the Department of Education.[2] He would hold the post for twenty-nine years. Seventeen degree-seeking education students were enrolled when Manahan became dean; when he left the post, they numbered 253.[3] During those years, significant steps were taken, describing a path for the Department of Education that continues to influence programs today.

Major accomplishments in Manahan's first decade of leadership included establishing new degrees and links between teacher training and state certification and licensure, creating a collaborative teacher training program with local public schools, and facilitating access for women to study at the University. Manahan valued state professional organizations and developed especially close ties with the state superintendents. He required that faculty members participate actively in state and national professional organizations such as the Virginia Education Association. Manahan consulted with schools throughout the state, regularly met with state administrators, served for sixteen years as secretary-treasurer of the Virginia Association of Colleges, and was ultimately elected its president.

In the wake of the Great Depression, enrollments in higher education dropped nationally starting in 1930. Throughout the decade, despite lower numbers, Virginia's education

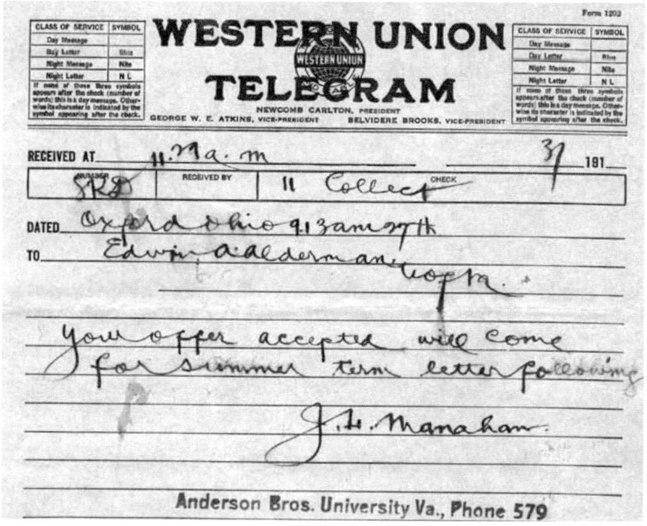
WESTERN UNION TELEGRAM

NEWCOMB CARLTON, PRESIDENT

GEORGE W. E. ATKINS, VICE-PRESIDENT BELVIDERE BROOKS, VICE-PRESIDENT

RECEIVED AT 11 Ma. m 31 191

DATED Oxford Ohio

TO Edwin A Alderman

Your offer accepted will come for summer term letter following

J. H. Manahan

Anderson Bros. University Va., Phone 579

Manahan's acceptance, March 1916

department continued to prepare administrators and secondary teachers for schools. New initiatives, especially in speech pathology and reading, gave a focus for future directions. Between women enrolled in Summer School and students in extension programs around the state, classes continued. World War II also brought a significant dip in enrollment, and indeed Peabody Hall was used for war-related preparations for a year. Dean Manahan led the Department of Education through these hardships, finally leaving the post in 1949.

First Steps of the New Dean

The newly organized Department of Education moved quickly to address administrative issues, such as the credits needed to enter the bachelor of science degree program. Manahan reported on enrollment to Alderman in late September 1920: seventy-six students in the ten courses offered that fall, fifty-two in five undergraduate courses and twenty-four in five graduate courses. Sixteen were degree seekers, three were women, and the majority of students were taking the courses as electives toward a college degree.[4] Manahan was eager to increase departmental enrollments: receiving a telegram requesting admission on September 24, he replied, "Not too late to enter University."[5]

When Harry Heck died in 1919, Manahan and his colleagues moved to establish a library in his name. Heck's widow, Anna Seely Tuttle, donated her husband's private library, "about 2000 well-selected volumes as a nucleus," and the newly formed Education Club began a campaign to buy furniture and equipment.[6] The Heck Memorial Library was dedicated on April 15, 1921.[7] In 1937, the collection moved from Peabody Hall to Alderman Library, making it the first departmental library to join the general University collection. The Heck library move created much-needed space in Peabody Hall, and funds were appropriated for renovation. The library collection ultimately returned to the education school when Ruffner Hall opened in 1973.

As Manahan developed the department, he needed a larger staff. He asked President Alderman for additional clerical help in October 1920, having also added the Bureau of Appointments and a Bureau of Tests and Measurements.[8] He identified the department's "immediate needs" as a "demonstration and experimental school" and endowments for a department of education research, a laboratory for educational psychology, and the new library.[9]

It was already possible to earn education credits for degrees in cultural studies from the College of Arts and Sciences, but early in 1921 the faculty and dean proposed that a bachelor of arts with an education major be offered in the college. After considerable debate, the resolution was passed on November 7, 1921.[10] The first such degrees were awarded in 1923, but the number of graduates earning them is hard to discern, since they were granted through the undergraduate College of Arts and Sciences.[11]

Women in Education

Women attended Summer School at Virginia from the first session in 1907 on, but only male students in Summer School received degree credit.[12] With such a large number of women enrolled, a network was created to work for other causes. Soon Charlottesville became a center for the suffrage movement, especially in the summer months. Along with other equity issues, women pushed for the right to matriculate at the University as degree recipients.[13]

Faced with pressure to admit women, debates ensued at the University, turning on the alternatives of coeducation or a coordinate college. On January 12, 1920, the Board of Visitors passed a decision intended as a compromise to full coeducation. Women could attend the professional and graduate schools as of September: "Only women more than twenty years of age on the date of registration will be admitted and in every instance two years of college work is a prerequisite," their provisions stipulated.[14] It was also resolved that degrees could be conferred on women students who attended Summer School and met the entrance requirements of the University. A third resolution related to coeducation and Summer School organized the Curry School into an official University department with the power to confer professional degrees. With these decisions, women could now receive training and earn degrees in education at the University of Virginia.

The education department's requirements for the admission of women were set forth in the 1920 *University of Virginia Record*: with thirty hours' credit from a state college or state normal school, a student could be authorized to enter a four-year course of college work. In 1921 the education faculty amended this rule by accepting graduates from a standard two-year normal school provided they had taught successfully for two years.[15] The next year, the department voted

Venable School classroom, Charlottesville, 1931

Nursing Education

Student nurses trained at the University of Virginia Hospital School of Nursing beginning in the fall of 1901, just as the hospital opened. The hospital's reputation for excellent medical and nursing care grew, and by 1918 both admission requirements and curriculum revisions had strengthened the program. Along with the recognition that nursing education needed improvement, many of Virginia's graduate nurses desired to create an undergraduate program in nursing education at the University. In 1923 the Graduate Nurses Association began soliciting for contributions. After several years of looking for an academic home, in the fall of 1928 the Sadie Heath Cabaniss Memorial School of Nursing Education became part of the Department of Education.

The new School of Nursing Education gained momentum as a result of efforts by the Graduate Nurses Association of Virginia (GNAV), which began in 1923 with the objective of providing graduate nursing education in the South. Concerned with the unavailability of nursing education in the South, as well as with the fact that many young nurses went north for nursing education and did not return to the South, the GNAV led a three-year fundraising drive to endow a chair of nursing named in honor of Sadie Heath Cabaniss, a pioneering Virginia nurse.[1] The GNAV presented President Alderman with a check for $50,000 in 1926 to begin the program. After several years of discussion among the faculty about where the program should be located, the Sadie Heath Cabaniss Memorial School of Nursing was opened in the Department of Education where it remained until February 1953, when a Department of Nursing Education was established.[2]

Louise Oates was appointed dean of this newly created program, and for the first few years, she struggled with its uneasy placement within the education department. Writing her in 1931, President Alderman reassured her he viewed her as a "clear-thinking, high minded woman doing your very best in a new and difficult pioneering post," adding that he would do his best to support her work in this "great undertaking" and that "we must not fail at it."[3]

The three-year program was designed to prepare administrators, teachers, supervisors, and head nurses to become nursing educators and administrators, combining courses in the Department of Education and the College of Arts and Sciences. Enrollment in the Nursing Education programs was always small and the relationship with the Department of Education somewhat uneasy; as early as 1935, the department was recommending the School of Nursing Education should be withdrawn from its administrative reach.

As of August 1953, a total of 153 B.S.N.Ed. degrees were awarded. In addition to on-Grounds courses, the school provided baccalaureate courses to more than 100 nurses in Richmond and Roanoke between 1946 and 1953.[4] The largest number of degrees were awarded in the late 1940s, when former nurses returned to school supported by the GI Bill.[5] The school was successful in meeting its goal of educating nurses who remained in the South. Many graduates became directors of schools of nursing, hospitals, and public health departments in Virginia and in other Southern states. As the quality of students enrolled in the school gained respect from faculty, an important step was taken toward recognition of the competence of women students.

Professor Oates served as the head of the Cabaniss Memorial School of Nursing Education, retiring after twenty-four years in 1952, when the nursing programs were consolidated in the School of Nursing. Lindley Stiles, then dean of the Curry School of Education, noted that "hers was never an easy assignment," as she struggled to improve the preparation of nurses engaged in educational efforts. "Upon the background of her efforts," he said, "the future of nursing education in the University of Virginia will be developed."[6]

Louise Oates, head of the Cabaniss Memorial School of Nursing Education

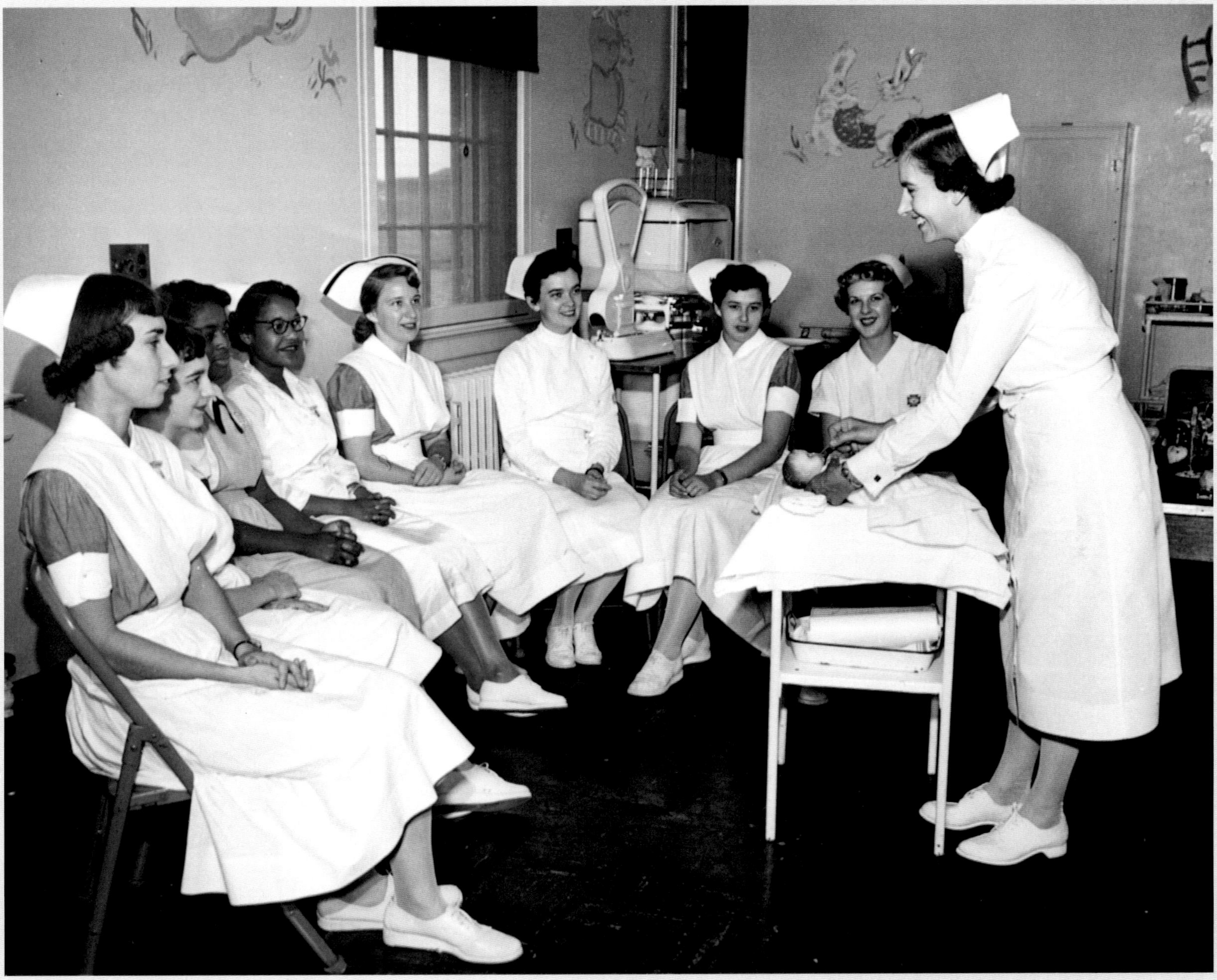

From 1928 to 1953, aspiring nursing educators enrolled in the Cabaniss Memorial School of Nursing Education, a part of the Curry Memorial Department of Education

Roberta Hollingsworth Gwathmey, Dean of Women at the University from 1934 to 1967

that twenty-five-year-old women could enter as special students even if without thirty college credit hours. These resolutions remained in effect through World War II, providing female enrollment at times when male student numbers declined. By 1925, 102 female students had enrolled in the schools or departments of education, engineering, law, medicine, architecture, commerce, chemistry, biology, and mathematics. More than half of the 102 were students in the Department of Education.[16]

Adelaide Simpson was hired by the University in 1921 as dean of women, a position critical to support for female students over the next fifty years. She soon reported that "it no longer causes a sensation for a woman to appear in a classroom or laboratory."[17] Simpson was succeeded by Mary Hamblin, then in 1934 by Roberta Hollingsworth (later Gwathmey), who held the position until 1967. As dean and active supporter for female students, Dean Gwathmey helped with academic problems and advised many young women. "Her guidance, advice, caring affected my life then and ever since," wrote one alumna, expressing a fondness shared by many.[18] In spite of Dean Simpson's early optimism, male students were far from welcoming to women into their classes. For example, a practice developed in 1928 called "stomping": Male students would stomp their feet when a woman entered a classroom or tried to speak.[19]

Education faculty acknowledged the needs of their female students, albeit somewhat grudgingly, when at a faculty meeting in July 1922 they moved that state teachers' scholarships could be awarded to women if men did not use all those made available. In 1929, again noting the particular needs of women students who wished to be teachers, Manahan specifically requested scholarships for women training as administrators in rural schools: "This, I believe, would be unusually important at this time," he wrote, "because the best women available for future rural supervisors are not in financial positions to spend the necessary time at the University to become adequately trained."[20]

In October 1923, 257 students enrolled in Department of Education courses, including seventy majors—forty men and thirty women.[21] Such swift change and growth was proving somewhat overwhelming for Manahan, who wrote President Alderman: "In the interest of my own health I feel justified in calling attention to my own heavy burden." Not only education school dean, Manahan was chair of the Bureau of Appointments, director of the Bureau of Tests and Measurements, and frequently a teacher in extension courses.

Manahan established the Bureau of Tests and Measurements in 1919 to provide tests as needed for schools. As stated in the 1920–1921 *University of Virginia Record,* faculty supervisors would train teachers in the use of testing instruments and would "direct the giving and scoring of" tests as requested, as long as "necessary traveling expenses" were covered. Bureau consultants also offered their services to school authorities interested "in the diagnosis and training of backward and gifted children," one part of their work in the field of educational psychology. The Bureau of Tests and Measurements continued to operate during Manahan's deanship.[22]

Early Women in the Department of Education

The stories from female education school students who graduated in the early years reflect their desires to become teachers and members of the University community. Some felt positive about their experiences; others felt deep disappointment with the lack of collegiality among their peers. In spite of the fact that women were a presence in education classes, there was no way to ignore their minority status in the larger University.

By 1930, 142 women had received a B.S. in Education. Through the 1940s, an average of thirty female students per year earned degrees.[1] At that time, only women over the age of twenty were allowed to enroll in the University, but many young women continued to apply for permission for waiver of the age standard throughout the 1930s, especially if they had completed the necessary coursework to qualify.

By the mid-1940s, once the coordinate relationship between the University and Mary Washington College had developed, the age requirement began to pose problems. Transfer women with two years of college credit were often not yet twenty years old. In 1951, President Darden deemed the age requirement unnecessary, and women were admitted to the professional schools on academic qualifications alone.[2] Before full coeducation at the University, close to half the degrees awarded in education went to women.[3]

"It was a well known fact that the women were resented," wrote Anne Snead, a 1940 graduate of the education department. "I was never treated rudely in any way, however."[4] Margaret Nye, a 1943 graduate, felt she never "belonged" and wrote that "UVA in the 1940s still upheld Thomas Jefferson's intent that it be a 'Gentlemen's University' and women, although accepted into the professional schools, were looked upon as interlopers by some professors, ignored, in general, by the majority of male students, and not welcome in 'The Commons.'"

Dorothy Eckford Wooster (B.S. '46), who entered the education school in 1943, describes her time at the University differently. She was one of "about 100 coeds," as she recalls, and she lived at home. There were no girls' dormitories yet, and female students from out of town had to room and board themselves. "Our social life was a different matter," she says. "With such an unbalanced ratio of girls to boys in the student body, we were never hurting for a date!" She remembers that wartime gasoline rations meant that all students walked, bicycled, or used public transportation.[5]

Members of Kappa Delta sorority including several education students, 1941

As late as the 1950s, female students continued to find the environment discouraging. "I was there to learn but found there was a pervasive negative atmosphere because of my gender—both by peers and professors," Anne C. Johns (B.S. '53) recalls.

"We women were a minority group and not too welcome by the majority of males," says Sarah Winn (B.S. '52). In the decade leading up to integration of women at the University, feelings intensified about the role of women in undergraduate life as they began to be more active in University life.

Throughout the 1920s, course offerings and degree programs expanded to support a B.S., an M.S., and a Ph.D. in education. The *Record* listed courses in education that could be taken to satisfy the cultural B.A. in the College and described the Collegiate Professional Certificate of the B.S.Ed. degree. Of the eight education degrees granted in 1922, five went to women. Of the thirty-one B.S.Ed. degrees granted in 1925, twenty-two went to women. More and more women received degrees at the end of the Summer Session as well. In 1927, twenty-five out of thirty-five degrees granted went to women, including a master of arts degree and the first master of science in education, a degree discontinued after 1937. In fact, close to half of the degrees awarded to women by the University of Virginia between 1920 and 1970—the year when women gained general undergraduate admittance—went to students in education.[23]

Between 1920 and 1927, education school enrollments grew from sixteen undergraduates and one graduate student to 105 undergraduates and thirty graduate students. Manahan had projected that the number of education graduates would exceed one hundred in June 1928, but in fact 156 students had graduated by that date.[24] Graduate degrees went primarily to those assuming administrative leadership positions in the public schools. Annual catalogs described many offerings, including a cooperative arrangement with the Albemarle and Charlottesville schools, called a "laboratory system of the Department of Education," which provided opportunities for teaching as well as for the study of school administration.[25]

The Dream of a Demonstration School

To create opportunities for students to develop teaching skills, Manahan sought a working relationship with the schools of Charlottesville and Albemarle County and also sought ways to found a demonstration school.[26] His colleague, William Smithey, had studied other laboratory schools connected with departments of education in state universities and, in April 1921, recommended that the University of Virginia follow the same "desirable organization of such work." Smithey urged a demonstration secondary school, but the faculty instead proposed a "School of Childhood"—a primary school—in Peabody Hall.[27] For the next year, Manahan attempted to raise funds, securing pledges from local donors and asking for University support from President Alderman. He wrote architect Sydney Fiske Kimball for remodeling ideas, and Kimball offered to do an initial feasibility study for no charge.[28] "For some time now we have recognized the need of a primary school as a part of a complete system of observation schools in our Department of Education," Manahan wrote in a draft of plans for the project.

> The purpose of such a school would be to afford an opportunity to school supervisors, superintendents and prospective high school principals to observe superior primary instruction by expert teachers. A careful study would be made of the capacities and needs of each pupil as an individual and appropriate methods and content employed to meet these needs . . . Estimated enrollment would be 45 pupils between the ages of 5 and 9 years for a term of 9 months.[29]

Manahan envisioned a school furnished with "modern equipment and materials." He was so optimistic that he told one interested party that "plans for a larger and more detailed program for the development of our program may occasion a delay," but he projected that the school could open in September 1923.[30]

On January 5, 1923, Manahan was disappointed. Faculty had met with President Alderman and determined "it would be unwise to attempt to launch our School of Childhood next September."[31] He continued corresponding with mothers of potential students, and in at least one case wrote that he still hoped the school would open in September 1924. The faculty continued to discuss a laboratory school into 1926, voting unanimously on November 17 to "communicate with the President of the University asking that the necessary steps be taken to set aside a site for such a school."[32] Ultimately it proved impossible to raise the necessary funds, and the faculty instead began work on cooperative schemes with the public school systems of the city and county.

"A Program of Experimental Education and Teacher-Training"

Education faculty formally designed a program for cooperation with the city of Charlottesville public schools in the spring of 1925 in a proposal authored by Professor Smithey, recommending a cooperative agreement between the University and the city for the sake of using Charlottesville schools as training grounds for education students. It was important to Manahan that the agreement be made by the University, not by the education department,[33] and that a link with Charlottesville's Lane High School and the other city schools be formalized in the person of a University faculty member, jointly hired by the University and the Charlottesville School Board.

Two types of cooperation were proposed: "one with reference to practice teaching and observation for students in education, and the other with reference to cooperation between the city school authorities and the professors of education at the University concerning professional matters."[34] A designated faculty member would supervise students, teach a secondary education methods course, and work with the principal to provide instructional supervision for the high

School room in Winchester, Virginia, 1920s

William Lambeth (back row, with mustache) and University gymnastics team, ca. 1896

Physical Education

The seeds for a program in physical education were laid in 1925 when Dr. William Lambeth wrote President Alderman, requesting permission to teach courses designed for students interested in coaching football and basketball. Lambeth, known as the father of athletics at the University of Virginia, received an M.D. degree from the University in 1892 and a Ph.D. in 1901. He joined the medical faculty as a professor of hygiene in 1898 and subsequently became director of athletics and physical education, then superintendent of buildings and grounds.[1]

Lambeth's request came just after the education faculty had approved a curriculum leading to a bachelor of science degree for teachers of health and physical education in 1923. At the time, other institutions in the state were shaping programs, combining health with physical education, but such programs did not develop in the University of Virginia's education department for another ten years. In 1937 a physical education program for prospective athletic coaches and intramural activity directors was approved by the Department of Education faculty.[2] It began the following year under the direction of Professor Norton Pritchitt.

On the faculty from 1938 to 1951, Pritchitt developed a series of tests to judge student fitness and offered undergraduate programs for body building, handball, boxing, acrobatics, and basketball.[3] In the fall of 1942, due in part to World War II, the University passed a requirement that "all physically fit male students of the College take physical exercise under the direction or with the approval of the School of Physical Education for a minimum of one hour per day at least five days a week."[4] The success of these offerings brought requests for more courses and led to a curriculum for a bachelor's degree in physical education, established at the war's end in 1945.[5]

Three faculty members who joined the Department of Education in the mid-1940s were to have considerable influence in developing physical educational programs. Raymond Heidloff and Lawrence Ludwig taught courses in health education, drivers' education, physical education, and recreation through the early 1970s. Edward (Butch) Slaughter directed intramural programs during this time, among numerous other athletic responsibilities. At one point, Slaughter had two offices, one in Memorial Gymnasium and one in Peabody Hall. Slaughter also served as assistant to the dean of the summer quarter. For that job, one of his responsibilities was to monitor campus fraternities, which earned him the informal title of "campus cop."[6]

The first degrees in physical education were awarded in 1948, and a total of forty-seven bachelor of physical education degrees were awarded by the Curry School between 1948 and 1955.[7] In 1951 the faculty voted to discontinue the degree, saying that all education students should earn a bachelor of science degree.[8] That same year, the programs of health, physical education, and intramurals shifted into the Curry School of Education from the College of Arts and Sciences. Dean Lindley Stiles saw in the move an opportunity to "integrate more completely the work in this area with the general

Edward K. Slaughter, known as "Butch," 1972

program of studies designed for the preparation of teachers for public schools."[9] University President Colgate Darden echoed the sentiment, saying that the transfer of intramural activities to the school of education would ensure the University's "first rate work" in physical education.[10]

The physical education programs continued to develop until 1967, when they became part of the newly formed Department of Curriculum and Instruction.[11] Dean Cyphert suggested that physical education be eliminated in 1969, and Slaughter fought to save the Curry School's health and physical education program, quoting Thomas Jefferson: "Give me about two hours every day to exercise, for health must not be sacrificed to learning. A strong body makes the mind strong." Butch Slaughter retired in 1973 after forty-two years on the University's athletic staff and sixteen years in charge of intramurals. At the time, the intramural program was said to be the best in the Atlantic Coast Conference, with thousands of participants in many sports.[12]

Patrick Bird, hired in 1972, became the head of the Department of Health, Physical Education, and Recreation. In 1975 the department received approval for a doctor of education degree, and the word "recreation" was eliminated from the department name. One of the first faculty members Bird hired was Linda Bunker, a specialist in motor learning and sport psychology. The recipient of many academic awards, Bunker served as director of the Motor Learning Laboratory, chair of the Department of Health and Physical Education, associate dean of student affairs, and then associate dean of graduate programs and admissions for more than twenty years.

A master's degree in athletic training was initiated in 1975 when Joe Gieck joined the department from the university athletics program. The nation's first doctoral program in sports medicine began in 1976. Both programs were supported by the University's director of athletics and the medical school's Department of Orthopaedics. With the School of Medicine, an exercise physiology and a cardiac rehabilitation program was jointly initiated.[13] The interdisciplinary projects allowed faculty members to collaborate with faculty from medicine, biomedical engineering, psychology, and nursing.

By 1981 the University of Virginia's Department of Health and Physical Education was nationally recognized. The graduate program was one of seven certified by the National Athletic Trainers Association, cited as the "best graduate program with a strong academic and research orientation." The undergraduate program was ranked in the top one percent in a national study of 236 schools and faculty.[14] In 1985, the department's programs were consolidated into the Department of Human Services. Today, as part of that department, the Kinesiology program area offers graduate degrees in Adapted Physical Education, Athletic Training and Sports Medicine, Exercise Physiology, Motor Learning, Sport Psychology, and Teacher Education, as well as an undergraduate degree in Sports Medicine.

school faculty. It was hoped that the school could provide a setting for students in educational psychology and school administration as well. The Charlottesville schools accepted this proposal.[35] The Department of Education proposed a similar arrangement with the Albemarle County schools beginning in the fall of 1926. These partnerships continued through the 1950s.

In 1928 the education faculty endorsed a program for "Maintaining and Developing a Superior Public School System" through cooperative programs with both the city and Albemarle County.[36] Part of the plan was to combine the two systems into one school division with its own school board. Manahan's correspondence with Alderman reflects that all was not working smoothly, but that he still had faith that this "great co-operative plan" could provide a "great educational laboratory for the improvement of all phases of school work, including the training of teachers, principals, supervisors, superintendents, and college teachers of Education."[37] Alderman proposed that the General Education Board fund the venture, resulting in $20,000 a year for two years, beginning in 1928.[38] After that, expenses were covered jointly by the University and the school systems, but for many years the publications from the Curry Department proudly announced program funding from the General Education Board.[39]

Curry professors of secondary education were actively involved in community schools for many years, teaching classes, supervising students, and carrying out research on instructional approaches. Edward Alvey's description of the early years of this collaboration provide a glimpse of the ways in which these positions evolved;[40] additionally, much of the work of these early teaching ventures was reported in the *Journal of Secondary Education,* published by the department for the next twenty years.

"Dr. Swindler's practice teachers" in the 1945 yearbook of Charlottesville's Lane High School

Robert Swindler joined the faculty as a professor of social studies, maintaining a joint teaching position with Charlottesville's Lane High School through 1953. Professor Arthur Jarman began a thirty-year association with the School of Education when he was appointed principal of Lane High School for the 1929–1930 year. He then taught English and worked as a "critic teacher," or supervisor, in the Charlottesville schools. Henry Acker, professor of school supervision and elementary school supervisor starting in 1929, became Albemarle County's director of instruction in 1941, a position he held until his death in 1944,[41] when Curry faculty member Francis Lankford assumed the position and led the county consolidation of seven high schools during the late 1940s.[42] The collaboration between these school systems and the Curry Memorial Department of Education formed the basis of student teaching through the 1950s.[43]

While local collaborations enhanced both Curry offerings and Charlottesville-Albemarle schools, the University's education department proudly reported the growth and improvement of secondary schools across the Commonwealth during the first twenty-five years of President Alderman's influence. In a report on the status of high school education in Virginia, William Smithey cited the changes from 1904 to

1930: In 1904, Virginia made "an inadequate gesture" toward public education, with fewer than ten high schools offering a four-year course of study free of charge to the public and with no state standards in place. By 1930, Smithey reported, there were 615 high schools across Virginia, 417 of which were accredited. Those schools graduated 8,149 students total in 1930; 45 percent of those students intended to go on to higher education.[44]

Extension Programs

In 1915 the Bureau of Extension was formally organized with Charles Maphis, professor of secondary education, as director. The first extension courses for college credit were offered in 1919.[45] In 1920 a University Extension Office opened in Richmond, and regional programs appeared in Lynchburg and Danville by 1924, Roanoke by 1926, and Petersburg by 1929.[46] In 1922, the name changed to the Extension Division. Maphis headed the Bureau, then the Division of Extension, until 1925, all the while continuing to teach education courses in the department. This Education-Extension connection continued in the appointment of George Zehmer, also an education faculty member who served as director then dean of the Division of Extension until his 1958 retirement.[47]

The University awarded extension programs their first appropriation, totaling $10,000, in 1925. Five years later, a staff of eleven managed extension activities serving thirty-five communities.[48] One outgrowth of extension program expansion was the Institute of Public Affairs, initiated in 1927 by Professor Maphis and President Alderman as a forum to discuss state and local governmental problems and their underlying economic and social questions. The institute grew rapidly, hosting national and international leaders including United States President Theodore Roosevelt, and its programs quickly became regular offerings at the University.[49]

Extension Division programs were constantly evolving. In the spring of 1934, a division committee sought clear rules for the role of extension credits in a University degree. The academic faculty determined that no more than one quarter of the credits required for a bachelor's degree could be earned in extension work; that students seeking such credits must satisfy regular entrance requirements; that extension courses offered for credit were to be approved by the appropriate school or department; and that degree credit would be granted only for course work equivalent to that offered regularly at the University. The majority of extension courses recommended for credit were in education; the majority of students attending between 1931 and 1934 were teachers from Virginia.[50]

The Bureau of Teaching Materials, another link between Education and Extension, began in 1928 as a repository for visual educational materials. By 1942, at the request of the Virginia State Board of Education, five regional bureaus had been established around the state, with greatly expanded lending collections, primarily for public schools. The Charlottesville bureau was housed in the Curry School, and under Dean Stiles was renamed the Bureau of Audio-Visual Materials.[51] Through the 1960s the bureau expanded, loaning textbooks to teachers and extension students. The bureau also built a collection of several thousand films, provided slide machines for schoolteachers and University faculty, and offered technical support and instruction.[52] Directed by Donald Shoemaker between 1969 and 1973, the bureau moved to Ruffner Hall in 1973, to Zehmer Hall in the 1980s when it was downsized, and closed soon thereafter, as public schools

Extension Division American literature class, 1930s

and universities assumed responsibility for their own collections and equipment in the growing field of audiovisual teaching.[53]

By the early 1950s, the Extension Division served 101 communities and administered two two-year colleges, Clinch Valley College in Wise and George Mason University in Fairfax, both founded in 1950.[54] Education courses still dominated division offerings, providing nonresidential instruction for those seeking teaching certificates as well as for those already teaching. When Education Dean Lindley Stiles was appointed Summer School director in 1950, it further reinforced the Curry School's presence in the Extension Division. When the Board of Visitors changed the division's name to School of General Studies in 1961, Ralph Cherry, dean of education, informed his faculty that "each member should expect to teach an extension class as part of their teaching load." Extension teaching was a very important part of the School of Education, he explained, as many prospective students were first contacted in these classes.[55] In 1971 the School of General Studies received yet another new name. Now called the School of Continuing Education, in honor of lifelong learning, it moved into a building large enough to encompass its many activities and named to honor the legacy of George Zehmer.[56]

Under the direction of education faculty members, two-year, off-Grounds master's degree programs in Counselor Education, Curriculum and Instruction, Social Foundations, and Administration were designed in the early 1970s. The first off-Grounds master's degree program, within the Department of Counselor Education, was approved in the fall of 1972 to begin in Windsor and London, Ontario, Canada.[57] Soon after that, a Curriculum and Instruction program began in Abingdon, Virginia, designed for sixty elementary education students who were required to complete comprehensive examinations graded by Curry faculty and eligible to graduate in Charlottesville with their peers.[58] The program included a four-week summer laboratory school, where students worked with elementary or middle-school children. During the next sixteen years, in locations around the state, up to 750 teachers graduated from this program.[59] The program was also offered in Roanoke and received high praise from the city council in 1987, which passed a resolution commending a "unique feature" of the program: Faculty and teachers worked with children in specially operated summer programs "in the locale" and thereby provided "a unique opportunity in cooperative fashion for designing and delivering an innovative curriculum for elementary schoolchildren."[60]

The Administration and Supervision program in Northern Virginia followed the Abingdon program, offering M.Ed. and Ed.S. degrees; it was the first to offer off-Grounds Ed.D. degrees.[61] These programs offered students the opportunity to complete required coursework necessary for the state administration and supervision endorsement. A master of education degree program, located in Quantico and designed especially for the Federal Bureau of Investigation, was initiated in 1978.[62]

The administrative link with the Curry School changed with the appointment of the chemistry department's James Cole as dean of the School of General Studies, an appointment he held from 1958 to 1968. Following Cole, the position was held by Andre de Porry, who had previously directed the Lynchburg and Central Virginia centers; by Bruce Nelson, from 1974 to 1977; and by Adele Robertson, who served through 1986. Thomas McKeon served as interim dean following Robertson's death. In 1988 Phillip Nowlen became dean of the school, now known as the Division of Continuing Education; he was followed by Sondra Stallard, appointed dean in 1996.

When Frank L. Hereford assumed the office of University president in 1974, he refocused University efforts on residential education. The Board of Visitors redefined the School of Continuing Education as a division and rescinded its degree-granting status. The Division of Continuing Education maintained its outreach efforts throughout the state, with continuing faculty discussions about academic oversight of its courses.[63] During this time, the Curry School remained a significant part of the division's operations and was especially influential with TEMPO, a reading outreach program begun in the 1980s through which several thousand teachers attained graduate credit at the same time they helped make significant advances in children's reading assessments.

The pendulum swung back toward commitment to educational outreach under the leadership of John T. Casteen III, who became president in 1990. A task force chaired by Curry School Dean David Breneman affirmed the need to offer University courses to citizens throughout the state and suggested careful study of a possible autonomous degree-granting school.

President Casteen observed in 1998 that the University had no way to offer bachelor's degree programs to part-time adult students, which prompted further discussions about the Division of Continuing Education. In 2000, the University of Virginia established the School of Continuing and Professional Studies as its tenth academic school, with Sondra Stallard as dean.[64] "We have made it possible for adults to earn master's and doctoral degrees from the Curry School of Education, the School of Architecture, and the School of Engineering and Applied Science," Stallard wrote in 2000. "We will continue such partnerships in the future."[65] As of 2005, eighty-two students had received the bachelor of interdisciplinary studies degree through a new continuing education program directed by Donna Plasket.[66] By the early twenty-first century, degree programs in engineering, mathematics, physics, reading, school administration and supervision/educational leadership, social foundations of education, instruction administration, and special education were offered through the School of Professional and Continuing Studies. Today courses are offered on-site at seven regional centers and at schools, businesses, and government agency offices, as well as through distance learning technology.

Living Up to the Legacy in Hard Times

Dean Manahan's 1929–1930 annual report reflected faculty publications as well as ways in which the department was responding to the state's educational needs. Summer school attendees, male and female, could now earn degrees. Three full summer quarters or their equivalent were deemed the residence requirement, and, according to the *University Record*, "the diplomas awarded at the close of the Summer Quarter are the same in character and value as those given at any other time."[67] By August 1930 nearly 300 education degrees, including 56 master's degrees, had been conferred.[68] The Department of Education's efforts to provide services for Virginia's future and practicing teachers and educational administrators were well established by the time of the Great Depression, providing a secure base through the hard times of 1930s.

Edwin Alderman, first president of the University of Virginia—a planner, dreamer, and educator whose impressive personality left its stamp on the school forever—died unexpectedly at the age of sixty-nine on April 30, 1931. John Lloyd Newcomb, dean of the engineering school since 1925, had been appointed assistant to President Alderman in 1926. He became acting president after Alderman's death and was inaugurated as president in 1933.

Newcomb brought administrative skills to the office: he had organized the University's centennial celebrations in 1921 and had represented the University in General Assembly discussions in Richmond.[69] His style was as different from Alderman's as could be. A member of the engineering faculty since 1909, Newcomb was modest and self-effacing, organized and astute financially. He took office at a time when state revenues were dropping and oversaw the University during a time of great austerity, steering through a 20 percent pay cut and other budgetary crises.[70]

John L. Newcomb, second president of the University of Virginia, 1933–1947

Enrollment in the Department of Education, as in the University as a whole, remained fairly constant through the 1930s. Extension Division offerings expanded considerably, providing education for those unable to come to Charlottesville as well as faculty employment opportunities. Requirements for admission and degrees were made more demanding, broadening degree requirements and bringing expectations in line with those of other schools. The faculty entertained the idea of offering courses in library practice. Courses in physical education greatly expanded, especially during the summer quarter.

A core faculty of six to eight taught undergraduate and graduate courses. The faculty roster often included some teachers in the public schools who were supervising student teachers, two nursing faculty, and, beginning in 1938, the University's director of athletics and physical education. William Smithey continued working with state high schools, rapidly expanding in number. He urged more collaboration with public schools, better liaisons with high school students, and broader career guidance for secondary school students.[71]

In 1931 education faculty participated in a series of radio lectures sponsored by the Extension Division and the Virginia Congress of Parents and Teachers.

Station W D B J at Roanoke, Virginia, is owned and operated by Richardson-Wayland Electrical Corporation Member Station of Columbia Broadcasting System

Broadcast live from WDBJ in Roanoke, lectures ranged in topic from "The Intellectual Development of the Child" to "Preventing Illness in Childhood" and from "Educational and Vocational Guidance" to "Teaching Habits of Thrift." It was a successful outreach effort, and the lectures were well received throughout the state.[72]

Professor Smithey and *Secondary Education in Virginia*

William Smithey, professor of secondary education, founded the quarterly journal, *Secondary Education in Virginia*, in 1927. Dean Manahan had earlier considered inaugurating a journal, which he wanted to title *The Virginia Education Research Review.* Smithey's journal filled the need that Manahan had seen. The journal was referred to as the "official organ of the Dept. of Education," and was "devoted to the encouragement of research in Virginia secondary school problems and to the reporting of research through its columns."[73]

Published quarterly through 1948 by the University's Extension Division, *Secondary Education* was inspired by the first annual meeting of the Virginia Committee for Research in Secondary Education, held at the University. As annual meetings on research in secondary education continued, the journal reported on them. The 1936 event attracted "about 200 superintendents, high school principals, teachers and students of education," according to Smithey, and included sessions standards, curriculum construction, and research findings related to instruction.[74]

The journal's appearance marked important work going on in the field of secondary education. Robert Swindler, Francis Lankford, Richard Meade, and Edward Alvey, all education faculty members, were developing units of instruction for secondary schools in social studies, mathematics, and English. *Secondary Education in Virginia* was useful in disseminating their ideas. The journal also provided yearly summaries of activities within the department. It helped connect faculty and practitioners around the state and encouraged professional collaboration as Virginia's public schools continued to develop.[75]

Administration and Supervision

From the beginning, the Curry School of Education has focused on preparing leaders for the schools of the state and the nation at all levels including building leaders, central office leaders and supervisors, and superintendents; and from its founding, the school has offered courses in educational administration and supervision. When John Manahan was hired as the first professor of school administration in 1916, a long tradition of academic concentration on issues related to educational administration began.

Forging relationships with the professional organizations that serve school administrators has been an equally important aspect of the department's mission, and over time, many of these organizations have been housed in the Curry School. Superintendents, principals, school board officials, and other professional administrators have maintained longstanding relationships with the School of Education. Two goals—to provide academic training for those desiring educational leadership roles, and to maintain working relationships with the state's professional

Teachers Preventorium

Plaque still hanging in University Hospital

In the spring of 1923, representatives of the State Board of Health and the state Teachers Association (precursor to today's Virginia Education Association) met at the University to discuss establishing a "preventorium"—a clinic and hospital unit—especially for teachers at the University of Virginia. First intended for women, if successful it would serve men as well.

The origins of this plan lay in an earlier initiative to build a cottage for teachers at the Catawba, North Carolina, Sanatorium for tuberculosis. Planners recognized, though, that teachers might not be able to afford paying for treatment for other medical needs as well, such as when they were "run down in health," and that it was important to provide more general health care—thorough medical examinations and treatment—at a cost "within the limited resources of these teachers." The University seemed an ideal place for such an arrangement.[1]

In 1923, Virginia teachers were asked to contribute a day's salary—four dollars—annually to support the cause.[2] The teachers did ultimately raise $31,524 toward their $40,000 goal, and the Teachers Preventorium opened in the Barringer Wing of the University of Virginia Hospital in March 1929.[3] A plaque was mounted to note the establishment of the unit, with William Smithey among those identified as the committee in charge.[4]

The hospital unit contained eighteen private rooms. Teachers who were ill were given priority in bed assignments, with the proviso that the University Hospital could use the beds for others if needed. Teachers paid a special rate of four dollars per day, which covered any professional, laboratory, or x-ray fees. The medical faculty donated their time for free. The early protocol was that a teacher coming in for diagnosis would be "subject during her sojourn to the control of the University and authorities, precisely as if she were a student occupying a University dormitory." By 1944, an estimated 5,500 teachers or more had made use of the preventorium hospital unit.[5]

Writing to President Darden in July 1950, Robert Williams, executive secretary of the Virginia Education Association, reported an increased demand for preventorium services. From July 1949 through May 1950, 339 new patients had been examined. Williams estimated that numbers would reach four hundred by July 1950, with half of the patients requiring hospitalization. A March 1950 article in the *Virginia Journal of Education* featured the preventorium, citing its importance for teachers in the Commonwealth but questioning the issues of eligibility for services and doctors' continuing willingness to provide services for free.[6]

Contributions were sought for the preventorium into the 1960s,[7] and in 1964 the VEA published a brochure explaining the benefits of the program.[8] By the late 1960s, the broader availability of health insurance mooting its value, the University of Virginia Teachers' Preventorium closed.

organizations—have guided administration and supervision programs to this day. Programs have been shaped in reciprocity with changing statewide professional requirements.

In the early years of the twentieth century, few requirements dictated one's eligibility to become a school superintendent in Virginia. In 1916 the state began to require that candidates be college graduates and hold teaching certificates. Officials at the 1925 annual Virginia Education Association conference founded a Virginia Department of Superintendents; its name subsequently became the Virginia Association of School Administrators. In December 1931 the State Board of Education raised the minimum requirements to become superintendents, setting September 1, 1935, as the starting date for the new rules. From that point on, superintendents needed a master's degree with at least fifteen hours in professional subjects and at least three years of administrative or professional experience and training.[76] Responding to this new standard, the education department began offering more courses for aspiring superintendents.

In 1930 John Manahan organized twice-monthly meetings for Central Virginia's division superintendents.[77] Registering for credit was optional. The plan was so successful that superintendents in eastern and western regions of the state wanted to meet similarly.[78] Manahan titled the course Problems of County School Superintendents,[79] but it quickly gained the nickname of the "Dean's Class." Early Dean's Classes focused on problems of the superintendency, providing valuable support for class members. This initiative led to superintendents' study groups in the 1950s and later.[80] When the groups expanded and became organized regionally in seven parts of the state, Curry faculty members worked with them to provide in-service education. Becoming dean in 1956, Ralph Cherry continued these groups and established summer seminars for superintendents. Manahan met with the Central Virginia group until his retirement in 1957.[81]

While courses on school administration had been offered from the school's founding, faculty work with state professional organizations spurred the formation of the Department of Administration and Supervision in the 1960s. Faculty members William Seawell and George Holmes, executive director of the School Board Association from 1958 to 1983, worked with the superintendents; their efforts strengthened ties between the School of Education and Virginia school personnel. Each chaired the Department of Administration and Supervision, Holmes from 1968 to 1972 and Seawell from 1972 to 1979. Frank Barham was chair from 1979 to 1985, at which time the department merged with Social Foundations and Higher Education to form the Department of Educational Leadership and Policy Studies.

For many years state superintendents belonged to the Department of Superintendents within the Virginia Educational Association. A new constitution in 1958 changed the department's name to the Virginia Association of School Administrators (VASA), but it still retained an affiliation with VEA. As of 1986, all 139 superintendents in Virginia belonged to VASA.[82] In 1978, with the appointment of Curry faculty member William Seawell as part-time executive director, the association moved its office to the Curry School.[83] Curry faculty members Frank Barham, Frank Flora, Vincent Cibbarelli, and Alfred Butler have held the director's position since then. Soon after Flora assumed leadership in 1988, VASA was renamed the Virginia Association for School Superintendents (VASS), designating it as primarily a superintendents' organization.[84] VASS continues to operate out of the Curry School, serving as an instructional and leadership resource for school administrators, education faculty members, and state organizations.[85]

The Department of Administration and Supervision has sponsored cohort and internship programs for school administrators—principals or assistant principals—for many years. The first developed under the leadership of Professor Lynn Canady, who in 1984 originated the School Improvement Project (SIP) to provide continuing education for administrators, both on Grounds and at centers across the state.[86] A cohort program for superintendents was developed in 1994 to address the need to create doctoral-level courses for students who wished to become superintendents. The program included courses in ethics and morals, curricular planning at a district level, and an internship.[87] Since 1998 a summer policy institute focusing on advances in technology for principals and assistant principals, superintendents, assistant superintendents, and aspiring superintendents has been directed by Alfred Butler.[88]

The Darden/Curry Partnership for Leaders in Education was instituted in 2003 when a Darden School alumnus created a foundation to support business and education leaders to work together to improve public schools in Florida. Education and Darden School faculty hosted an initial summer Executive Leadership Academy for Florida educators.[89] An outgrowth of this partnership, the Virginia School Turnaround Specialist Program (VSTSP) was initiated with a $1.4 million grant awarded by Virginia Governor Mark Warner and supplemented by a commitment of up to $3 million over five years from the Microsoft Corporation beginning in the fall of 2004. The program now offers programs for school leaders in Virginia year-round, designed to help education leaders with a business model for developing school programs and, more specifically, to raise student achievement by mirroring high-performing organizations, by strengthening personal leadership and by developing school turnaround plans. The first ten specialists were trained in the summer of 2004 and received further coaching during the following school year.[90] The program has continued to expand its outreach in 2005.

Another organization, the Virginia School Boards Association—part of the Virginia Education Association from 1927 to 1957[91]—formally affiliated with Curry during the Kellogg Foundation Project (or Cooperative Program in Educational Administration, CPEA).[92] In 1952, B. J. Chandler joined the Curry School to work with the Kellogg Project, a nationally funded, five-year initiative to support new program development and academic collaborations among school administrators across the country. Chandler became VSBA's first executive secretary and edited the *Virginia School Boards Association Newsletter*. He clearly saw the association's potential for educational leadership in the state and organized regional meetings similar to the superintendents' study groups for school board members.[93]

When the VSBA withdrew from the VEA in 1957 for political and professional reasons, it needed another home base. With Dean Cherry and President Darden's approval, the VSBA office formally moved to the School of Education. Curry faculty members have worked in the VSBA administration through 1992, when Frank Barham left the University to become VSBA's first full-time director.[94] A cooperative arrangement continued through the mid-1990s until the organization moved to a home of its own in Charlottesville. The VSBA–Curry School relationship formed an important nexus of educational leadership in the state.[95]

Other professional organizations under the umbrella of the Virginia Education Association were housed in the Curry School for many years. The Virginia Association of Secondary Principals (VASSP), with Frank Flora as advisor, operated out of the Curry School until 1982, as did the Virginia Association of Elementary Principals (VAEP), under the supervision of Lynn Canady. Ultimately both organizations hired full-time directors and established offices in Richmond.[96] In 1986 the Virginia School-University Partnership was created[97] as part of the National Network for Educational Renewal initiated by educator John Goodlad, who believed that collaborations among public schools and professional schools of education promised the best model for change in American education. Still housed in the Curry School in 2005 under the leadership of Andrew Stamp, the Virginia School-University Partnership holds regular member meetings, hosts student and teacher leadership conferences, and provides resources for professional development.[98]

Over the decades, the graduate courses and programs of the Department of Administration and Supervision have fostered ongoing relationships with state personnel, offered ways for students to participate in school issues, and provided avenues of employment for many Curry School graduates. By the mid-1990s, the majority of Virginia's superintendents—as well as a significant number of school-level leaders—held degrees earned through the department. In the last ten years, close to 300 students have completed degree programs in the department.[99] In 2005, department programs focused on administrative leadership at all levels, with classes provided both on Grounds and at locations around the state.

Charles Maphis with Summer School participants, ca. 1930

Curry faculty, Summer 1931. Front row from left: Wingfield, Phippins, Ivy, Swindler, Smithey. Back row from left: Broadwater, Windes, Alvey, Rorer, Eutsler

CHAPTER 4

Developing Education Programs

John L. Manahan, 1930–1949

The rapid development of educational science and practice has made it necessary that ample provision be made for the professional training of those who expect to teach or to administer school affairs. The Department of Education, therefore, aims to provide the following:

1. *An opportunity for the study of Education as an important function of society;*
2. *To give the necessary technical training for teaching and administration;*
3. *To develop scientific methods of testing school work and to furnish demonstrations of the way in which these methods may best be applied, thus developing a spirit of observation and experimentation tending to increase our knowledge of the science and art of education;*
4. *To become a center of educational influence to which teachers of all grades and kinds may come for information and educational guidance;*
5. *To furnish to the general public information on any phase of school organization, administration, and supervision, thus helping to create a clearer understanding about Education and the State.*

— *University of Virginia Record*
Curry Memorial Department of Education,
through the 1930s

In the early 1930s, the department's relationship with the state strengthened. The Virginia State Board of Education established a committee, including Manahan, to study "educational practices and pupil learning under present school conditions in Virginia" for students in grades four to seven. They were to oversee student testing in the fall of 1931, then retesting in the spring of 1932, providing data that could determine how well students learned that year. A "new type of field experimentation," the study focused on what was being taught in the classrooms ("practical working conditions in the schools, as they now are") to determine student achievement. The stated goals of the study were to "assist teachers in finding, understanding, and correcting poor work habits in very slow or exceptionally bright children," to "enable teachers to compare the educational advancement of their pupils with the average score made by pupils of like age and grade placement," and to "stimulate teachers and pupils to make a good record of progress during the year."[1]

Facing the Challenges

In 1932, Dean Manahan reported eighty-three students enrolled in the Department of Education, the same as in 1931.[2] Numbers did not grow, but students sensed the personal commitment of their professors. William Knight (B.S. '29) recalls that Dean Manahan helped him pay for school by hiring him as a babysitter. Recalling those days, Knight writes, "The first time, he pointed to a room where the infant was sleeping. Even after many sittings, I had never seen the infant. To this day I have *not*. I figure that the 'infant' is about 74 years old!"[3]

In 1934 Manahan reported to University President Newcomb, "We have also been exceedingly fortunate in placing practically all of our former graduates in good positions at a time when most teacher-training institutions have found great difficulty in placing even a major portion of their students."[4] The total number of degrees awarded remained consistent during the entire decade of the 1930s, but in that period the department granted its first Ph.D.s—ten, all to men.[5]

During the 1930s, though, concerns emerged about relatively static offerings in education and a perceived lack of vitality in the department. Calls for changes came in 1934, and a committee formed "for the purpose of studying ways of extending and improving the usefulness of the department of education," as expressed in the resulting 1935 report. Existing courses were to be studied, with professors asked to justify their content at a faculty meeting. The department was urged to find ways for faculty to "feel more vitally related to the activities of the department" and to help develop "a better morale" among the students in the department. Regular faculty meetings, at least once every two months, announced in advance, and standing committees on specific administrative subjects were suggested as a way faculty could "stimulate more intensive professional zeal" among their students.[6]

Discussions about the department and its enrollments continued within the education community and the University as a whole for several years.[7] In many ways, the conversation

Band members, Venable School, Charlottesville, 1947

Classroom displays, 1930s

reflected national trends in education schools. The debate between a vocational and an academic approach to education had been ongoing since early in the century. In the first half of the twentieth century, in their quest for legitimacy, education schools increasingly focused on issues of scientific research and educational leadership, while continuing to prepare teachers for the public schools.[8]

In response to departmental concerns, committees on rules, courses, attendance and scholarships, publications and library, articulation with academic departments, and student morale formed. Faculty members were urged to host students in their homes and in "other ways cause students to feel kindly" toward the department.[9] In 1936, education students voted to revise their constitution, separate from the college governing body, and create their own self-determining governance. Those motions, however, were denied, based on student numbers: compared to 1,400 students in the College of Arts and Sciences, the Department of Education had eighty and the next smallest department had two hundred.[10] To form connections with other departments of the University, education faculty proposed to organize public lectures by prominent speakers, airing contrasting views on education. In 1938, enrollments rose by three compared to 1937.[11] By 1938, President Newcomb appeared to be considering new leadership for the department. That search was not completed for another ten years.[12]

Further Scrutiny

A letter written to the editor of Charlottesville's *Daily Progress* in 1932 had expressed concern that the public school system was paying four University faculty as critic teachers while potential teachers were struggling to find work. The writer also noted that, despite the promise of the collaboration, "During the five years in which this yearly contribution has been made, the city has not employed a single teacher trained with this money to fill any of the vacancies in the high school faculty." The *Progress* responded by interviewing Superintendent James Johnson, who said that the University not only contributed to critic teachers' salaries but also helped pay for instructional supplies. There were other advantages to the collaborations between University faculty and public school teachers, Johnson asserted, but he agreed to pay more attention to hiring graduates trained in the local schools.[13]

Even before that dialogue, Curry faculty member Henry Acker had noted that graduates who had trained for secondary education were having trouble finding work and accepting positions as elementary teachers instead. Detecting an oversupply of candidates for secondary positions, Acker urged that elementary school training be offered at the University of Virginia as well.[14] The faculty moved in October 1935 to "enter upon a critical study of the whole offering of the Department, including degree requirements, looking to an improvement and enlargement of the program."[15] The faculty strongly recommended a "full program of Education in both

Sailors on the Lawn during World War II

Elementary and Secondary Education" that would include practice teaching and other elements required by Virginia's Department of Education and by accrediting agencies of the South. They also called for provisions to train teachers in music and art.[16]

The faculty suggested revising degree requirements for students in education to coordinate with those in the College of Arts and Sciences. Complicating the issue was the longstanding tradition of antipathy between faculty members in Arts and Sciences and those in professions, especially education. University President Newcomb called for a department-wide study of the existing education curriculum and asked for suggestions for change. Professor Smithey was appointed chair of the President's Committee on the Reorganization of the Department of Education at the University of Virginia, which included many education faculty members as well as several representatives from other divisions of the University.

An initial committee report was drafted in October 1939. It recommended continued undergraduate programs in education and the professional training of teachers and principals. The draft stated that the undergraduate program should not include a curriculum for training elementary schoolteachers, however, since both the University's summer quarter program and the state normal schools already provided for this. State Superintendent Sidney Hall actually approved that decision, but the tide turned before the final report was issued.[17]

On February 2, 1940, the committee presented its final recommendations to President Newcomb. The recommendations specified requirements for graduate work leading to a master of arts or a doctor of philosophy in education awarded from the Department of Graduate Studies. Master's degrees were offered for administrators, for secondary-level teachers, and for elementary-level teachers and supervisors. The departmental curriculum was to be reorganized to provide courses in general psychology, educational psychology, history of education, principles of teaching (elementary and secondary levels), and school administration, along with practice teaching and training in special methods.[18] The faculty endorsed continuing cooperative programs with the city and county schools. Physical education courses in coaching, nursing courses, and a health course were all endorsed, while courses in music and related fine arts were suggested for students planning to be elementary teachers. Events followed on the state level. The

Chemistry class, Lane High School, Charlottesville, 1949

Commonwealth of Virginia stopped granting the Normal Professional Certificate in 1942. From that date forward, all teachers had to be college graduates. These statewide changes affirmed the new curriculum of the Curry Memorial Department of Education, now designed to attract prospective teachers into its programs.

The events of World War II eclipsed many efforts at the University, including those in the Department of Education. "Men came and went," recalls alumnus William R. Dudenhausen (B.S. '47), who left after his fourth year to fight in the war, then returned to finish his degree later.[19] In 1942 Peabody Hall was evacuated, as the University was prepared as a possible hospital evacuation center for Washington, Baltimore, or Norfolk.[20] The School of Education "practically folded up," recalled Richard Meade.[21] Several faculty members taught in military schools established at the University during this time; William Smithey taught mathematics in the engineering school, Butch Slaughter taught physics, and Richard Meade taught air navigation.[22] Smithey also advised high schools on curriculum materials appropriate to wartime efforts.[23]

Many students went off to serve in the war and enrollments dropped, as did the number of degrees granted. The few who completed education degrees during this time were women in the B.S.Ed. program.[24] In the wartime climate, the department's struggles for funds reflected the University's condition as a whole. In spite of cutbacks, several programs developed in the 1940s that were to have a long-lasting effect on the curriculum overall, including programs in speech and hearing and the McGuffey Reading Clinic. At the same time, a significant state report on the future of teacher training in Virginia identified the University of Virginia's Department of Education as the state's leading unit responsible for establishing graduate programs in education. Referred to as the Denny Report, after the chair of the committee, George Denny, it would wield an influence in the reshaping of the department during and after the war years.

Developing Specialized Degree Programs

National attention was turning to children with special needs, and by the middle of the century, many states had made provision for educating handicapped children and certifying

McGuffey Reading Center

In the mid-1930s, Curry faculty began discussing the need for a reading clinic. It should be a laboratory for training teachers, they decided; it should provide clinical services for students nearby and enhance elementary education offerings.[1] A clinic began in 1937, continued to operate during the war, and was reconfigured in 1946 as the McGuffey Reading Clinic, directed by Ullin Leavell, a reading specialist on the faculty.[2] Its new name honored William Holmes McGuffey, professor of moral philosophy at the University of Virginia from 1845 to 1873 and author of the famous *Eclectic Reader,* adopted as a standard text in thirty-seven states and estimated to have sold 122,000,000 copies. While at Virginia, McGuffey revised and further developed his readers, a series of six books with a spelling book and a high school reader that went through many editions during the late nineteenth century.

Ullin Leavell was a pioneer as well in the teaching of reading. He recognized many causes for reading difficulties, not always associated with intellectual ability. His research on eye movement suggested a physiological approach to reading. He also believed that high-quality reading materials could influence the attitudes and minds of children. Of his two reading series, the second—*The Golden Rule Series: The New McGuffey Readers*—was highly influential, adopted by forty-one states as standard reading texts during the late 1950s.[3]

Leavell's impact was felt so strongly that department faculty drafted a 1947 proposal for the "Projected Program for the Reading Clinic in the Department of Education."[4] The resulting clinic offered services in the diagnosis and remediation of reading problems to children in surrounding school systems. A move in 1948 from Peabody Hall to buildings on Dawson's Row enabled the clinic to expand services. For a while, the clinic operated out of the basement of faculty apartments on Rugby Road; it then moved to Ruffner Hall in 1973.

The McGuffey Reading Clinic trained teachers and worked with parents, teachers, and administrators "regarding the educational stimulation of children." Plans for the clinic included a public school demonstration forum for diagnosis and remediation of reading problems. Between January and December 1949, clinic staff worked on 611 cases.[5] Highlighting education department activities, the 1948 *Corks and Curls* yearbook included several pictures of sessions in the reading clinic.[6]

When the clinic moved to Ruffner Hall, its name changed to the McGuffey Reading Center, reflecting the more comprehensive nature of its work. Coming to the University in 1969, Professor Edmund Henderson directed McGuffey programs for twenty years. Henderson emphasized the developmental nature of reading and decoding, a new philosophy and approach to reading that had long-lasting influence in the field. He believed that children invented spellings as a natural stage in their growing knowledge of written language,[7] and supervised numerous doctoral-level research projects that investigated the relationship between specific aspects of invented spelling and reading achievement. These dissertations, seen as important contributions to the literature in reading education, have come to be known collectively as the "Virginia Studies." Henderson's own texts on the developmental and cognitive aspects of spelling are critical mileposts in the history of reading education.

By the 1980s, as demand for reading instruction was growing across the state, Henderson took Reading Center activities off Grounds through a program he named TEMPO, Teaching Educators McGuffey Practica Off-Grounds. Supported by the School of Continuing Education, the TEMPO program benefited from the installation of a new satellite antenna that broadcast to all parts of the state and to many who otherwise could not have participated. Henderson and other on-Grounds faculty taught live from the University, their presentations delivered via satellite.

At the same time, Curry School doctoral students or alumni with advanced degrees in reading education were on site at each receiving facility, guiding the new technology-assisted classroom experience. The program grew at a rapid pace and in 1989, Professor Mary Abouzeid began creating program cohorts in all parts of the state. Today, in addition to facilitating off-Grounds master's degree programs in reading, the TEMPO program offers graduate-level professional development courses to fifty school districts in the state. After participating in what is now called the McGuffey-TEMPO Outreach, many students have entered the Curry School's doctoral programs in reading.

Joining the reading faculty in 1986, Professor Marcia Invernizzi soon developed intervention programs for children

Tutoring session, McGuffey Reading Center, ca. 1970

with reading needs, so highly effective that they have achieved national and international recognition. The Book Buddies program, launched in 1991, grew out of the *America Reads Challenge,* prompted by the ESEA Act of 1965. *America Reads* asked all Americans to support teachers and help ensure that every child could read well and independently by the end of third grade. Book Buddies provided an infrastructure for one-on-one community involvement with children learning to read in the local schools. Today it is the model program for *America Reads,* successful in helping children read and training work-study students as tutors.

In 1997, legislation in the state of Virginia called for school districts to identify kindergarten and first-grade children in need of additional instruction, then provide them with early services. In response, Invernizzi, along with Professor Connie Juel, led a McGuffey Reading Center team in developing the Phonological Awareness Literacy Screening (PALS) diagnostic tool, an array of screening instruments that measure children's knowledge of literacy fundamentals including phonological awareness, alphabet knowledge, word recognition, and oral comprehension. PALS results provide teachers with explicit information about their students' literacy, and the PALS program provides instructional information for teachers. By 2005, PALS services were in use by 98 percent of the school districts in Virginia, by school systems in thirty-eight other states, and in at least eleven countries internationally. Originally designed for kindergartners and first-graders, it has now expanded to include students up through third grade.[8]

In 2001, legislation passed in Virginia required the state to provide ways for teachers to improve reading achievement for students in low-performing schools. Called Reading First in Virginia (RFIV), a contract to carry out these programs was awarded to the Curry School in 2003. RFIV services include Teacher Reading Academies in the summer along with academic support for teachers and other personnel during the school year. In the summer of 2004, two thousand teachers were trained in four-day academies around the state.[9]

Successful research contributions and outreach programs by reading faculty members have formed the groundwork for further steps in the field of reading education. Reading program graduates now hold significant faculty positions. They have written major spelling and reading texts and play key roles in educational policy–making efforts throughout the country.

Walter and Elizabeth Burnley Smith, both B.S.Ed. 1941

special education teachers.[25] In Virginia, Superintendent of State Instruction Sidney Hall had written President Newcomb in 1939, urging special education training at the University. "Since handicapped children are in greater need of assistance and guidance than other children," argued Hall, "it would appear that some recognition of this need would be appropriate in terms of courses in education of teachers along these lines."[26] Over the next ten years, the department developed programs to prepare teachers for work with children with special needs. Specialized programs developed in speech and hearing and in reading as well.

The origins of today's Communications Disorders Program began in 1941 when Karl Wallace, professor of speech, and Fletcher Woodward, professor of otolaryngology, received University approval to establish a Speech and Hearing Center. A "free clinic for speech faults" associated with the center was the first of its kind in the South, dedicated to aid "regularly enrolled students who may have such speech problems as stuttering, lisping, or other sound substitutions, hard-of-hearing speech, abnormal pitch levels, or general articulation problems," according to an article in *College Topics.* First located in Cocke Hall, the clinic then moved to 58 East Range, quickly establishing itself as an important part of the educational community.[27] The clinic also served community children and coached teachers.[28] Its success led to courses in speech pathology and speech correction, then to a degree program in speech education in 1946. When James Mullendore joined the faculty in September 1945, the speech and hearing program extended its reach out through the state. Soon courses supporting a speech correction program were offered by the Department of Education, the extension department, and the summer school.[29]

The postwar years saw renewed vigor in the Curry Memorial Department of Education, expressed in the desire for a variety of new programs. Manahan hoped to expand Peabody Hall, add an auditorium and classrooms to the building, and work toward closer links among the summer program, the extension division, and the education school's professional programs.[30] A summer institute for mathematics teachers, continued Saturday classes, broader access to audiovisual materials, and improved career placement—all new efforts—were put into place to expand the services rendered to Virginia teachers and administrators by the department.[31]

There was a strong sentiment toward creating a master of education degree, to be granted by the Department of Education, as distinct from the College-granted master of arts degree. Many American universities already granted the M.Ed. degree by 1946, since language requirements for a master of arts were difficult if not inappropriate for education students.[32] A committee report reiterated the needs for more scholarships, new faculty—especially to run new graduate centers around the state—and more students. In stating the request for the M.Ed., the faculty cited the 1920 Board of Visitors' resolution that the department had the power and obligation to confirm professional degrees.[33] Especially in the wake of the Denny Report, the M.Ed. seemed

Lankford and Meade

Richard A. Meade (above)

Robert Swindler, back left, and Francis Lankford with Sylvia Horwitz (from Lane High School), front right, and two unidentified women, 1930s (right)

Two early Curry faculty members were to have a great influence in state and national educational practices: Francis Lankford and Richard A. Meade. Their research contributions on the secondary-level teaching of two critical subjects, mathematics and English, paved the way for many twentieth-century developments in each field.

Lankford joined the department in 1931 as an instructor in the teaching of mathematics and a critic teacher in the Albemarle County schools. He left the University several times—including the decade of 1955–1965, when he served as president of Longwood College in Farmville—but returned to the Curry School of Education in 1965 as director of the University's newly formed Office of Institutional Analysis, today the Office of Institutional Assessment and Studies. Lankford authored or co-authored numerous articles and mathematics textbooks; many stayed in print for more than thirty years, including his pioneering work in consumer mathematics.[1]

With a longstanding interest in the process of children's mathematical thinking, in 1972 Lankford used the new technique of oral interviews with pupils as they solved mathematical problems. "We interviewed 176 seventh-grade students in several middle schools in the state as they were working with fractions and decimals," he recalled in 1976. "The students said out loud what they were doing [and] we had plenty of data to analyze."[2] Lankford's research formed evidence for mathematicians and scholars as they reexamined and revised procedures for teaching mathematics.

Meade joined the faculty in 1935 as an instructor in the secondary-level teaching of English and a critic teacher in the Albemarle schools. He enjoyed a long and distinguished career as one of the Curry School's earliest English educators. A faculty member for forty-seven years, he directed the English Education program and chaired the Department of Curriculum and Instruction between 1968 and 1972. He actively led state and local professional organizations. In his work, including several textbooks, he exerted a great influence in English Education by encouraging students to find books they enjoyed and teachers to portray literature as part of life, not as a collection of monuments to be "passed by as in a museum."[3]

Meade frequently consulted for school systems, helping redesign curricula. "Gently, he started me on the way to discovering that teaching is helping, guiding, urging, caring," remembers one of his many students, "not dictating, forcing, dominating."[4] In 1976, Richard Meade received the first Curry School Outstanding Professor Award.

appropriate. President Newcomb hesitated to grant the request, since his presidency was coming to an end. Ultimately the request was granted by the next University president, Colgate Darden, together with the next education dean, Lindley Stiles. The first master of education degrees were awarded in August 1950.[34]

Defining the University's Role in Statewide Education

The 1944 Denny Report contributed significantly toward solidifying the mission of the Curry Department of Education, offering a view of the University of Virginia as central in meeting expanding needs for education in a modern society. "Through its graduate training and an efficiently operated bureau of educational research," read the report, the University was in the position of "setting the pace and standards for the entire public school system of the Commonwealth." Establishing a strong graduate center in education at the University, said the report, was key to "strengthening the teacher training phase of the school problem, both in the instructional and administrative spheres of its operation." Such a center would have "prestige equal to that of centers of this kind now generally conceded to be outstanding," and "other Virginia institutions concerned with teacher training will look to the University of Virginia for guidance and leadership." The commission recommended that state teachers' colleges continue to improve the training of public schoolteachers.[35]

The Denny Report recommendations no doubt influenced Manahan in 1944 as he wrote University President Newcomb about what it would take to establish a graduate school of education. One would need to consider vocational education, guidance, library science, music and the fine arts, and physical and health education, Manahan listed. The surrounding public schools could provide "superior laboratory facilities for research and experimentation in all fields of instruction and training for teachers," he continued. "The desire on the part of the public school people in this area for such cooperation with the University is exceedingly strong."[36] In early 1945 the education faculty again endorsed cooperation between the department and the schools of the City of Charlottesville and Albemarle County, to "provide an opportunity for the University to train teachers and to carry out research methods and demonstrations of methods and materials and for the county the opportunity to benefit from professional services of the Department."[37] In August 1946, President Newcomb appropriated funds for a secretary to work with faculty members in the mornings and with school officials in the afternoons.[38]

Public school classroom, Charlottesville, late 1940s

In essence, President Newcomb interpreted the findings of the Denny Report as a directive. He wrote Dr. Wilson Gee, executive director of the Virginia Education Commission, saying that the proposed graduate center would require funding for seven new positions and other related expenses.[39] He took the report to mandate that the Department of Education should be responsible for teacher training at the graduate level and should continue to provide leadership in other areas of graduate education. With this new direction in mind, Newcomb actively began pursuing nominations for a new departmental leader.

Postwar growth in public school enrollment paralleled the continuing debate over the role and reputation of schools of education. Were they to serve only as research institutions? Or should they continue to educate teachers for the nation's schools? With few substantive changes in the curricula of teacher education programs, skepticism about education schools persisted in the minds of many academics. Some even felt that in the field of education, there was no cohesive body of knowledge, hence education was not worthy of being termed a substantive field of study. In this context, education as a field of study suffered in comparison to other professional fields. It is an issue with a history almost as long as that of teaching itself. At the University of Virginia, only after the close of the Second World War was the department able to adopt a fully developed plan of teacher education for all levels. Under Dean Lindley J. Stiles, who took the post in 1949, standards for education students rose and curriculum requirements expanded, advancing the Curry Memorial Department of Education to a new status within the University and the state.

A New University President

In the spring of 1947, Colgate Darden was inaugurated as third president of the University of Virginia. Darden's credentials made him uniquely aware of educational issues: While not an academic by training, he had a long career in politics and was especially interested in social issues and educational policy. He had been chancellor of the College of William and Mary, governor of Virginia, and a member of both the United States Congress and the Virginia House of Delegates. This history gave Darden wide visibility in the state, a broad perspective on public issues, and an understanding of how the University fit into the larger public sphere. One of his missions from the beginning of his tenure as president was to increase the number of public school students entering the University.[40]

As Darden arrived, faculty in education continued to be concerned with the fate of their department. In the spring of 1948 they submitted a "Statement to the President of the University of Virginia from the Faculty of the Curry Memorial Department of Education," asking Darden to clarify what changes he intended for the department and citing their "constant and prolonged state of uncertainty as to the future of the department due to . . . the incessant rumors throughout the state of impending reorganization of the department."[41] No steps had been taken to address issues raised in the Denny Report, the statement added, although other colleges in the state were already doing so.

For the second year in a row, the student yearbook, *Corks and Curls,* gave a page to the department's activities, quoting Dean Manahan and featuring the reading clinic, work in visual education, Saturday courses for teachers, and the popular conference for teachers of mathematics. The upbeat page ends by expressing the hope that more "cooperative undertakings may be expanded to include all important teaching fields, both in secondary schools and colleges. The University is the logical place for such leadership and service."[42] Marjorie Taite Austin (B.S. '51) recalls arrangements made by the deans of education and engineering for herself and her

The Virginia Education Association

Athena Angelus at the annual Virginia Education Association meeting in Richmond, 1966

The Virginia Education Association (VEA) was established in 1863 as the Educational Association of Virginia, with a membership of teachers, administrators, and higher education faculty from across the state. Its second annual meeting, in July 1866, convened in Charlottesville. Annual meeting sites circulated around the state until 1913, when the organization settled on Richmond as its primary meeting location.[1] For many years, annual meetings took place around Thanksgiving. Attended regularly by education faculty, the meetings provided a way to keep in touch with graduates and to participate in statewide school decision-making and related activities.

In November 1925, University of Virginia President Edwin A. Alderman addressed the annual meeting, speaking on "The Present State of Higher Education in Virginia." Alderman expressed concerns about the state's poor level of funding for higher education, remarking that Virginia had the lowest per capita allocation of any state in the union except Georgia.[2] He cited increased attendance at Virginia's "nine institutions for the white race and the Virginia Normal and Industrial Institute for the Negro race," but noted that appropriations had not kept up with enrollments. Alderman's address received much publicity statewide and inspired newspapers to support his pleas for more education funding.

The VEA met in Charlottesville in April 1927 with 402 registered attendees. Speakers addressed the need to upgrade the certification of teachers. William Smithey spoke on the state of secondary education in Virginia. On the topic of the state's small-sized high schools, Smithey said bluntly, "Let's stop talking about it and do something about it." He proposed a committee to develop plans for coordinating research in secondary education. Charles Maphis welcomed meeting attendees, urging each one to "'sell'—an abominable but necessary word—the public school system to the community in which you work, and overcome criticism by seeing that all the facts about the system are made known." Maphis urged the teachers of the state to "get together and help to make a state program that will be satisfactory."[3]

Under Dean Manahan, all faculty of the Curry Memorial Department of Education were expected to attend meetings and serve on committees of the VEA. Manahan himself was elected president of VEA's District J and held that position for several years in the mid-1920s. He wrote President Newcomb in 1935, distressed that the University no longer paid for VEA membership, leaving faculty to pay the $1.50 annual membership fee out of their own pockets.[4]

Still, departmental faculty stayed active. In 1949, Dean Stiles began hosting a Curry alumni breakfast at every annual VEA meeting. Almost one hundred alumni attended the first such breakfast, and "enthusiasm for the continuance of this activity was generally expressed by all."[5] Into the 1960s, Dean Cherry frequently encouraged the faculty to join, attend, and participate in association activities.[6] But by the early 1970s interest declined, in part due to the proliferation of national and international professional organizations in which the faculty participated, and the department's chapter dwindled.[7]

A student chapter of the VEA was organized at the school in 1959. In 1966 Athena Angelus was elected president of the local chapter and the statewide organization as well, the first woman to hold the local post.[8] The Curry School chapter of the SVEA is still active in the early twenty-first century, earning awards and recognition for its excellent programs. In 2004–2005 the president of the SVEA, for the first time in many years, was again a female Curry School teacher education student, Lianna Moss.

husband, allowing them to enroll in courses on alternate days so that both could pursue degrees with two children at home. "When my education courses were not available, I was allowed to take courses in the College to keep up our G.I. Bill allotment," she says.[43]

How best to focus programs of study so the Curry Memorial Department of Education remained a strong presence in the University and a leader in the state? This was the challenge that Colgate Darden hoped to address by appointing a new dean. John L. Manahan resigned as dean in June 1949 after twenty-nine years in that office, leaving the department at a critical point in its history. Manahan could point to important programs and services established during his deanship, such as the McGuffey Reading Clinic, the Speech and Hearing Clinic, continuing collaborations with the public schools, and the involvement of many faculty in matters important to the schools in the state and, increasingly, the nation. After his retirement as dean, Manahan remained a professor of educational administration, working particularly with the superintendents' programs, until his retirement in 1957, thus becoming one of the longest-serving faculty members in the school's history, with forty-one years of service.[44]

As one historian of the University has said, the Curry Memorial School of Education was regarded with "decided skepticism by faculty members in other disciplines"[45] during its early years. Yet the school—its leaders, faculty, students, and the many teachers and administrators who benefited from its courses and counsel—persevered, withstanding many challenges in the first half of its century. By 1949 the department was ready to carve out a new path—still poised, given strong leadership, to assume a more public role in statewide educational developments, to develop nationally influential advanced degree programs, and to generate a body of research on theory and practice that might make a difference in educational practice in the second half of the twentieth century.

Extension Division evening class, Hampton, Virginia, 1950

Aerodynamics lesson, Charlottesville public school, 1950s

CHAPTER 5

Raising Confidence and Enhancing Visibility

Lindley J. Stiles, 1949–1955

In the School of Education, we take the point of view that the University of Virginia must educate teachers, not the School alone. We see our function as making the resources of the University available to prospective teachers and to teachers in-service. [I advocate] the all-university approach to teacher education: Professionals must have liberal arts backgrounds if they are to make schools better.[1] — Lindley J. Stiles, 1953

In 1948 University President Colgate Darden and faculty in the Curry Memorial Department of Education began the search for a new, "alert and dynamic" dean. Among the qualifications listed for this position were the ability to "recognize the need to understand public education" and the "zeal for improving public education." The new dean should also have the ability to work effectively with other University departments, with the State Department of Education, and with other state institutions of higher education.[2]

After a national search, Darden appointed Lindley J. Stiles in 1949. Coming from the College of William and Mary, Stiles understood the need to make the University of Virginia "truly a state university by linking it to the elementary and secondary schools of the state."[3] In his six-year deanship, Stiles led the Department of Education through advances that solidified its direction and presence in the University and in the Commonwealth. Stiles's accomplishments were many. He raised academic standards, created the first graduate professional degree programs, established strong professional ties in the state, and addressed school desegregation, a critical issue in Virginia. He strengthened education department ties to the summer school and the extension division, both of which enjoyed increased enrollments. These efforts were made in the time when a shadow of increasing criticism of education schools fell on education schools in general,[4] and Stiles was ever mindful of the challenges facing the profession in the 1950s.

Becoming a School of Education

The vigor with which Stiles redirected the Department of Education in his first year as dean did much to lay the course for its future growth. He worked closely with President Darden, who

Art class, Lane High School, Charlottesville, 1950s

evinced concern over the department's future. He began by initiating regular monthly faculty meetings,[5] at which he presented his goals, sought faculty approval, and created committees in key areas. He met with administrators to determine the status of the department within the University.[6] Presenting recommendations to President Darden in November, Stiles said that the "Department of Education of the University of Virginia exists for the purpose of extending and improving the quality of educational experiences that are accorded to the children and youth of Virginia." Then he articulated three goals. First, he believed that the department ought to clarify and make explicit its status as an independent and professional division of the University of Virginia, "defined and developed largely by people who are themselves professionally prepared and who are acquainted with and sympathetic to the professional purposes of teacher education." Second, he intended to establish an undergraduate four-year program of teacher education. Finally, he considered it essential that the department continue to grant professional graduate degrees to students at the University and throughout the state to in-service teachers.[7]

One of Stiles's first initiatives was to establish the Department of Education as a professional school within the University. It began functioning as a "separate professional department of the University, enjoying a status similar to that accorded to the Departments of Engineering, Law, and Medicine."[8] With this change in name and status, approved in 1950, the department could award its own professional degrees—the M.Ed. and the Ed.D.—along with the existing graduate degrees—the M.A. and the Ph.D. In 1951 the education faculty formally requested that the "department" become a "school," a change soon to be applied to all professional divisions of the University in recognition of their autonomy.[9] The new course and degree offerings distinguished between the degrees awarded by the Department of Education and those offered by the Department of Graduate Studies. The master of arts degree and doctor of philosophy degree programs involved "the development of competency for research in a specialized aspect of education," while the master of education and doctor of education degree programs focused on "the improvement of competence for educational leadership and the application of knowledge to the solution of educational problems."[10]

President Darden urged the department to pay "particular attention to the development of courses calculated to increase and broaden the knowledge of those in the teaching profession." He added, "There has been, I think, for many years too much emphasis upon method here in Virginia as well as elsewhere."[11] When Stiles reported a 19 percent enrollment increase in winter 1950, Darden cautioned that he hoped the department "may not become a refuge for those unable to carry on in other fields." He admonished Stiles to "maintain high standards" and "place emphasis on substance rather than method" in order to "perform a service of incalculable worth to the public school system of Virginia."[12]

The School of Education gained representation on the Student Council in the fall of 1950,[13] and Stiles sought faculty representation on the University Senate as well, beyond the seat he held by virtue of his administrative rank.[14] The dean created an advisory committee that included representatives from teachers' organizations and administrators from across the state as well as graduate and undergraduate students.[15] The group met several times in the spring of 1951. As part of a project to improve the education of school administrators sponsored by the Kellogg Foundation, visitors observed that the "transformation that has taken place in the Department of Education over a two year period is nothing short of remarkable," and that it "has been transformed into an active, aggressive and dynamic agency that is beginning to make itself felt throughout the state." The report commended Darden and Stiles for their leadership.[16]

Soon the department was exerting more control over education courses taught in extension and summer school programs. George Zehmer resigned as dean of the summer school in October 1951.[17] Succeeding him in 1952, Stiles allowed his faculty more control over course content and increased their influence in hiring decisions. He shortened the summer term to six weeks, making it more feasible for teachers.[18]

Stiles's influence was felt statewide. A Roanoke editorial commended the reorganization he spearheaded, noting that it brought the University of Virginia in line with forty-one institutions around the country offering the same degrees. Quoting President Darden, the essay stated, "We intend to build the University's teaching program directly around the problem of improving the education program of the public schools." It closed by saying of Darden, "It is good to know that at the University he is able to put his ideas into practice."[19]

Paralleling degree and curricular reforms, Lindley Stiles sought to strengthen courses and requirements for the undergraduate degree. Courses on counseling and degrees in physical education were recommended. Graduate seminars were to include "live research" in schools that would benefit from research findings.[20] The faculty voted to admit first-year students directly into education, but that practice ended in 1962 when faculty concluded students were not ready to choose a teaching career that early.[21]

In his first year as dean, Stiles reported 250 undergraduates and 79 graduate students in the department. Undergraduate numbers included 61 students in the nursing education program (soon to leave the department), 71 in physical education, and 107 in secondary education. In

Speech and Hearing

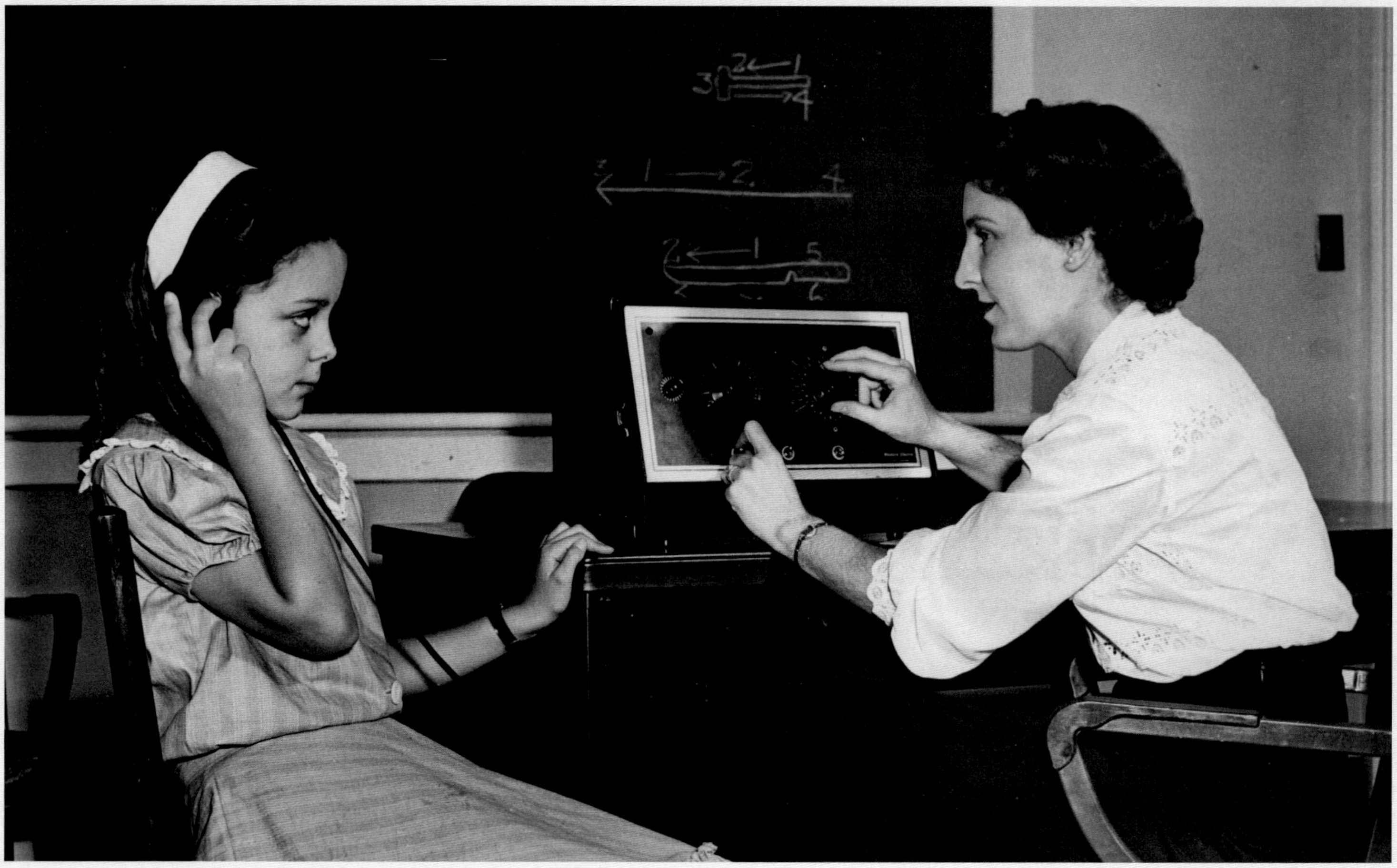

Auditory testing in the Speech and Hearing Clinic, 1950s (top)

Speech and Hearing outreach efforts, 1960s

Programs in speech, hearing, and related communications disorders were housed first in the School of Public Speaking, then in the College's School of Speech and Drama. Finally, in 1960, the Department of Speech Education was moved to the Curry School and the programs were consolidated in the Department of Speech Pathology and Audiology. The first grants for summer work in speech correction were awarded in 1948, establishing a long-term University association with Easter Seals. In 1953 a cooperative plan with Mary Washington and Longwood Colleges brought more statewide involvement with the Speech and Hearing programs. A uniquely effective public outreach program developed in the 1950s and 1960s under Professor James Mullendore and Dr. Fletcher Woodward, chair of otolaryngology at the University, who also created a self-supporting and nonprofit foundation to finance their efforts. Gifts and grants to the foundation helped send faculty and graduate students around the state, offering diagnostic clinics and conducting speech and hearing surveys to the children of Virginia.[1]

Beginning a career that spanned more than thirty years, Helen Gunderson Burr joined the Speech and Hearing Clinic in 1953, directing it until 1968; she joined the education school's Department of Speech Pathology and Audiology in 1961, directing it until 1978. In 1966, Burr became one of the first women promoted to full professor from within faculty ranks at the University of Virginia. Thanks to her leadership, the University became one of the South's first accredited centers for speech-language pathology and audiology. Professor Burr retired in 1988.[2]

When the program in speech pathology and audiology was transferred to the Curry School of Education in 1960, a doctoral degree program in Speech Pathology was established.[3] A master's degree program in the education of the deaf—the only such degree in the state—was founded in 1967, thanks to a fellowship from the U.S. Office of Education.[4] These programs coalesced into one of six School of Education departments,[5] but have never shared physical space with the Curry School, moving out of Cabell Hall into offices on Emmet Street in 1986, then to present offices on Fontaine Avenue.

In the late 1980s, the program for educating the deaf was discontinued, and a Communications Disorders Program was established in the new Department of Human Services, offering a preprofessional undergraduate degree and graduate degrees in speech-language pathology.

The Speech-Language-Hearing Center had been offering clinical services to the public since 1942, serving as a research laboratory for students and faculty, and celebrated its fiftieth anniversary on April 3, 1992.

Through its sixty-year history, the Speech and Hearing Program has led advances in the field: drug therapy for stutterers, protocols for detecting hearing loss in young children, devices for measuring speech abnormalities, hearing therapy for children with cochlear implants, and the use of computers in speech therapy. Course offerings expanded from the initial one and a faculty of one in 1941 to forty-three courses taught by seven faculty members, with additional supervisors, by 1991.

The long history of outreach in communication disorders continued through the Speech-Language and Hearing Center's Summer SPLASH program. Begun in the 1990s, SPLASH (SPeech and LAnguage Summer Help) provides services for preschool through early school-aged children, working to improve articulation, language, preliteracy, and social skills. Other new programs include a voice laboratory and a distance education program. The lab was founded by faculty member Aliaa Khidr in 1998 to offer diagnosis and treatment for adults with communication and swallowing problems. Graduate students work with clients in speech retraining and voice therapy, employing state-of-the-art technologies. The distance education program, sponsored by the Virginia Department of Education, uses videoconferencing to help professionals working with the schools obtain a master's degree in speech-language pathology without leaving their jobs.[6]

Dr. and Mrs. Walter Ridley at commencement, 1953 (top)

Walter Ridley, 1988

elementary education, only 11 were enrolled.[22] "I think we can take a great deal of courage from the fact that members of the faculty of the department are now carrying their full responsibilities within the institution," he wrote to Darden the next fall. "I might say the staff members are working six days a week in order to carry the teaching responsibilities incident to this large enrollment."[23] Programs operating under the Curry School's auspices included the Teacher Placement Service, the McGuffey Reading Clinic, and the Bureau of Audio-Visual Services, all "providing services for the people of Virginia."[24]

Stiles assumed leadership among deans of education in the Commonwealth when he spearheaded a statewide cooperative plan for graduate education. In part a response to the Denny report, this plan would allow students to take courses from any state institution, degree-granting or not, and transfer those credits toward a graduate degree at one of the four graduate education schools in the state. To eliminate course duplication around the state, the University of Virginia Extension Service would serve as a clearinghouse. While the plan was never implemented, it created productive discussion among Virginia's education departments.[25] Stiles advocated higher qualifications for pre-service teachers and graduate training for in-service teachers, as he expressed in the speech he gave at the November 1950 meeting of a division of the VEA in Charlottesville. Graduate education programs, he asserted, should be designed to

> produce teachers who possess a background of broad general education, a sound professional education, and a thorough understanding of the fields of knowledge to be taught. . . . A period of supervised internship is essential to all professions . . . We must look forward to a time when, as a minimum, a five-year program of pre-service collegiate preparation for teaching will be followed by a full year of internship.[26]

Throughout his career, Stiles emphasized the advantage of a teacher education program within a larger university, where students acquire knowledge in both the liberal arts and educational pedagogy.[27]

Making History

In September 1950, Walter Ridley, an educator on the faculty of Virginia State College—an all-black institution—applied for admission to the doctor of education degree program in the Curry Department of Education.

The historically segregationist policies of Virginia's higher education institutions had just recently been tested. In July 1950, the University of Virginia Board of Visitors had rejected the application of Gregory Swanson, a practicing lawyer and a man of color seeking admission to the graduate-level law program. Identifying the applicant as a "colored man," the Visitors referred to

Virginia's laws and constitution, which "provide that white and colored shall not be taught in the same schools." Supported by lawyers for the NAACP—including future Supreme Court justice Thurgood Marshall—Swanson appealed to the state attorney general's ruling that Negroes could attend all-white institutions to pursue study in areas not available at the all-black state college.

On September 5, 1950, the District Court of Charlottesville found that since Gregory Swanson possessed all necessary scholastic and moral qualifications, he was denied admission solely because he was a member of the Negro race.[28] The decision made it possible for Ridley—a black man highly qualified for graduate studies—to apply and gain admission into the Curry Department of Education, as Virginia State College did not offer a doctoral degree in education.[29]

Walter Ridley received his Ed.D. in Educational Administration from the University of Virginia in 1953, becoming the first African American to earn a doctorate at a major white Southern university.[30] Twenty-five years later, in 1988, Ridley was recognized as a distinguished alumnus on the Curry School Foundation's Education Day. Interviewed for the *Curry School of Education Newsletter* at the time, he stated he had always been treated with respect at the University. He added that several times during his days as a graduate student, both black workers and white university students told him how proud they were of his achievement.

In his years as dean at Virginia and after, Lindley Stiles worked for school integration. Virginia's public schools of 1950 followed the separate-but-equal system, as did offerings in education at the University. Black and white teachers continuing their education at the University attended identical workshops, but on separate days. To circumvent the system, Stiles brought in guest speakers for a day at a time. By expecting all workshop participants to attend a one-day presentation, he ensured that black and white teachers came together.

Stiles testified at the controversial school desegregation hearings in Prince Edward County, Virginia, in the fall of 1951. "Segregation is not a matter of personal preference but rather a social cancer which is eating away at the heart of America," he stated publicly. "At a time when so much needs to be done to develop good schools for all," Stiles testified, "the principle of providing an equally excellent education for children of both races . . . should take precedence over the proposal that 'identical educational experiences' be provided for all."[31] The Prince Edward case was one of three sent to the Supreme Court, resulting in the historic *Brown v. Board of Education* decision in 1954 to end school segregation. Many believed that Stiles's arguments articulated fundamental principles essential to the decision.[32] The court ruling angered many state superintendents, a stance for which they apologized later.[33] In years to come, Stiles recalled how the struggle for integration monopolized the energies of the Commonwealth of Virginia in the early 1950s. Although his involvement was critical, he reported that it had hampered his efforts in other directions.[34]

McGuffey Reading Clinic, 1960s

Building a Community

In 1952 the Bureau of Educational Research was established as a division of the School of Education with Frank Lankford appointed as director.[35] President Darden viewed the bureau as essential for improving practices in schools and strengthening the University's research base in education. The bureau's original mission was to funnel information to state officials responsible for making decisions about Virginia schools. Its role expanded rapidly, though, and by 1957, the Curry School endorsed educational research as an area of specialization for an M.Ed. degree.[36] Under the bureau's aegis, Lankford and graduate student assistants conducted small-scale, service-oriented research projects, such as a two-year study of fifth-grade mathematics teaching, a study of pupil performance in public schools, and a summary of statistical information about Virginia schools.[37]

Stiles continued to promote his broad view of teacher preparation. "We see our function as one of making the resources of the University available to prospective teachers and to teachers in service," he wrote Darden in 1953, emphasizing that the University of Virginia, not just the School of Education, should prepare teachers. "To carry out such a role effectively professors of education must work harmoniously and closely with those in academic departments who are helping to prepare teachers."[38]

Following these principles, the school participated in developing a program in music education, jointly appointing a faculty member in the music department, Bernard Busse, in 1954. Busse presented a curriculum—a collaboration between the Department of Music, the College of Arts and Sciences, and the Curry School—that led to a B.S. degree in music education. The faculty approved four new courses in music education and an M.Ed. degree program in music

The Bureau of Educational Research

Established in 1952, the Bureau of Educational Research swiftly became an influential center, inspiring and administering research training and projects within the Curry School.[1] The Bureau provided consultation services to public schools and received governmental funding including a $48,000 multi-year research contract with the Air Research and Development Command.[2] Another study, completed in 1959, surveyed science departments in twenty-eight Virginia high schools and, based on findings, conveyed information and advice to science teachers and education school faculty.[3]

Succeeding Lankford, Ralph Banghart directed psychophysiological and psychological studies funded by the Air Force and Navy.[4] He left the post to join the University's medical school. Then, under the two-year leadership of William Hedges, Bureau research shifted to science education and a large-scale developmental effort in programmed elementary-level science instruction was launched. Milton Jacobson joined the faculty in 1964. He expanded the Bureau staff to three full-time faculty members and, emphasizing information technology, connected with the University's growing computing facilities. He maintained traditional service-oriented activities in the Bureau as well: consulting with individual Virginia schools, conducting surveys of instructional offerings in various fields, and analyzing test validity.[5]

In 1961 Curry School Dean Ralph Cherry sought ways for the Bureau to act more autonomously.[6] Cherry believed this structure would encourage an interdisciplinary approach to the study of educational problems and would create an office better able to compete for funds.[7]

The Bureau attained status as a separate unit within the school in 1965, and by 1971 there were six full-time faculty and a support staff numbering up to twenty-five. The Bureau remained a separate, non-academic unit from this time on, and its faculty also formed the Department of Educational Research as an academic unit of the school. Donald Medley joined the department from the Educational Testing Service

Bernard Busse and student, 1970s

education.[39] Busse went on to serve as acting chair of the music department, a coordinator of extension programs, and a professor in elementary curriculum and instruction through his years at the University of Virginia.[40] The music education program continued jointly with the music department through the 1970s.[41]

Alumni relations was another strand woven in to strengthen the fabric of the Curry community during the Stiles administration. In 1952, the first *Curry School Newsletter* was published and distributed to teachers and alumni in the state.[42] The December 1953 issue noted programs in teacher education; reported on the school's first social studies conference—including an address by the noted historian Henry Steele Commager—and its first physical education conference. It also announced conferences for teachers of science, mathematics, and language arts scheduled for the spring of 1954.[43]

While University enrollments had recently fallen, in the fall of 1954 they took an upward turn as nearly 3,600 students attended.[44] In the School of Education, the total number of resident undergraduates remained stable between 1949 and 1955, yet their academic records exceeded those of students before, reflecting strengthened entrance requirements. Graduate programs increased thanks to summer school and extension offerings. Fifteen M.Ed. degrees were awarded in August 1950; by August 1955, Stiles's last summer at Virginia, a total of 545 master of education degrees (almost half to women) and 19 doctor of education degrees (four to women) had been granted.[45] Between 1949 and 1955, enrollment in resident graduate education programs increased from 79 to 221, and

in Princeton, New Jersey, in 1970. Medley brought a strong quantitative background, from which he drew knowledge to apply to the analysis of many educational approaches.

The passage of the Elementary and Secondary Education Act of 1965 and subsequent federal educational grant legislation changed the entire field of educational research and affected the work of the Bureau between 1966 and 1971. This legislation established new planning, design, and evaluation components for grant programs and provided expanded funding both for program operations and research activities. State and local educational agencies often had difficulty meeting new mandates, accelerating the need for consulting assistance and researcher training. Private research organizations became eligible for contracts with the Office of Education and other federal agencies and, in general, the research contract requirements became more complex, decision-oriented, and extensive. The Bureau embarked on one particularly relevant project in 1969 when it collaborated with Virginia's Department of Education in a needs assessment designed to aid state leaders in determining future policies and practices related to student achievement. Jacobson served as director of the Bureau beginning in 1968 and was succeeded by Malcolm Provus. Michael Caldwell was appointed chair of the Bureau in 1975, also serving as chair of the Department of Educational Research and Evaluation through 1985.

Bureau activities continued through the 1980s, providing large-scale surveys of educational practices, both national and statewide.[8] One program headed by the Bureau, the Beginning Teachers Assistance Program (BTAP), was developed in response to legislation passed in the mid-1980s to assess beginning teacher competence and to provide teachers with specific feedback on classroom skills. The Bureau took the lead in Virginia to develop the program's assessment instrument.[9] State budget cuts and changes in University funding led to the decision to close the Bureau of Educational Research in the early 1990s.

Kindergarten class, Suffolk, Virginia, 1960

in the graduate program of the extension division from 457 to 642. Total student enrollment in education programs advanced from 229 in 1949 to 1,086 in 1955. Similarly, the total number of resident and extension classes offered by education faculty grew from 79 in 1949 to more than 930 in 1955, an increase of more than 300 percent.[46]

During these years, the Curry Memorial School of Education gained a valued ally in University Bursar Vincent Shea. A 1935 graduate of the University of Virginia with a background in public administration and finance, he was appointed bursar in 1947, replacing Elmer Carruthers, who had held this position since 1912. Shea was also administrative assistant to the president and secretary to the Board of Visitors. He was appointed comptroller in 1954 and vice president for business and finance in 1970. Deans from Stiles on considered Shea's advocacy critical to their efforts to hire new faculty, increase faculty salaries, enhance scholarships, and build new programs in the Curry School.[47]

Teacher education continued to be a point of controversy during the 1950s, not only in Virginia but nationally. In September 1953, Virginius Dabney, influential editor of the *Richmond Times-Dispatch,* called for higher standards of teacher preparation and better quality in education courses. He urged University faculty members—those in academic subject areas and those in professional teacher education—to address the issue together. Stiles responded, noting current changes in the Curry School and plans for continuing improvement.[48]

The *Cavalier Daily,* the University of Virginia student newspaper, picked up on the debate, running the headline: "Education School Held Weak Sister of University: Degree Factory Produces Athletes, Teachers and College Cast Offs." The school had become a "means of escape for the majority of undergraduates who cannot, or more frequently will not, muster up the necessary knowledge and effort to hurdle the few required courses set down by the college," wrote Corky Hawthorne. He concluded that the only students justified in enrolling in the School of Education were the athletes.[49] Education faculty and students retorted vigorously, and Hawthorne published an apology the following day, saying he had not been informed of recent changes in the school's academic requirements—although his tone was still somewhat dismissive. The school was, he wrote, "of course, only in existence to prepare students to become educators in some manner," but the "present move [to raise standards for admission] is in the right direction and is recognized as such."[50]

To serve as conduits between the faculty and his office, Dean Stiles formed a faculty council, a group of appointed and elected faculty members to advise him on important policy issues. Stiles felt this innovation was critical to creating a sense of ownership among faculty members. The Council was to exist in various permutations for the next fifty years until, during David Breneman's deanship, it became an autonomous faculty body. At the same time, the school lost the three faculty members who had been most involved in early work with county and city schools. Robert Swindler, professor of social studies, died in 1954; Frank Lankford, professor of mathematics, became president of Longwood College in 1955; and William Smithey, professor of secondary education, retired in 1952. All had been on the Curry School faculty for twenty-five years or more.

Another side of Lindley Stiles was reflected in his consistent praise of faculty and staff who worked with him during this time. He said that Mary Rush, longtime secretary for the school, shouldered many responsibilities for him. One anecdote Stiles tells of Miss Rush illustrates the times: "At Commencement Services, when I as Dean, had to call out the names of each graduate," Stiles recalled, "she coached me on the pronunciation of each. I remember her saying, 'That's John Smith III, and don't forget the "Third"; it is important down here.'"[51]

Stiles's vigor in attacking the issues he viewed as central laid the groundwork for many developments in the Curry School's future. He inherited a school that had been rudderless and sought to bring back a sense of direction. He established the school as a professional unit that granted master's and doctoral degrees and oversaw development of an elementary teacher preparation program.[52] He increased the size of the faculty to twenty and challenged them to broaden their outlook, to become involved at the state and national levels. He worked to bridge the gap between the public schools and the University and publicly supported school integration at a key time in the nation's history. He broadcast a weekly series of radio shows, which gave him a chance to share education school developments with teachers and administrators across the Commonwealth. Education faculty and students must have been pleased with the attention given the school in the 1954 *Corks and Curls,* with summaries and pictures of ongoing activities. All these changes reflected Stiles's willingness to challenge established patterns of behavior. He was not always an easy man to deal with. His zeal to reinvigorate the education school sometimes left ruffled feathers in its wake. "Dean Stiles listened to what students had to say but he made sure that we knew that major changes were needed in public education," one student of his recalled. "There was no question that Stiles was a change agent."[53]

Mary Rush, Curry School secretary from the mid-1930s to 1970

Early in 1955, it became clear that Stiles was looking for other career opportunities, especially something in which he could further develop the field of educational research. He accepted a position as dean of the education school at the University of Wisconsin in late May. The education faculty, the education advisory board, and President Darden all urged Stiles to stay at Virginia, but he felt that the Wisconsin offer better suited his future goals.[54] He was dean of the Curry School for only six years, but unarguably Lindley Stiles heightened the school's visibility, establishing a presence in Virginia and the nation that proved essential to its future.

McGuffey Reading Clinic, 1960s

CHAPTER 6

The Challenges of Growth and Expansion

Ralph W. Cherry, 1956–1968

One of the major responsibilities of the University is the preparation of teachers and other professional workers in education. The School of Education plays a leading role in planning and conducting programs designed to serve this purpose . . . A second function of the School of Education is research. . . . A third responsibility of the School of Education is to provide information, advice, and assistance to individuals and groups seeking to improve educational programs.[1]

— Ralph W. Cherry, 1963

When Lindley Stiles resigned his position as dean of the School of Education in the spring of 1955, Douglas Ward was appointed acting dean. After the 1955–1956 academic year, Ward left to become dean of the School of Education at Miami University. In his annual report for 1955, he anticipated critical issues facing the nation and Virginia, given the Supreme Court decision on integrating the public schools. It is "incumbent upon the University to spare no effort in maintaining the highest possible quality of programs for the preparation of teachers for the schools of the Commonwealth," Ward wrote.[2] Maintaining quality education while grappling with the complexities of integration was a challenge that occupied many Curry School faculty members for the next decade.[3] Behind them in their efforts stood Colgate Darden, University president and former governor of Virginia, who supported integrating the public schools.[4]

In February 1956 the education faculty voted to appoint Ralph W. Cherry as dean.[5] This Tennessee native had already been approached for the deanship in 1949, but he had just accepted a new position at the University of Texas.[6] With a doctorate from the Columbia University Teachers College, Cherry had been a high school teacher and athletic coach. After four years' service in World War II, he became a school administrator, ultimately superintendent of schools in Owensboro, Kentucky, then professor of educational administration at Texas. At Virginia, Cherry also assumed the leadership of the summer school. By all accounts he was a fair-minded man, committed to the social aspects of education and not afraid to make decisions. Cherry's "straight and firm" leadership style, as departmental minutes called it, promised that he could continue and cement the initiatives of his predecessor.[7] Cherry entered an institution "quite

Art education, 1980

unlike any I'd ever been associated with," as he put it: The University student population was still overwhelmingly male by law, and public education in the state of Virginia still faced turmoil surrounding issues of desegregation.[8]

Cherry began by hiring five faculty members, strengthening the school administration program, and suggesting appointments in guidance, science education, reading, and elementary education, positions that were filled in 1957. He had inherited a faculty still wrestling with change. Like Stiles, Cherry maintained a commitment to teacher education, steering a path midway between a strictly graduate, professional, and research-based school and a school focused exclusively on the undergraduate preparation of teachers. Thanks to this focus, the Curry School avoided the problems faced by many other schools of education in mid-century when they abandoned the mission of preparing teachers and focused only on training administrators and educational research.[9]

Teacher Preparation in the Cherry Era

During the Cold War—and especially when the Russian launch of the Sputnik satellite led to fears of American educational inferiority in the late 1950s—teaching and teachers underwent intense public scrutiny. Among lay critics, beyond a consensus that more intensive academic training was needed, there was no agreement on how to train teachers. In the words of one educational historian, "There were no models."[10] Writing in 1963 in *The Miseducation of American Teachers,* James Koerner delivered a scathing attack on the teaching profession and teachers' academic preparation, critiqued those entering teacher education programs and the content of education school courses—a judgment not uncommon at the time.[11] By the 1960s, research on teacher education programs became central to the debate about the nature of teacher preparation. The 1973 *Second Handbook of Research on Teaching* concluded that while no empirical research informed teacher training, "it is of current concern."

One route to improving teacher education was the newly conceived master of arts in teaching degree, first proposed by James Conant in 1936 as a way for liberal arts graduates to prepare to teach.[12] M.A.T. degree programs were funded primarily at Northern and Eastern institutions and rarely at the larger teacher preparation institutions. Well aware of this national initiative, the Curry School faculty approved an M.A.T. program in 1959.[13] The Curry School M.A.T. differed from others around the nation in that the program drew experienced, licensed teachers, not recent liberal arts graduates with no prior teaching preparation. Between August 1960 and May 1994, 257 M.A.T. degrees were awarded from the College of Arts and Sciences.[14] The degree was discontinued with the establishment of the five-year teacher education program leading to the Master of Teaching degree.

In 1960 the school sought accreditation by the National Council for Accreditation of Teacher Education,[15] which would validate offerings and ensured the survival of the teacher preparation program. The resulting NCATE review described undergraduate enrollment as traditionally small, between 200 and 250, and stated that "a limiting factor has been the policy concerning admission of women students . . . who are admitted only after they have completed two years

Counselor Education

Robert Pate

In 1951, Dean Lindley Stiles and Professor Richard Meade initiated an introductory class in counselor education, Theory and Practice of Guidance. This course represented the first step toward the Curry School's present-day degree program in counselor education, and soon the school was offering courses for those who wanted to be school counselors, thanks especially to the early work of Richard Beard, hired by Dean Cherry in 1958, who helped establish a Counselor Education program. Beard, who held degrees in English and counselor education, remained on the Curry School faculty for almost thirty years, serving as the first chair of the counselor education program from 1968 to 1973. Four others played important faculty roles in the program: Paul Walter, hired in 1959; Robert Pate, hired in 1968 and later becoming associate dean for administrative services; Ken LaFleur, hired in 1970; and William van Hoose, hired in 1972. Jeannette Brown initiated the first elementary counselor education program, in 1969. In 1972 counselor education became the Curry School's first off-Grounds degree-granting program, established in Windsor, Ontario.

Under the leadership of William van Hoose, the school developed a program of courses in school guidance counseling as well. Van Hoose founded and directed the Center for Professional and Career Development, which served the Charlottesville community. In 1979, the Curry School's counselor education program was one of the first four in the nation to be evaluated and approved by the Association for Counselor Education.[1] The program continues to provide graduate training at the University of Virginia as well as classes, workshops, and service placements throughout the state.

Helen Burr, Director of Speech and Hearing Clinic, working with children, 1960s

of college elsewhere. Since the possibility of effecting a change in this policy is slight and since men are not entering the profession in great numbers, the emphasis in recent years has been on the development of graduate programs." The report noted the increase in degrees awarded since the 1950 authorization of professional degrees and a 317 percent increase in budget allocations for the Curry School, compared with an overall University increase of 225 percent between 1949 and 1960.[16]

Full accreditation for all programs for ten years was granted in 1964.[17] The teacher education programs have been fully accredited by NCATE through 2005 and, in 2000, were fully accredited by the new Teacher Education Accreditation Council (TEAC). Under the leadership of Professor Sandra Cohen, Curry School's was the nation's first teacher education program to receive TEAC accreditation and thereby achieve the status of being accredited by both organizations.

Special Education

In 1939 Sidney Hall, the superintendent of state instruction, had written President John L. Newcomb to emphasize how important it was for the University of Virginia to offer courses in special education.[18] Through the 1940s, the department had developed several programs that prepared people to work with children with special needs, in speech and hearing and in reading. Nationally, more people were recognizing that only a small percentage of children who were identified as "exceptional" were being educated. Handicapped children were receiving inadequate educations. Attention was turning to children with special needs and to the quality of teacher preparation for those children. By the middle of the century, a majority of state legislatures had passed provisions to improve the education of handicapped children and to solidify certification requirements for special education teachers.[19]

In 1953 the Virginia General Assembly adopted a resolution recommending comprehensive special education programs in schools, adding that teacher training for such programs should be provided. Dean Stiles petitioned for a faculty position in special education. In May 1954 a committee report, *Program to Prepare Teachers for the Handicapped on the Grounds of the University of Virginia,* followed.[20]

The School of Education offered summer school courses on teaching exceptional children between 1947 and 1956. In May 1957 a comprehensive plan for a program in special education was presented to the faculty.[21] This proposal identified the categories of disability requiring teacher preparation: "Mentally Retarded, Gifted, Crippled, Emotionally Maladjusted, Deaf, Hard of Hearing, Blind, Partially Seeing, Speech Defective," and those with "special health problems such as being Epileptic, Diabetic, Cardiac, or Arthritic." Education school programs should coordinate with medical school clinics, the report suggested, and a Children's Rehabilitation Center should be built to serve children with special needs. Priorities listed were "mental retardation" and work with the "crippled, speech defective, hard-of-hearing and the gifted."[22]

Virgil Ward, colorful and controversial, joined the faculty in 1956 and established a program of education for gifted students, part of a program for exceptional learners that expanded under Cherry's leadership. Ward helped develop nine new courses in special education, including Exceptional Children, Mentally Retarded Children, Crippled Children, and Gifted Children.[23]

University Presidents Edgar F. Shannon (1959–1974), left, and Colgate Darden (1947–1959)

Changing Times

Responding to increasing student interest, Cherry proposed doubling allocations for the Reading Clinic and recommended a University committee on teacher education. He also shared Stiles's belief that the whole University, not just the School of Education, bore the responsibility for preparing teachers. In January 1957, the faculty moved to recommend the admission of first-year women students beginning in the fall semester.[24] Agreeing with Cherry, President Darden appointed a University-wide committee—with three members from the education school, four from the College, and chaired by Joseph Vaughan—to "make a careful study of the relationship of the College of Arts and Sciences and the School of Education."[25] Darden's concern was course redundancy, but Cherry felt that committee results could help his school move through a "difficult time" of transition.[26]

The school was challenged by organizational issues as it expanded. Program areas were evolving; more courses in various disciplines were being offered. Faculty discussions eventually resulted in the establishment of a departmental structure within the school. In advance of formal departmentalization, Cherry established four area committees: Administration and Supervision, Curriculum and Instruction, Educational Psychology, and Physical Education. He also assigned his twenty-six faculty members to three committees to guide operations: Undergraduate, Graduate, and Student Personnel, each designed to oversee courses, programs, and administrative tasks.[27] Faculty morale improved, relationships with professional organizations in the state strengthened, and a counselor education program was emerging.[28] Additionally, a student chapter of the National Education Association was established in 1957.

Rumors about Colgate Darden's retirement had been circulating for a year before his formal 1958 announcement. Phi Delta Kappa, the Curry School's educational professional organization, wrote the retiring president to commend his efforts on behalf of their school. "When you arrived, the field of Education was a small field indeed. At that time we were merely a Department," they wrote. "You built us into a School, for which we owe you much."[29] Edgar Shannon, a professor of English, was appointed fourth president of the University of Virginia early in 1959. His appointment was fortunate for the School of Education, given his longstanding interest in education. President Shannon would continue to be most supportive of education school efforts throughout his tenure.

The Vaughan committee issued its report in the spring of 1958. Cherry assured his faculty that the "committee and President are most sympathetic and not hostile."[30] The report focused first on the need to coordinate course offerings between the Curry School and the College of Arts

Special Education and Gifted Education

Federally mandated improvements in education for handicapped children in the 1960s prompted rapid changes in special education offerings. Faculty member James Beaber led the Curry School's efforts in that era, and his significant contributions in the field of mental retardation brought attention to the Curry School.[1] In 1964 the department received the first of many federal grants to educate teachers planning to work with children with special needs,[2] specifically mentally retarded children, children with crippling conditions, and children with emotional disabilities.[3]

In 1967, as part of the restructuring of the school, a Department of Special Education was created with its own budget, with Beaber as chair, and with eight faculty and two clerical staff members.[4] John Mesinger headed the program for teachers planning to work with emotionally disturbed children. In 1967 he and his colleague, Eleanore Westhead, received state funding to start Charlottesville's first Emotionally Disturbed and Learning Disabled Resource for teachers.[5] William Carriker, another noted expert in the field of mental retardation, chaired the department between 1969 and 1978. The department later merged with other areas to become the Department of Curriculum, Instruction, and Special Education.

Special education faculty collaborated with University of Virginia Medical School faculty on a 1966 grant proposal to develop a Research and Training Center for Exceptional Children, an initiative that ultimately resulted in the building of the Children's Rehabilitation Center at the University.[6] James Kauffman and Daniel Hallahan joined the department in the early 1970s, enriching the collaborative possibilities that have resulted in significant work in the field of special education over the past thirty years.

In 1977 the University of Virginia was selected as the site for one of five new learning disability institutes in the United States, funded by the U.S. Office of Education. Co-directed by Hallahan and Rebecca Kneedler, the five-year grant supported teachers, pre-service students, schoolchildren, and evaluators, whose goal was to systematize the work of teachers with children identified with learning disabilities.[7] Many faculty became involved, including Ann Loper from educational psychology in the Curry School and others from Arts and Sciences's Department of Psychology. John Mesinger obtained funding for an "educateur" program, through which students were trained to understand adolescent behavior and counseling techniques in addition to the instructional techniques used in special education. They worked in residential programs and held internships in the Charlottesville and Albemarle County schools. The program continued into the mid-1980s.[8]

Special education faculty received significant funding for training grants for both master's and doctoral students. Bill Carriker and Jerry Wallace were successful in securing training grants for doctoral students from 1986 through 1997. In 1987 the department received a three-year grant to study children with severe emotional disturbances; at that time the department ranked third among eighty-one U.S. doctoral programs in special education.[9] From 1997 to 2000, through the Center for Minority Research in Special Education, a cadre of doctoral students conducted research

Exhibit on Curry School special education programs, 1965

Special Education Rehabilitation Center, 1968

on minority students in special education classes. Another three-year initiative began in 1997: the Multicultural Special Education Leadership Training Grant. Professor Marti Snell's work with children with severe disabilities has inspired a consortium with other institutions for training special educators.

The Curry programs in special education continue to rank high nationally: fourth in 2004, in part because of the significant research and publications of the faculty. Kauffman and Hallahan authored *Exceptional Learners*, now in its ninth edition and one of the most widely read texts in special education. Faculty members consult nationally and internationally on issues related to children with special needs. The debate over inclusion—teaching children with special needs in the regular classroom with assistance—has been of particular interest in the Curry School. Snell's research has done much to advance the concept through identifying the benefits for all children of including children with special needs in classrooms. Other faculty members believe it is important to assess each situation to determine the least restrictive environment in which an individual child will learn.

From the 1960s on, developments in the field of gifted education have paralleled those in other fields of special education. Virgil Ward, professor in the educational psychology program, published a 1961 text, *Educating the Gifted*, an early contribution to the field.[10] Joining the department in 1973, Carolyn Callahan spearheaded many innovative programs. In the late 1970s, gifted education became a specialty in educational psychology, evolving to include a doctoral program.

Under Callahan's leadership, in 1980 a residential summer enrichment program for children in grades five through ten was established. It continues today, attracting students from all over the country for three two-week sessions. Another enrichment program for children in or near Charlottesville was created in the mid-1980s. The Saturday Enrichment program, operated during the spring semester each year, provides education for elementary school children in areas ranging from science to the arts, staffed by many students and teachers in the Curry School.

In 1985 the first National Research Center on the Gifted and Talented—a consortium of the Curry School, Yale University, and the University of Connecticut—formed to involve educators in research on topics ranging from the identification of gifted students to studies of Advanced Placement courses. Carol Tomlinson became a leader in the center, developing her work on differentiation as part of her involvement. Her research and publications on differentiating instruction have widely influenced the nature of teaching, nationally and internationally. Other initiatives of the gifted education faculty are the Summer Institute on Academic Diversity and the Best Practices Institute, both of which draw educators to the Curry School to explore instruction design for varying student needs.[11]

Dean Cherry dictates a letter

and Sciences; then it addressed teacher education, urging the school to scout out unnecessary course duplication, drop inactive courses from the catalog, and strengthen both the undergraduate and graduate programs. These calls motivated the faculty to make some changes. They increased to thirty the number of hours of education courses required for an undergraduate degree in elementary education and, in a selected field, for an undergraduate degree in secondary education. Requirements for the master's and doctorate of education degrees were clarified, and offerings in health, physical education, music, and exceptional children programs were reexamined.[31]

1958 was the year of massive resistance to school integration in Virginia. Ralph Cherry and other education school faculty often addressed school groups during this contentious time. An outspoken advocate of integration, Cherry received much publicity; only one out of four state superintendents supported his position.[32] Cherry actively worked to keep the Charlottesville City Schools open at a time when other school systems shut down entirely. He served as acting superintendent of the Charlottesville school system in the summer of 1966 and later headed the Consultative Resource Center in the Curry School.[33]

At an alumni breakfast in Richmond, scheduled during the annual VEA meeting in the fall of 1961, plans began for regional alumni meetings. These events quickly proved successful and represented another effective link between state educational leaders and the Curry School, leading to the development of the Curry School of Education Foundation.

By 1962 the education faculty had increased in number to thirty-four. Undergraduate enrollment was static—in part, Cherry reported, due to tightened admission standards and the recent retraction of first-year admission opportunities.[34] To encourage and model educational research among graduate students, the Curry School began publishing the *Education Review* in 1963. The journal continued for the next twelve years and highlighted contributions made to the field of education at the University.[35]

Developments in the Curry Memorial School of Education during Ralph Cherry's time as dean reflected developments in the University as a whole. During Edgar Shannon's fifteen-year presidency, from 1959 to 1974, the University of Virginia doubled in size, added many buildings to support new programs, addressed issues of integration and coeducation, and faced the challenge of student protests against the Vietnam War. Throughout all this, the quality of education in the nation's schools was also receiving wide public attention, focused increasingly on schools of education.

Programs had grown so that it became necessary to organize the school into departments. After much debate, in the fall of 1967, Dean Cherry brought nine new faculty members into a school now organized into six departments: Administration and Supervision, Counselor Education, Curriculum and Instruction (which included the former Department of Physical Education), Foundations of Education, Special Education, and Speech Pathology and Audiology.[40]

Old Dominion Humanities Institute

In 1966, a six-year program designed to broaden teachers' knowledge of the humanities was instituted under the sponsorship of the Old Dominion Foundation in the Virginia schools, staffed by faculty from the engineering school's Division of Humanities. The Old Dominion Humanities Institute, a four-week Summer Session course, began without direct association with the Curry School but soon involved many Curry faculty. The program grew out of extended discussions with the education honorary society, Phi Delta Kappa, and was designed to connect humanities scholars with secondary schoolteachers, "creating a meaningful interchange from which both scholars and secondary schools will benefit."[36] The institute developed newsletters for state educators. By 1970, 272 teachers and 25 school divisions had benefited from its assistance in developing interdisciplinary programs.[37] Although tangential to Curry School offerings, the institute's underlying philosophy and interdisciplinary approach to learning resonated within the Curry School's teacher education faculty, many of whom were associated with the institute during its planned six-year lifespan. School of Education faculty adopted the program,[38] and in 1971 it became the University of Virginia Humanities Institute, offering six hours of credit for an anticipated sixty attendees.[39]

Institute leaders joined with Curry faculty in 1970 to seek more funding, especially in response to the state of Virginia's new Standards of Quality, which mandated the "humanizing of instruction in classrooms," which meant providing for individual differences and using materials that addressed an array of student skills and attributes. Funds were not renewed, however, and in 1972 the Humanities Institute saw the end of its "temporary but exciting life," as a newsletter article termed it.[40]

Student protests affected the University from the late 1960s into the early 1970s

A New Education Building

Departmental reorganization solved one of the Curry School's mid-1960s crises—complexity of governance—but it still needed larger and more modern quarters to accommodate its growing needs.[41] The entire University had grown tenfold since the days when Peabody Hall was first built, and Curry School programs were scattered all over the Grounds. Based on the recommendation of School of Architecture Dean Thomas FitzPatrick, the Houston firm of Caudill, Rowlett and Scott was selected to design a new education school building.[42] As associate architects, Rawlings, Wilson and Fraher of Richmond, Virginia, created final working drawings, approved by the state in 1967, and construction was carried out by the Charlottesville firm of R. E. Lee.[43]

Siting the building was a challenge. No room contiguous to the central University Grounds remained, so a site was chosen that could connect to the Grounds by a bridge over Emmet Street. Budget issues resulted in several construction delays. The frustration of the architects was apparent in a letter written to President Shannon during an impasse in negotiations in 1968. "So many of our dreams and ambitions" were

The Consultative Resource Center on School Desegregation

Nathan Johnson and James Bash, 1967 (above)

Mothers bring children to Venable School, Charlottesville, on first day of integration, 1959 (opposite)

In 1967, to facilitate school desegregation in Virginia, the Curry School of Education established the Consultative Resource Center (CRC). Funding came from Title IV of the Civil Rights Act of 1964, by which the federal government could provide technical assistance and training to help public schools solve problems remaining after desegregation.[1] Announcing the center, founding faculty member James H. Bash described that school involvement with it was voluntary: Programs would help school systems "develop their own solutions to their own problems so that the tensions resulting from these problems will not disrupt the educational function of the schools." The center referred specialists in sociology, law, and psychology to schools as needed.[2] Over its fourteen years, the CRC provided resources to school systems in Virginia, Maryland, West Virginia, and the District of Columbia. The work of the center was extremely important, but much documentation has been lost over the years—a reflection, perhaps, of the ambivalence felt by many at the University toward school desegregation in general and the center in particular.[3] Center offices moved frequently during its fourteen-year history, too, which undoubtedly contributed to the loss of records.

James Bash wrote the first funding proposal, hired the first staffers, and directed the center until 1972. Bash had been the principal of the white high school in Farmville, Virginia, an office from which he publicly opposed closing the Prince Edward County schools. His position alienated him from other whites in the community and eventually led to his resignation as principal. Nathan Johnson, a former principal of George Washington Carver High School in Fieldale, Virginia, served as associate director through the entire existence of the center. Professor Johnson holds the distinction of having been the first African American appointed to the University of Virginia faculty.[4] Both men's public school backgrounds helped them develop successful school contacts. After Bash, the center was directed by Dean Ralph Cherry for a year, followed by Professor Howard Allen.

In 1972 the "Deseg Center," as many tagged it, changed its official name to the Consultative Resource Center on School

Integration. The new name reflected a "new emphasis," reported the Charlottesville *Daily Progress,* moving away from "direct work on immediate problems involved in desegregation" and toward "long-range work dealing with larger problems in the integration of schools."[5] School participation was voluntary, so the center could contact districts to publicize its services but could not require any school system to work with it. Center representatives had to be persuasive in order for staff to be invited into the schools. Bash employed George Copenhaver, a former superintendent of schools from Clifton Forge, Virginia, reasoning that superintendents would respond better to invitations that came from one of their peers.[6] Once a superintendent did request assistance, the staff planned workshops and seminars for that school district, covering issues such as curricular reform, minority student counseling, discipline in the integrated classroom, and analysis of the treatment of minorities in textbooks.

The center's philosophy was based on the belief that dialogue across racial lines would smooth the desegregation process. "We were bringing blacks and whites together for the first time—our job was to get black and white people to talk," said Allen and Bash when interviewed together in 2002.[7] The center sponsored two- or three-day regional meetings, statewide conferences, and retreats on topics such as curriculum revision and strategies for hiring more African American professionals. The center also held two-week summer institutes at the University. Faculty members published several texts that developed out of their work through the center, in particular James Bash's *Effective Teaching in the Desegregated School,* published in 1966.[8]

In 1973–1974 the center worked with eighty-five school divisions in Virginia, West Virginia, and Washington, D.C.,[9] ran seventeen two-day workshops and thirteen one-day workshops, and organized a seven-weekend Educational Leadership Institute attended by more than 350 school personnel. The institute's goals were to build understanding on work issues in multiethnic settings and to increase the pool of schools using its services. Among institute participants, twenty-five stated

they would be doing further work at the University.[10] The CRC consistently sought feedback from participants and educational leaders around the state, although much of this documentation is lost. One research project associated with the center was carried out by Curry professor Herbert C. Richards, who developed and validated a survey instrument to measure attitudes toward race and change.[11]

In response to Title IX of the Education Amendments of 1972, which prohibited gender discrimination in educational institutions, the center turned to gender equity issues as well. Racial equity continued to be the central focus, however, and the center lost Title IX funding in 1981 to a gender equity center at American University in Washington, D.C.

Many center activities were staffed primarily by graduate students, who traveled throughout the state and region. What documentary materials exist, combined with oral histories of those involved, portray a complex operation and diligent outreach efforts to a broad geographic area. The Deseg Center contributed significantly to the integration of the public schools, yet its impact is now, sadly, difficult to measure.[12] Mention of the center, though, continues to evoke impassioned memories from those who worked to bring about change in the schools of Virginia and the surrounding states.[13]

Rendering of proposed School of Education building, ca. 1968

embodied in the plans, wrote the architects. "We so wanted to put a first-class building on the University of Virginia campus."[44]

By the time problems were solved and ground was broken, in 1970, the school had already outgrown the plans. Education faculty sought funding from the Kresge Foundation in Birmingham, Michigan, proposing to establish a Kresge Center for Educational Experimentation and, to house it, a wing to the building under construction. The proposal envisioned a two-story experimental wing "where we will be able to invent and/or reproduce virtually any setting in which learning and education take place" plus videotaping facilities, a Multiprofessional Education Diagnostic Laboratory, and a Communications Complex, all sending Virginia's School of Education to a vanguard position in educational technology.[45] Two architecture faculty members even drafted plans for the wing, but funding failed and the center never came into being.

Since 1970 critics have assailed the design and construction of the new education building, but at the time CRS was considered one of the finest architectural firms designing school buildings and had just completed two junior high and the senior high school buildings for the city of Charlottesville. They were particularly noted for innovative plans in classroom design, and many believed that such an approach would express the Curry School of Education's interest in new directions in education.

Retiring from the Deanship

Ralph Cherry announced his intention to step down as dean of the Curry School as of July 1968. In his letter to President Shannon, Cherry expressed pride in the school's growth and development through the twelve years of his leadership. Pleased with the present direction of the school, he also felt that much credit should be given to others, including Shannon himself: "Certainly

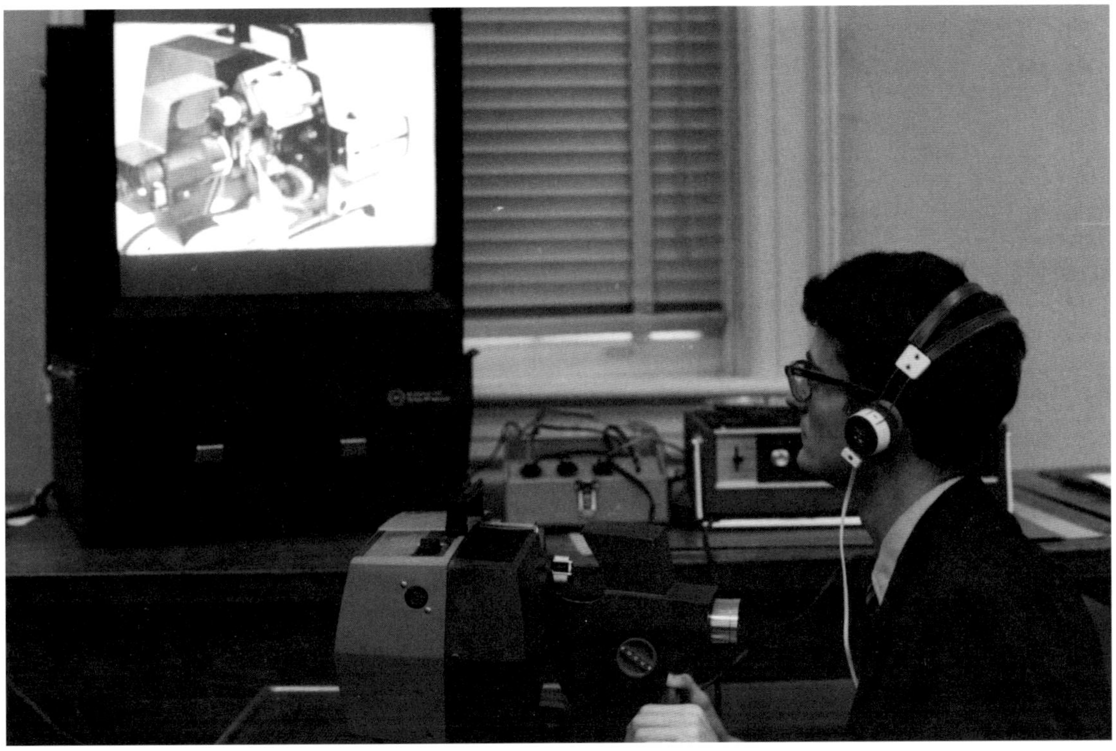

1960s-era audiovisual technology

we could have done little to improve the situation without your wholehearted support."[46] He felt "optimism" about the future, he wrote, but it was time for new leadership.[47] Cherry stayed on as an active faculty member until his retirement in 1976. He became chair of the Department of Special Education within a year, remained dean of the Summer Session, served as acting dean of the Curry School during the summer of 1974, and directed the Curry School Foundation.

Ralph Cherry saw the school through a tempestuous time in the country's history. Fending off criticism both local and national, he steadily solidified programs in the Curry School and raised standards for entering students. Visions did not fail him: In his last annual report, he requested eight additional faculty members, although he had already doubled the faculty to nearly forty full-time and thirteen part-time members. He left a school that offered more than 120 courses in the areas of education (including teacher education, administration, special education, counseling, and foundations); health; physical education and recreation; and music education. At the same time, his guidance had helped the school coalesce these disparate programs into a logical departmental structure.

"Summarizing my life as dean of the School of Education," said Cherry when interviewed in 1976, "I'd say it was a constant race between demand and supply of services."[48] Ralph Cherry developed programs and instituted structures that were emerging under Stiles's tenure. He brought order and substance to the school's offerings. At the time of his retirement, many believed that his greatest contribution was to raise the stature of the Curry School of Education within its own community at the University of Virginia.[49]

Civil rights rally, 1968

CHAPTER 7

A Vision for the Role of Educational Research

Frederick R. Cyphert, 1968–1974

The best professional schools are characterized by a pervasive theme . . . which permeates their approaches to scholarly endeavors. The School of Education seeks to be known as the leading exponent of the point of view that educational phenomena can be approached scientifically. . . . We are more than ordinarily committed to enlarging and strengthening the knowledge underlying professional practice and to seeking better strategies for applying such knowledge. Our chief business is extending knowledge and communicating understanding.[1]

— Frederick R. Cyphert, 1971

In 1968, Frederick R. Cyphert of Ohio State University was selected as the fourth dean of the Curry School of Education. Cyphert—called Ted by all who knew him—came to the Curry School with a background in curriculum and instruction and a particular interest in teacher education. As dean, however, his primary goal was to establish the school as a research institution, and many of his efforts went toward this end. He believed that lessening the divide between theory and practice was critical to the Curry School's growth as an institution of importance.[2] His emphasis on research reflected a desire for legitimacy in an era when schools of education continued to be under fire, and Cyphert was anxious to create a leadership role for the Curry School. During his six-year administration, he advanced faculty efforts in educational research, supported the expansion of many programs, and nearly tripled the size of the faculty.

The 1960s saw increased funding for educational research. President Lyndon Baines Johnson designated education as a priority of his "Great Society," and federal funds to improve educational practices became available as never before. Both qualitative and quantitative studies of education were part of the agenda.[3] Increased funding for educational research came from the National Science Foundation, the U.S. Office of Education, and other agencies as well, all seeking ways to improve and encourage educational attainment in the nation's schools.

What Should Be Done?

Cyphert wanted to create a vision for the School of Education. While the school had grown and standards had tightened in both undergraduate and graduate programs, many questions still had to be addressed. One of Cyphert's first initiatives was to survey more than four hundred educational, political, and organizational leaders in Virginia, asking their views on the future role of the Curry School of Education. Study results would help shape plans for the school through the next decade.[4] The survey utilized the Delphi Technique, with four occasions for respondents to answer questions and provide feedback.

Respondents said that the school's main priorities should be to increase the quality of its graduating educators, recruit talented people into teaching, and improve the curriculum of the education school. Secondary priorities expressed were to use research to improve teaching methods, to prepare educators for work in "innovative programs that deal with constantly changing educational problems," and to develop nationally acclaimed programs. Survey respondents did not emphasize outreach to school divisions or leadership among Virginia's other schools of education.[5] These findings gave impetus to Cyphert's plan to strengthen research on effective educational practices and to strengthen the undergraduate program of teacher education.

Cyphert put his stamp on the school, much as his predecessors had, by encouraging faculty to seek out grants, by actively cultivating state and national contacts, and by expecting faculty members to publish and participate in national professional organizations.[6] He was able to recruit a substantial number of new faculty members each year. In the fall of 1969, seventeen new faculty members taught in the school. He added twelve more each for the academic years of 1970–1971 and 1971–1972.[7] He hired recognized leaders in their fields, especially in special education, reading, and counselor education. Concerned with faculty and student perceptions of the Curry School, Cyphert met with individual groups regularly. He heard that they were satisfied with programs "but not excited" about their work. He felt that in his six years as dean, he managed to reverse that trend.[8]

From Peabody to Ruffner, Winter 1972–1973

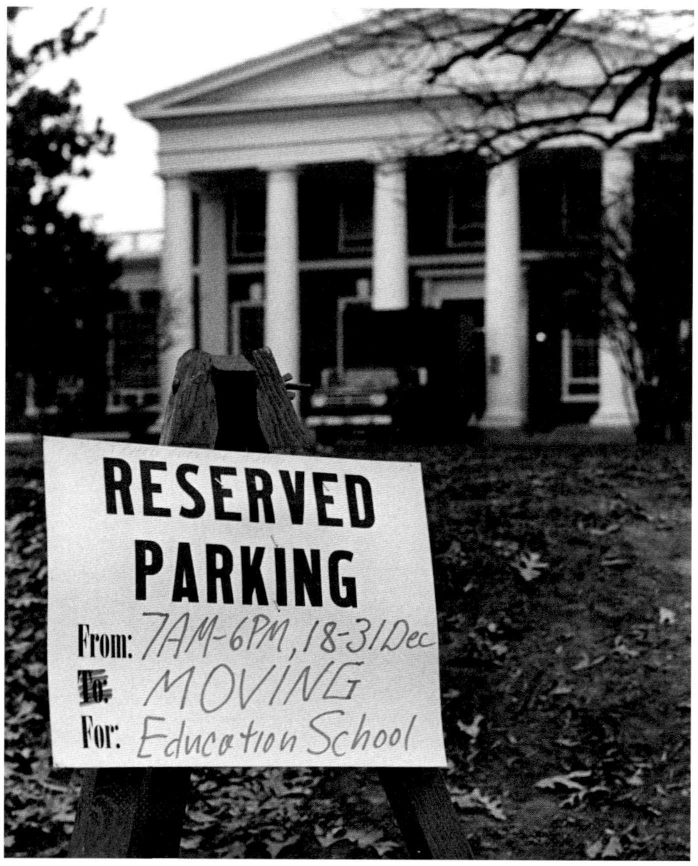

Cyphert enjoyed close relationships with President Shannon, Provost David Shannon, and University Bursar Vincent Shea, important connections as he sought to develop programs and to recruit outstanding faculty. A number of handwritten notes, many in red ink, from Cyphert to Shannon can be found among the University president's papers from this time, suggesting a level of informality and ease of communication not enjoyed by other deans. In his 1969 annual report, Cyphert stated that he was "committed to making this the nation's best school of education."[9] A national accreditation team visited in the spring of 1970 and noted how a "renewed commitment to professional education" was spurring the present administration and faculty to "rapidly develop programs which will have an impact on the field of professional education." Faculty and administrators told them that "if they don't succeed in becoming one of the foremost leaders in the field of professional education in the next decade, they will have only themselves to blame."[10]

"Experimental education" class, ca. 1970

Broadening the Community

The historic 1970 admission of women to the University of Virginia "on the same basis as men" had great impact on the Curry School as well as the University as a whole. Coeducation had been under consideration for many years. Interim solutions had included establishing a coordinate college for women, Mary Washington, in Fredericksburg in 1945.[11] In 1967 President Shannon recommended a study "of the need to admit women to the College of Arts and Sciences" and formed a committee led by T. Braxton Woody, a professor of French and Spanish. The Woody committee studied all aspects of the coeducation issue, arousing both negative and positive responses from alumni. In November 1968 the committee recommended that women be admitted to the University on an equal basis with men, and the Board of Visitors directed that President Shannon should oversee the transformation.[12] Education school faculty considered coeducation especially important for their school, since it would make it possible to screen out those not seriously interested in teaching before their last two years of college—a factor quoted in the Woody commission report itself: "The future of the undergraduate program within the School of Education is very dependent upon the University becoming coeducational."[13]

Cyphert focused on finding outside funding, bolstering faculty research, and working to strengthen Curry's graduate program, but inadequate facilities continued to thwart his efforts. At the end of the 1969–1970 academic year, Cyphert cited sixteen areas in which the Curry

The Center for the Study of Higher Education

Curry School faculty interest in the emerging field of the study of higher education found its expression when, in 1969, Dean Cyphert hired Professor Jay Chronister from the University of Pittsburgh to direct a new Center for Higher Education (later renamed the Center for the Study of Higher Education). The rapid growth of Virginia's community college system helped stimulate the center, and it quickly became a lively and integral part of the Curry School.[1] First a "one-man operation" in the basement of Peabody Hall, it moved into a converted classroom the next year and expanded its activities.[2] A doctoral program in the study of higher education received approval from the School of Education in 1970 and from the State Council of Education in 1971.

The center became a nexus to which faculty from different departments contributed time and effort. Robert Pate of counselor education taught several courses and went on the road with Chronister to offer workshops and to recruit students. Jennings Wagoner of the foundations department developed a course on the history of higher education, which became a core offering for center students. Faculty from beyond the Curry School also worked with the center, including Alton Taylor of Institutional Research, later director of the Summer Session, and Lawrence Simpson of Career Planning and Placement. Annette Gibbs, appointed associate dean of students by University President Edgar Shannon in 1970, requested appointment to the center faculty as part of her assignment.

Samuel Kellams, a Curry faculty member for thirty years, helped run a fellowship program for preparing community college teachers. With the University of Virginia Graduate School of Arts and Sciences, between 1969 and 1974 the center received $170,000 in fellowship aid for community college teachers and administrators. The center has offered courses in organizational theory and legal aspects of higher education, developed a strong program in student affairs administration, and maintained a long-term relationship with Charlottesville's Piedmont Virginia Community College.

Early on, many students at the center worked as interns in the community college system. Over time the program expanded to include placements in many of the University's top administrative offices, in other universities and colleges, and in higher education agencies in Richmond and Washington, D.C. These internships built networks and brought financial aid that gave the Center an advantage over similar programs elsewhere. By 2005, well over one hundred higher education professionals had benefited from the center's internship program.

The Center awarded its first three doctoral degrees in 1973. Within a decade, fifty more Ed.D. or Ph.D. degrees had been awarded. With an average enrollment of eighty students per year—most of them part-time—from the 1980s onward, the Center had awarded more than 150 doctorates by the first years of the twenty-first century.[3]

In 1977 the *International Encyclopedia of Education* listed the Center one of the world's "institutions of major significance in the study of higher education." It has more recently ranked in *U.S. News & World Report* among the top higher education programs in the country. Over the years, the center has drawn prominent visiting scholars, including David W. Breneman—then a scholar at the Brookings Institution—who ultimately became dean of the Curry School—along with David Riesman, Howard Bowen, Patricia Hollander, James S. Coleman, and Malcolm Knowles. For years the center published addresses by these and other scholars in its *Occasional Papers* series. Faculty led summer workshops for the center between 1982 and 1988, drawing participants from across the country. Topics under discussion included higher education management strategies, faculty evaluation, faculty employment issues, pathways to the community college presidency, managerial perspectives on women in administration, and changing perspectives on student affairs and the law.

In 1985 Dean James Cooper implemented a new organization, combining the center with the Department of Educational Leadership and Policy Studies, with Jennings Wagoner as chair of the newly formed department and Annette Gibbs center director. Under their leadership, the center continued to build its emphasis in policy studies along with preparing students for leadership in higher education institutions.

School could claim accomplishments: recruitment of outstanding faculty, improvement in the quality of undergraduate students, the largest percentage of school budget increases across the University, successful NCATE reaccreditation (he called it "survival"), more outside funding than ever before, progress in construction on the new building, and the increased national stature of the faculty.[14]

New education building, outside and inside, 1974

Graduate program enrollments increased in 1971, up 300 from the year before to 994 applicants, of whom 746 were accepted. A total of 744 education degrees were awarded at the spring and summer graduations in 1971. Faculty productivity increased as well, with outside funding that included several grants over one million dollars. The faculty approved a new education specialist degree program in 1972, offering school personnel a degree beyond the master's without having to commit to the lengthier process of earning a Ph.D.[15] Cyphert reported a 206 percent faculty increase in five years: "greater than any other academic unit in the University," he proudly stated, "which has resulted in a better faculty-student ratio since the student population has not grown at this rate."[16] At a July 1971 meeting, Cyphert complimented the faculty for their efforts, noting the "high influx of positive statements" he had received about the school's courses and teaching.[17]

Faculty fall retreats continued during Cyphert's years, and a faculty council provided the dean with faculty input on administrative decisions. The council drafted mission statements and debated student admission policies. When the Student Education Association was revived in the fall of 1971, it had a membership of 150, compared to 21 in 1970. While faculty membership in the Virginia Education Association declined, alumni receptions still took place at the annual fall VEA meeting in Richmond.

In an effort to broaden the reach of public education, in 1971 the C. S. Mott Foundation funded fifteen community education regional centers across the country. One of them, the Mid-Atlantic Community Education Consortium, was located at the University of Virginia and directed by the Curry School's Professor Larry Decker. Serving as a nexus for six higher education institutes and four state education departments, it focused on improving community education in Virginia, Maryland, Delaware, the District of Columbia, West Virginia, North Carolina, and South Carolina. Initially, the center offered seed grants to selected school systems to develop events for the benefit of their local community members. Later the emphasis shifted to establishing a consortium of cooperating centers covering the region. By 1976, the consortium consisted of twelve centers, including state departments of education and institutions of higher learning, and provided training and consultation to keep community education programs thriving. Community education centers became a way to encourage schools to improve community outreach.[18] The consortium publicized ways to integrate the public schools into the community, such as the pamphlet "Public Schools: Use Them Don't Waste Them," which offered ways to use school buildings for community-based programs.[19] Consortium newsletters, published several

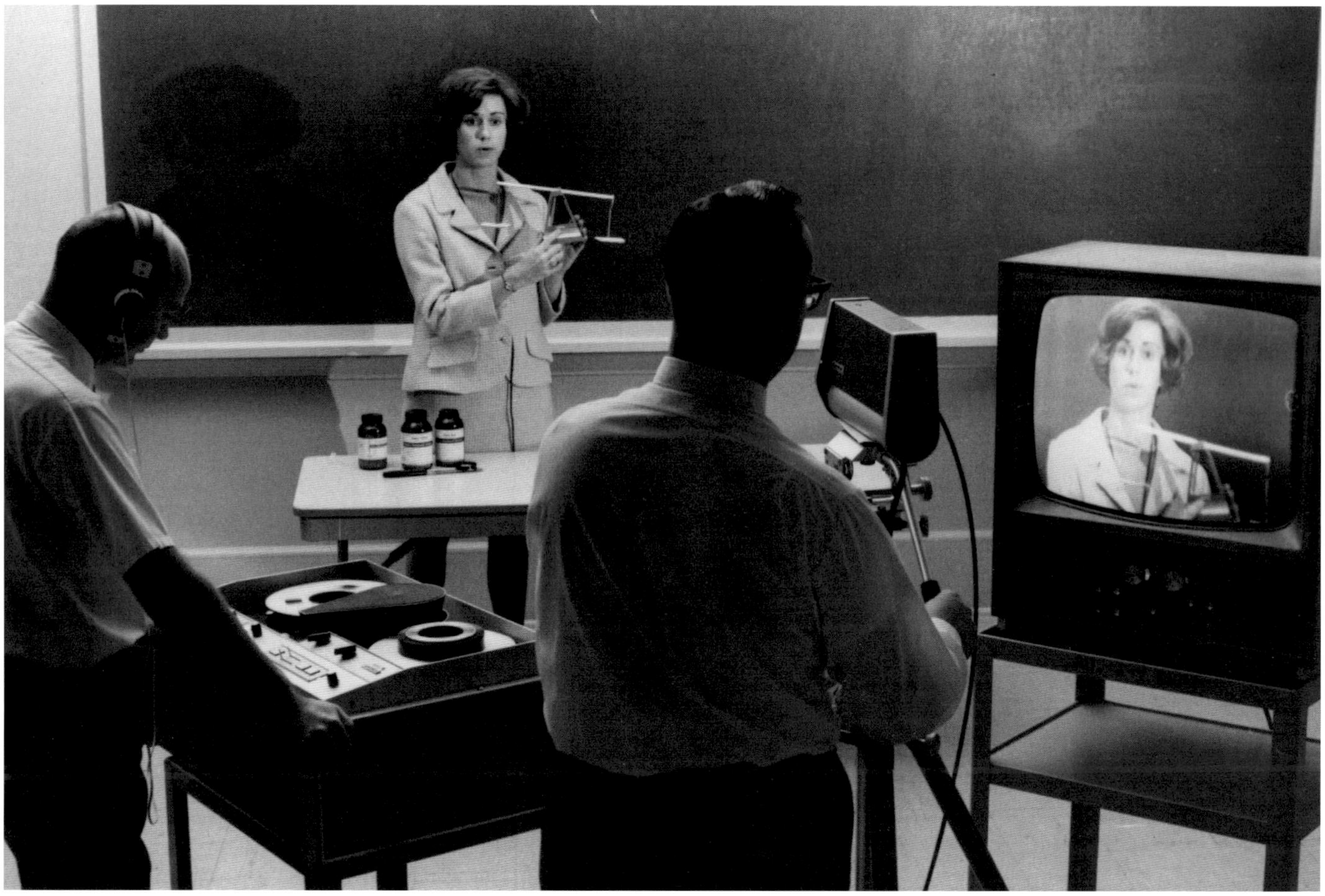

New audiovisual possibilities, 1970s

times a year, gave suggestions on how to break down barriers in communities between social agencies and the public schools.[20]

Ruffner Hall

When Ted Cyphert arrived, he found a faculty demoralized by their working conditions. He minced no words in his first annual report about the decaying atmosphere of Peabody Hall and wrote to the University's building and grounds personnel: "Peabody Hall is used by students from several areas of the Grounds and by hundreds of part-time students . . . neither the building nor the School of Education is identified in any visible manner. As you would expect, this lack of identity causes considerable confusion."[21] The 1972 *Corks and Curls* highlighted space problems in Peabody Hall by showing a picture of a computer punch card alongside existing classrooms—a graphic statement that the school needed more room for computers. Assistant Dean Michael Caldwell promised that the new building would accommodate "apparatus for modern audio-visual aid equipment," specialized labs containing one-way mirrors for teaching observations, and rooms for studying children in "realistic class situations." The long-anticipated move took place over the Christmas holidays in 1972. It was not without its problems. Faculty complained about space allocations. And soon after its completion, structural problems developed.[22]

The issue of the name for the new building was a topic of debate, but the decision was finally made to honor William Henry Ruffner, an influential proponent of public schools in the late nineteenth century.[23] Born in Lexington, Virginia, in 1824, Ruffner was the son of the president of Washington College (now Washington and Lee University). After graduating from Washington College in 1842, he briefly attended the University of Virginia, where one of his professors was William Holmes McGuffey, the famous author of the *Eclectic Readers*. Ruffner prepared for the ministry and served as chaplain at the University of Virginia from 1849 to 1851. Poor health forced him to retire from the ministry, and Ruffner farmed for a number of years. In 1870 he returned to public service and was appointed Virginia's first superintendent of public instruction in 1870. In this role Ruffner oversaw progress toward a system of public education in the Commonwealth.

Ruffner knew the importance of competent teachers. "The world always knew there was a difference in teachers," he wrote in his second annual superintendent's report, "but it was a long time in finding out that a poor teacher was doing harm and not good."[24] He repeatedly urged the legislature to establish a normal school for the preparation of teachers, and that pressure finally resulted in the bill, written by J. L. M. Curry, that established the State Female Normal School in Farmville. Ruffner was its first president, Curry the first chairman of its board. Of normal schools, Ruffner said, "The chief value of these schools is in showing to our teachers, and to the public generally, the importance of professional study and our own deficiencies." Ruffner also had a longstanding interest in teachers' institutes, and he secured approval for a six-week state teachers' institute at the University of Virginia in 1879.[25] In naming the new building for Ruffner, the University again honored the intertwining history of its education school and the state public school system.

In the spring of 1973, Cyphert brought in thirteen new faculty members for a total of 124. All the school's programs were fully accredited nationally. Faculty publications had increased fourfold, grants threefold since Cyphert arrived. The school's twenty-two approved degree programs offered forty-nine degrees and several off-Grounds master's degrees.[26] Sponsored research had increased by 300 percent over the past three years, from $659,008 in 1970 to $2,135,423 in 1972.[27]

Despite such progress, Cyphert expressed frustration with the lack of funds appropriated for the school for 1973–1974, reflecting statewide budget cuts for the 1974–1976 biennium. Edgar Shannon had announced his intention to step down as president in 1972, and as the budget tightened, Frank L. Hereford, Jr., was appointed the fifth president of the University of Virginia. A professor of physics, Hereford had served as vice president and provost under Shannon until 1971 and had chaired the Committee on the Future of the University.

Cyphert invited President Hereford to address the Curry School faculty in the fall of 1973. "We in the School of Education believe that we must constantly be looking ahead, clarifying our goals, planning and bringing our actions in line with our aspirations," Cyphert wrote in his invitation. "We also desire to be a prime contributor to the momentum and impact of the University. We eagerly anticipate your leadership." Interviewed at the time on his views for the future, Cyphert urged more centralized communications, pointing to the University's need for a central planner. His position was as a "futurist," Cyphert said: Not only did he keep an eye on the needs of his "own shop" but he also looked out for "how my own shop impinges upon other facets of the University."[28] Cyphert continued to be an advocate for the Curry School and its leadership in educational research even as he made plans to step down as dean and return to Ohio State as the new dean of education there. He announced his resignation in January 1974 and left the Curry School in May.

In the fall of 1973 the Curry School faculty had participated in a self-study as part of a University-wide initiative. The faculty approved a report on the "Future of the School" in February 1974. Among other things, the report noted that the faculty looked for a future not "of comfortable mediocrity, but rather one that is based on exceptionally competent teaching, research, and service"—a future based, in other words, on the gains of the previous five years. The report concluded with the statement that the Curry School of Education would remain primarily a graduate institution.[29]

"I'm a pot stirrer for better or for worse," Cyphert said in 1996, reflecting on his years at the Curry School. "I think we accomplished many things, making it a different kind of school of education. . . . We were more scientific, we were more database-oriented, and I'm confident that we had much more national visibility than we did before."[30] During the six years of Ted Cyphert's deanship, the number of faculty publications and the dollar amount of grant funding both increased five times. Student numbers increased by 60 percent, and their entrance scores improved nearly a full standard deviation. Many programs were initiated or consolidated during his tenure.

Rapid growth in the school's faculty and programs had caused problems not initially understood, however. Administrators and faculty grappled with the issue of criteria for promotion over the next decades, together with the problem of overlapping functions and responsibilities among the plethora of programs created during the 1960s. While some viewed Cyphert's legacy

Social Foundations of Education

The Curry School's program in the social foundations of education began in 1968, when Jennings Wagoner and Peter Hackett joined the faculty. Wanting to provide more advanced work in their field and strengthen the school's service offerings, Wagoner and Hackett made the case for hiring two more faculty members, one of them Harold Burbach, who came in 1970. This group taught large lectures and specialized courses in their fields of scholarly interest: international and comparative education, sociology of education, philosophy of education, and history of education. The College of Arts and Sciences first offered master's and doctoral degrees in the field, and the first Ph.D. in Social Foundations was awarded in 1973. In the mid-1970s Hackett helped establish an off-Grounds program in the Northern Virginia Center for Continuing Education for students from the greater Washington, D.C., area. Today the Social Foundations programs in Charlottesville and in Northern Virginia provide academic and humanistic perspectives on education. Graduates of the program have gone on to provide leadership in schools, educational agencies, museums, and government offices as well as in other fields related to education. The program is now part of the Department of Leadership, Foundations, and Policy.

as controversial, he had served during an era—and under a University president—that actively supported education and willingly provided a sound financial basis for a newly configured School of Education.[31] Cyphert's emphases on expanding programs, on increasing faculty, and on developing research-based educational practices—and the decisions that they led him to make—were bound to provoke tensions. His eagerness to propel the Curry School to national and international prominence left a somewhat complicated legacy in its wake. Perhaps the most positive element of that rich legacy is the list of faculty members whom he personally hired. While Cyphert left the University in the early 1970s, many of the people he recruited remained on the faculty for decades after, guiding programs of the Curry School of Education into the twenty-first century.

Dean Cyphert, ca. 1970

Student teaching, early 1970s

CHAPTER 8

Creating a Base for Private Financial Support of Education

Richard M. Brandt, 1974–1984

I hope to promote openness and candor in personal relationships; integration and congruency of activities, both amongst themselves and in relation to relevant outside needs and pressures; and a sense of real enjoyment and satisfaction in fulfilling our academic and professional roles.[1]

— Richard M. Brandt, 1974

When Dean Cyphert announced his plans to leave the University of Virginia in 1974, President Hereford appointed a search committee to select a new dean of the Curry School of Education. Ralph Cherry returned to the dean's office during the summer term of 1974. After a national search that included 107 candidates, the committee recommended that the president appoint Richard M. Brandt, already a faculty member in the school, as dean. Brandt assumed the position in September 1974.

Brandt graduated from the University of Virginia's engineering school in 1943. After serving in the Navy and teaching for a year, he earned an M.A. in secondary education from the University of Michigan, then a doctorate in human development from the University of Maryland, where he taught until 1965. After coming to the Curry School as an associate professor in 1965, he served as chair of the Department of the Foundations of Education from 1968 until his appointment as dean in 1974.

By the time Richard Brandt became dean, the Curry School had undergone tremendous growth in faculty, resources, programs, and quality of students. A faculty of 127 was divided into eight departments with many overlapping allegiances—an issue that would soon prove problematic. Brandt's ten years as dean also coincided with a time when education schools were under fire across the nation. By the middle of Brandt's second term, after his 1979 reappointment, national enrollments in schools of education were dropping, many universities were reducing the size of their education school faculties, and schools of education were routinely being criticized for much of what was wrong with the public schools. Critics charged that education schools allowed below-average students to become teachers. They argued that teacher preparation programs

Science class, 1970s

overemphasized methods of teaching at the expense of coursework with traditional academic content. Education professionals responded; Brandt wrote a text in which he discussed the state of public education based on his work with state administrative leaders and research into national trends.[2]

Against this backdrop, the Curry School of Education faced intense scrutiny by University administrators. In his first meeting with the faculty, Dean Brandt discussed the importance of the recent self-study report, saying he intended to build on the achievements of his predecessor, Ted Cyphert. He wished to address the organization and operation of the dean's office; the departmental and committee structure of the school; issues related to promotion and the reward system in general;[3] space allocations and physical resources ("Only two years in the new building and we are already bulging at the seams," he commented during a faculty meeting); alumni relations; relations with continuing education programs and state school divisions; and the question of rigor in grading and course requirements.[4] It was a broad, complex list of challenges that were easier to pose than to meet.

Celebrations and Concerns

One of Richard Brandt's first initiatives was to establish a private foundation to provide support for school initiatives. Under the leadership of President Hereford, the entire University was seeking ways to increase private giving toward University projects, and Brandt asked Ralph Cherry, the former dean, to head up this effort at the Curry School. Cherry, who had already established strong alumni ties, organized an exploratory meeting in April 1975.[5] Howard Allen, director of the Consultative Resource Center, also contributed to the early planning of a foundation for the Curry School.[6] A board of directors was assembled and first met in October 1975. Brandt asked board members to use the new foundation to raise funds to help make the school outstanding in relation to its peers. On April 12, 1976, the University of Virginia Curry School of Education Foundation was formally incorporated, stating its mission as "providing alumni and friends a means of assisting the School of Education . . . in achieving its objectives and in promoting and facilitating the active involvement of alumni and friends."[7] Board members identified five areas needing support: development for the School of Education, student support, faculty development, in-service research and scholarship, and the Distinguished Alumnus Award.

Seizing the opportunity to make a significant event out of the dedication of the new education building, Dean Brandt declared April 23 and 24, 1976, the first Education Days at the University. The first Education Days coincided with bicentennial celebrations at the University of Virginia and around the country and established the tradition of annual awards presentations to students and faculty in the Curry School. At dinner on the first night, Professor Richard Meade delivered a "Brief History of the Curry Memorial School of Education." Education Day also marked the publication of a newly designed *Curry School of Education Newsletter,* including announcements about the Child Development Center (a new preschool in Lambeth House), the McGuffey Reading Center, and the Mid-Atlantic Center for Community Education. During the formal dedication of Ruffner Hall, President Hereford took note of changes since the building was originally planned in the mid-1960s—student enrollment had risen from 674 students to 1,562, or 130 percent and the faculty had grown by 135 percent—yet the new building increased education space by only 75 percent over that in Peabody Hall.[8]

Foreshadowing a concern that continues in the twenty-first century, Brandt formed a committee on student minority affairs early in his term and charged it with coming to understand the situation of minority students in the school and to review how well programs prepared teachers to work with minority students.[9] Statistics assembled in August 1976 showed that among Curry School students, there were 107 black students, 61 female and 46 male, comprising 3 percent of the undergraduate population and 8 percent of the graduate.[10] Even fewer minority faculty taught in the education school: only three out of more than 110 faculty, a ratio far lower than that of the state population.[11] Faculty members designed courses in multicultural education open to all University students, as well as summer institutes for in-service instruction. Under the guidance of Robert Covert, these courses continue to provide resources for many today. The Multicultural Pavilion, a web site of teaching resources developed by Curry graduate Paul Gorski, provides information on current research and practices in multicultural education.[12]

Preschool activities, mid-1970s

Other issues, some related to programs, faced Brandt early in his tenure. When grading practices came under question, a faculty advisory committee moved that the school conform to the practices of the College of Arts and Sciences in March 1975. As enrollments declined, Brandt told the faculty in October 1977, "We are being looked at to provide some of the needed leadership" to recruit qualified students actively.[13] Off-Grounds degree programs in Wise, Abingdon, Roanoke, Quantico, and Northern Virginia were designed as one solution to increase the student body. The school also took first steps to bring the Ph.D. in education, a program historically administered by the Graduate School of Arts and Sciences, over to the Curry School. This effort was not resolved until June 1996.[14]

As part of a new research effort in early childhood education, Dean Brandt approved the establishment of an experimental nursery school. First housed in 1973 in Ruffner Hall, the preschool moved into Lambeth House in 1974. Planned as an "observation and training laboratory" for graduate students majoring in psychology and special education and in early childhood education, the school enrolled about twenty-four children aged two through five, who attended for two and a half hours each day, either morning or afternoon.[15] Soon called the Child

Development Center, the school continued operating into the late 1980s. Another program was initiated in 1981 that continues to this day: the summer program for young writers. A residential Young Writers' Workshop led by Professor Margo Figgins, the program attracts students from all over the country and provides intensive instruction for aspiring writers.

A Time of Many Challenges

In the mid-1970s a University-wide committee met sporadically to examine teacher education programs in the Curry School. Amid concerns over the emphasis on method over content, the committee considered a dual-degree program between the Curry School and the College but

Clinical Psychology

In 1967 Richard Abidin was recruited by Richard Brandt to develop a doctoral program in school and clinical psychology. At the time, clinical psychology was a relatively new applied profession, and the Curry School's program offered the first applied psychology doctorate offered in the Commonwealth.[1] By 1972, Brandt was writing to President Shannon, outlining developments in the field to explain why the Curry School should establish a separate clinical psychology Ph.D. program. One of his arguments was that at the time, the University's Department of Psychology was primarily committed to training research psychologists.[2]

In 1976 the State Council on Higher Education in Virginia (SCHEV) authorized a Ph.D. degree in clinical psychology to be granted through the Curry School. Abidin designed the program's structure and curriculum. He also built supporting library holdings and linked with community agencies and schools to establish clinical placements for students.[3]

Professors Ronald Reeve and Peter Sheras were hired in 1975 to work in the school and clinical programs. In 1979 the combined clinical and school psychology program received approval from the American Psychological Association.[4] It was the first such program nationally, and its model of an integrated clinical and school psychology graduate degree now prevails nationally.

By 1980, coordination efforts began among faculty from the Curry programs and the psychology department in the College of Arts and Sciences. Discussions led to the formation of the Institute of Clinical Psychology, headed by Abidin and including eight Curry faculty, eight psychology department faculty, and four faculty from the medical school's Department of Behavioral Medicine and Psychiatry. All held joint appointments in their schools and the Institute. By 1988, the programs were proving complex to oversee, and the decision was made to separate them and dissolve the institute. Today, programs in the psychology department have a research focus, while Curry programs in clinical psychology focus on children, families, and schools. The program is headed by Ann Loper today, and competition for the doctoral program is steep: typically several hundred applicants vie for eight slots each year. The Curry School operates a Center for Clinical Psychology Services—a training facility offering therapy, evaluations, and consultations to families and individuals for sliding-scale fees.

Faculty members in the program have made many significant contributions to the mental health field. Abidin has developed four published psychological measures, including the Parenting Stress Index, now translated into twenty-eight languages and used for research and in clinical settings around the world. Dewey Cornell and Peter Sheras's study of youth violence has led to significant changes in policy issues, both in the Commonwealth and the nation,[5] and Sheras is presently studying issues related to school bullying.

Ann Loper's work with incarcerated females is leading to changes in rehabilitation practice. Edith Lawrence has developed the Young Women Leaders Program for local middle and high school girls, pairing them with University undergraduates as mentors. Robert Pianta, another program faculty member, has established a national reputation in the areas of early child care, student-teacher relationships, and interventions and consultations designed to support preschool and elementary school teachers and staff. Pianta is currently involved with several other Curry programs linked to the at-risk initiatives.

abandoned this idea in 1975 due to the complexities related to creating such a program.[16] In the late 1970s and early 1980s, the cry for higher-quality teacher education programs rang out across the nation. One critic, B. O. Smith, went so far as to say, "Nothing short of a thorough overhauling of pedagogical education will do."[17] In Virginia, a series of articles in the *Richmond Times-Dispatch* in December 1980 highlighted the differences among teacher preparation programs throughout Virginia. The articles publicized the low standards met by applicants who gained acceptance into these programs and the low test scores of students presently enrolled.[18]

In response to these concerns, the Virginia State Board of Education proposed to take administrative control of all teacher preparation programs, bringing them under its standards for accreditation—a move that posed a threat to colleges and universities. One argument used to rationalize the centralized control of teacher credentialing was an anticipated shortfall in teaching positions, making it necessary to limit the number of teaching candidates. Brandt, then president of the Virginia Association of Colleges for Teacher Education, countered this argument by noting that the oversupply was not as severe as projected and that a "state of healthy competition among institutions of very different size and character is responsive to the overall need of our public schools for a diverse teaching staff."[19]

It was the late 1970s, and the Curry School found itself challenged from many directions. Its faculty and programs had tripled in size during the previous fifteen years. The school had moved into a new building that almost immediately proved too small for its activities. Enrollment was beginning to level out, the undergraduate teacher education program was deemed inadequate, the relationship with the School of Continuing Education had its own challenges—and the relationship between education school faculty members and the rest of the University faculty was tenuous at best. External visiting committees between 1977 and 1981 reviewed all schools and units within the University, and the Curry School was among those studied first. The visiting committee, headed by John Corbally, president emeritus of the University of Illinois, included James Banks of the University of Washington and Patricia Graham, then dean of the Harvard University Graduate School of Education.

Annette Gibbs and student

Their report served as a critical starting point for discussions about the future of the Curry Memorial School of Education. The report noted a disjuncture within the University: "For whatever reasons, the bridge which one must cross to go from Ruffner Hall to the Lawn is not readily used to integrate faculty, students and programs of the School with those of Arts and Sciences and of the other schools of the University." While the School of Education could not "address all of the issues in professional education," the committee believed it could "be a leader in seeing to it that they are addressed." The report talked of "extreme fragmentation" and departmental autonomy, which among other things led to differing standards for doctoral degrees granted by the same school. The report cited positive results from a poll of students, who said that if given the choice again, they would choose the Curry School.[20]

Edgar and Mary Alice Gunter with student award winner, Suzanne Esterson, 2003

The Curry School Foundation

When he initially established a foundation for the Curry School of Education, Dean Richard Brandt spoke of two main goals: to strengthen loyalties to the school and to develop an awareness of the school's need for private support.[1] James Bash was appointed the first executive director, a post he held until 1985.

During the foundation's first years, efforts went mainly to encourage alumni to give annually to the school and to establish special recognition opportunities to generate further alumni support and highlight students and programs. In 1976, 83 donors gave a total of more than $6,000. Three years later, in 1979, 256 donors contributed twice that. Today more than three thousand donors give annually to the Curry School, with gifts totaling more than $500,000. In one early year, 1978, the foundation provided $5,000 to the school for discretionary use. Today, in 2005, discretionary funds going to the school from the foundation exceed $100,000 annually.

The foundation organized its first phonathon in 1982 as a means to contact alumni and to broaden the list of those giving unrestricted annual funds. A Curry School case statement was developed in 1982, one of the first such documents developed at the University.[2] Efforts that year also brought in the first major gifts to the education school since the 1905 Rockefeller grant with which President Alderman founded the school. Two contributions of $100,000 each allowed the Curry School to establish the William C. Parrish, Jr., Chair and to endow the John and Florence May Fellowship. The foundation continued to grow during the years of Dean Brandt's administration, and when he left office in 1984, its assets totaled more than $86,000. During the following thirteen years, the Curry School Foundation's assets grew to more than $2 million.[3]

Since its beginnings, the foundation has found many ways to support Curry School students directly. By 1988, private gifts helped the foundation offer fourteen scholarships and awards. As of 2005, the foundation administered sixty-five monetary awards, scholarships, and fellowships, with a value of more than $192,500.[4]

Mary Alice Gunter became executive director of the foundation in 1985, a position she held for ten years. Gunter was followed by John Rice, then Margaret Unsworth, who served as foundation director through 2003. When James Cooper became dean in 1985, he increased the scope of foundation efforts by organizing the Dean's Council—alumni and friends contributing $1,000 or more over a three-year period. The initial goal was to greet one hundred charter members into the council by 1999. The campaign was so successful that one hundred members had joined by 1993. A new all-University capital campaign began in 1993, and the Curry School set its fundraising goal at $14.5 million. All told, more than seven thousand alumni and friends contributed. A total of $22.4 million was raised by 2001.

Funds raised by the foundation find a multitude of uses in the school. Each year the foundation allocates $5,000 from its unrestricted annual fund contributions each to the three departments. The funds are used at the discretion of the department chairs, but they usually finance student travel to professional conferences and support student and faculty research, projects, and other pressing initiatives. The

Alumni gathering at Pavilion I, home of Dean David Breneman and his wife, Donna Plasket, 2003

foundation also designates $100,000 from its unrestricted annual fund to the dean's office for use at his discretion. This money has helped fund a variety of projects, including feasibility studies and concept plans for a new building and created an additional tenure-track faculty position as of 2005.

The Curry School Foundation keeps ties with alumni alive by organizing events such as a buffet before the Homecoming football game, an honors and awards luncheon, a fall donor recognition dinner, reunion weekend gatherings, and regional gatherings around the state. More than 22,000 alumni form the foundation's alumni database, joined by non-alumni friends and donors to the school. Informational mailings such as the *Curry School of Education Newsletter* communicate developments in the school. A board of directors, comprised of school and University administrators, faculty members, business people, and philanthropists, meets three times a year. The foundation today is headed by Jane Urbaska, executive director. Jane Buck is associate director for foundation operations and donor relations, and Jay Jackson is director of development and alumni communications.

Foundation outreach efforts have resulted in important friendships, such as the one between the Curry School and Boston businessman Daniel Meyers. Meyers came to know David Breneman when the two collaborated to find ways to help students finance higher education loans. Soon Meyers expressed his longstanding commitment to higher education by making several significant contributions. He has joined the foundation's board of directors and is currently head of the board. In 2004 he pledged $22,000,000 toward a new education building, to be named in honor of his longtime friend, Anthony "Wally" Bavaro, who taught children in the greater Boston area public schools for forty years.[5]

The Corbally report indicated the need to reorganize, to write a new mission statement, and to redesign the teacher education programs in the Curry School. All these concerns were already under discussion, raised pointedly during a series of faculty retreats during the spring of 1979.[21] A summary of notes from those retreats listed similar needs: clarifying the overall direction of the school; providing leadership for program, faculty, and research development; coordinating an integrated teacher education program; and reorganizing so that teaching, research, and service efforts were integrated throughout the school.[22]

Dean Brandt invited Robert Howsam, dean of the University of Houston's education school, to spend the 1980–1981 year at the Curry School, consulting with faculty on redesigning teacher education. One of Howsam's primary recommendations was to hire a director of teacher education; Robert McNergney was hired for this position. The faculty continued to work on restructuring programs and departments.[23] One committee, headed by Professor Annette Gibbs, found that as of 1980–1981, the Curry School was one of the nation's largest producers of master's and doctorates in education.[24]

As president of the Association of Colleges and Schools of Education in State Universities and Land Grant Colleges, Brandt participated in the national debate over the quality of education school programs. He was instrumental in organizing a conference on "Improving the Quality of Education" in July 1982, coordinating the national Parent-Teachers Association and inviting speakers including Governors Robert Graham of Florida, Charles Robb of Virginia, Lamar Alexander of Tennessee, plus Earnest Boyer of the Carnegie Foundation, Marian Wright Edelman of the Children's Defense Fund, and other outstanding educators.[25] Brandt also oversaw a 1982 report that found that 18 percent of all education schools across the country were currently reorganizing significantly in ways that included the elimination, consolidation, or transferal of programs to other university units. "In almost any academic corner of any major university, whether in the business schools or the humanities and the sciences, there is a substantial opinion that the preparation of [educators] is not warranted as a function which requires so much of the university's resources," concluded the report.[26] Furthermore, the document reported that education schools had done little to address the problems identified.

Dean Brandt at his desk

As the debate continued within the University of Virginia, Provost Edwin Floyd addressed a March 1983 Curry School faculty meeting, affirming that the school must remain "pivotal" in the state. "Education is not an isolated field and cannot exist apart from the larger University community," said Floyd.[27] On March 31, Brandt responded to this charge with a seventy-two-page "Academic Plan," supported by an additional seventy-six pages of self-study reports. The report summarized the present status of the school and identified the steps that had already been undertaken to address the needed changes,[28] such as creating a mission statement and consolidating the school's many programs.

Richard Brandt announced his intention to retire as dean of the Curry School in the fall of 1983. When the *Richmond Times-Dispatch* suggested in late fall that the University of Virginia's School of Education might be closing, Brandt quickly refuted the rumor. "The University will consider ways to strengthen the undergraduate programs of the School of Education, but is not planning to close it down," he wrote. "We're reassessing and planning how far we can strengthen the program. As far as preparing teachers, the University's commitment is as strong as ever." Provost Floyd supported Brandt in his statement. There was "no possibility of closing," he told a student newspaper: "We are looking hard at the mission and organization only with the intent of strengthening the school."[29] Writing to alumni in the Spring 1984 *Curry School of Education Newsletter,* Brandt reassured them of the steps being taken to ensure the future of the School, including efforts to improve teacher education and to stanch declining enrollments.[30]

As Richard Brandt prepared to leave the deanship, he acknowledged the severity of issues he had faced while dean. He asked the faculty to fully support his successor, James Cooper. The school was still a fragmented and decentralized organization, Brandt believed, and many changes were yet to come. His administration had faced many controversies and he hoped for a smoother path for the dean coming after him: "Dissent is inevitable in any social entity," he said in a statement to the faculty,

> but I would hope that the voices of support will be stronger than in the past. . . . I think if we do not support the new leadership vocally and visibly we will ultimately be downgraded within the University community in status, size, and resources. . . . I am proud to be associated with such a fine faculty . . . I feel that the school is stronger than it was when I came into office, but I feel it has much greater potential than we have yet realized. . . . I say these things to urge you individually and collectively to do whatever you can to insure a new and constructive attitude toward a new Dean and whatever his leadership efforts will be.[31]

During his ten years as dean, Richard Brandt steered the Curry School of Education through serious challenges to its programs. He did so without losing faculty positions or academic programs. When he left office, the School of Education was divided into eight departments—1) Administration and Supervision; 2) Counselor Education; 3) Curriculum and Instruction; 4) Foundations (Educational Psychology, School and Clinical Psychology, Institute of Clinical Psychology) and Social Foundations; 5) Health Education and Physical Education; 6) Research and Evaluation; 7) Special Education; and 8) Speech Pathology and Audiology. In addition to the departments, the school included other related centers and programs. These included the Child Development Center, the McGuffey Reading Center, the Evaluation Research Center, the Bureau of Educational Research, the Mid-Atlantic Center for Community Education, and the Center for Higher Education. During Brandt's deanship, the Curry School of Education Foundation was soundly established, providing financial support for the school's future and creating a long-lasting network among students, faculty, and alumni. Highly supportive of choosing a new dean with a background in teacher education, Brandt urged the faculty to seek innovative responses to the school's future challenges. "A dean cannot build a great school by himself," he reminded his colleagues. "It has to be done by an administration and faculty working together."[32]

Curry student teacher and two students, 1995

CHAPTER 9

The Five-Year Teacher Education Program

James M. Cooper, 1984–1994

The Curry School of Education has two major missions. The first is to prepare personnel to work in America's educational system . . . and to conduct research and scholarship that address problems and issues of importance to our educational system. . . . The second . . . is to enhance human potential and performance by preparing personnel and conducting research in such areas as psychological/ emotional development, physical development and fitness, and speech/language/auditory development.[1]

— Curry School mission statement, 1992

James W. Cooper was appointed the sixth dean of the Curry Memorial School of Education in the spring of 1984. A professor of teacher education at the University of Houston, Cooper's background was of critical importance to the decision, made when many schools of education had shut down undergraduate teacher education programs and the University of Virginia was examining its own. Among his other professional affiliations, Cooper soon became a member of the Holmes Group, a consortium of education school deans from twenty-eight major research institutions, joined through their dedication to high standards for teacher education programs.[2]

Cooper arrived with a charge from Provost Edwin Floyd to strengthen the school's and the University's leadership role in public education, both in Virginia and the nation, and to enhance communications among the Curry School, the College and Graduate School of Arts and Sciences, and the other schools of the University.[3] The education school was to focus on a mission statement, consolidate departments and program areas, and reorganize the teacher education program. During Cooper's first year as dean, President Hereford left the presidency. He was succeeded by Robert O'Neil, a legal scholar with a deep-seated interest in public education. O'Neil proved highly supportive during efforts in the Curry School to make substantive changes to programs and curricula.

New Beginnings

The coauthor (with Kevin Ryan) of *Those Who Can, Teach,* one of the most widely used foundational texts in teacher preparation, Jim Cooper knew the key issues in teacher preparation and saw how they might be addressed at the University of Virginia. His first action was to organize a retreat for faculty in the fall of 1984, inviting them to discuss and prioritize the issues facing the school. "A line attributed to Freud asserts that 'changing a university is like trying to rearrange a cemetery,'" Cooper said during the retreat. "Although I wouldn't go that far, I do believe that . . . making the changes necessary to take advantage of our opportunities, overcome problems, and become a School of Education of the first class means, then, changing ourselves—our attitudes, beliefs, and our behaviors."[4]

The faculty took that challenge to heart. Out of the retreat came the commitment to reorganize the school into more manageable departments, to create a unified sense of mission, and to restructure the undergraduate teacher education program. Vitalizing the school's identity, Cooper received permission to drop the word "memorial" from the school's name, changing it to the less cumbersome Curry School of Education.[5] Eight departments were reorganized into four: Curriculum, Instruction and Special Education; Educational Studies; Educational Leadership and Policy Studies; and Human Services.[6] Out of that initial faculty retreat came another critical step. While talking with Professor Glen Bull, Cooper decided to designate technology use as a strand in the newly designed teacher education program.[7] This decision opened up the possibility of technology instruction for pre-service students, as well as opportunities for doctoral students to work with these students.

In 1983 a University-wide committee began studying the Curry School's teacher education programs and their relationship to offerings in the College of Arts and Sciences. The committee recommended more liberal arts coursework for education students and suggested eliminating the undergraduate education degree. During 1984–1985, a Curry faculty committee chaired by Cooper worked on revising the curriculum, eventually recommending a five-year teacher

Jerry Short, Glen Bull, and James Cooper with the Curry School's first microcomputer, acquired in 1977, on top of the IBM mainframe, acquired in 1987

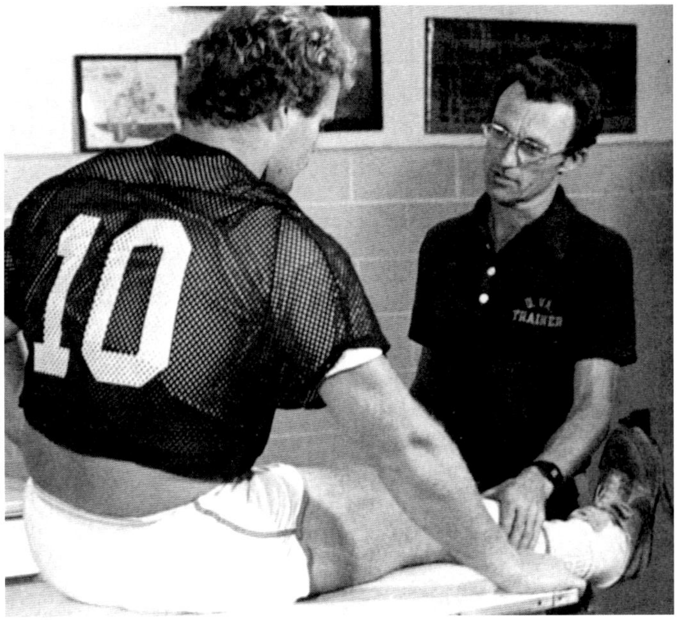

Joe Gieck tends student athlete

education program, approved by both the Curry School and the College of Arts and Sciences in December 1985.[8] Integrating a liberal arts major with a master's degree in teaching, the curriculum included three specialized instructional threads—technology, special education, and multiculturalism—and led to a B.A. or B.S. in an Arts and Sciences field and a master of arts in teaching degree (M.T.) at the end of five years of studies.[9] In 1986 the M.T. degree program became the standard for all students preparing to be teachers, whether heading into elementary, secondary, or special education. All other four-year programs were eliminated except two, in health and physical education and in communications disorders.

The theme of the five-year, dual-degree program was "Teacher as Decision Maker," based on the principles that "knowledge and skills are the important substance of this model, and the planning process is the 'dynamic' that brings action to the model."[10] The logistics of creating such a program were considerable. Education school faculty collaborated with Arts and Sciences faculty to work out many details. Additionally, while most of the courses were offered through the Department of Curriculum, Instruction, and Special Education, several were offered by faculty members in the other Curry departments, creating an all-school involvement in the program. For two years, the new program ran in parallel with the old, stretching the school's resources. Jerry Moore, professor of curriculum and instruction, was appointed the first director of the new teacher education program. Moore was followed by Greta Morine-Dershimer, a teacher education scholar, then by Sandra Cohen, a professor of special education, who heads the program today.

Today's five-year teacher education program nearly replicates the original design. Students apply during the second year in the College of Arts and Sciences. During the next three years, they complete liberal arts requirements, take core courses in the Curry School as background for certification, and participate in field experiences. They apply for graduate status in their fourth year. Enrollment in the program has nearly doubled during its twenty-year history, from approximately one hundred students when it began to 188 in the Class of 2006. The program also includes a two-year master of teaching degree, designed for students with a bachelor's degree in the liberal arts who wish to become licensed teachers.

The five-year program was the key to the Curry School's future in many ways. It brought Curry's teacher education offerings in line with the most current national research findings and policy recommendations. It depended on connections with the College of Arts and Sciences, validating the school and the teachers it produced in the eyes of the Arts and Sciences faculty. The new initiatives gained public attention, too. An April 24, 1985, article in the *Cavalier Daily* heralded the new program, noting that the Curry School had raised admission standards and applauding the new program's potential for improving the education of teachers. Amidst the accolades, Dean Cooper said that the Curry School would warrant the teaching ability of its graduates and would provide mentoring assistance to any beginning teacher in Virginia if requested by a school

Technology in Education

Early television classroom (above)
Exploring microscopic botany, 2005 (opposite)

Today we associate technology with computers, but instructional technology came into use long before computers arrived on the scene. From the early application of films and filmstrips, overhead transparencies and overhead projectors, the Curry School has provided students with support and information about technologies for teaching. As a field of study, audiovisual education—the precursor to technology education—was established by 1954, but its place in teacher education programs varied over many years, nationally as well as at the University of Virginia.[1] Curry School courses in audiovisual education were offered for many years and provided an important resource for undergraduate and graduate students.

In 1977 the school acquired its first microcomputer and, ten years later, an IBM mainframe computer, promptly named Jabez, in honor of Jabez Lamar Monroe Curry.[2] Soon Curry faculty members were finding innovative ways to integrate computers into teaching. Professor Harry Strang developed a microcomputer-based educational simulation in 1978; in 1980 the first course in instructional computing was offered; and soon a computer education committee formed, led by Professor Jerry Short. In 1985 an internal school newspaper was developed, known as "On-line with the Curry School" to signify the development of information links with all members of the Curry community. Dean Cooper's 1984 commitment to making learning and teaching technology a central emphasis in the new teacher education program brought increased attention to computer and multimedia possibilities in teaching. By 1988 most faculty members had computers at their desks.

Faculty members who specialized in educational technology began urging a computer network linking school personnel. In 1986, under the leadership of Glen Bull and John Lloyd, the Curry School received a $2 million IBM grant for Teacher-LINK, a project facilitating computer communication between the Curry School and teachers and students in surrounding school districts. The program began as electronic mail for communication, but those using it quickly realized its potential as an instructional tool as well. In one initiative funded under this grant, for example, Jennings Wagoner—a Thomas Jefferson scholar—assumed the third president's persona and used the computer to answer questions posed by elementary school students about his life.[3] Teacher-LINK also led to the creation of the Virginia Public Education Network (VPN) in 1987, linking more than two thousand schools. Other grants

have followed, including Project Impact in 1996, a project to design computer-based modules to be integrated into courses on teaching methods. In 1994 the Congressional Office of Technology Assessment identified the Curry School as one of four schools of education judged exemplary for the integration of technology into its curriculum; that year the National Council for Accreditation of Teacher Education (NCATE) cited the Curry School for similar reasons.

Curry's Center for Technology and Teacher Education was established in 1998 to support doctoral students and offer resources to help all Curry faculty members integrate technology into their teaching. Staffed by several full-time faculty members, the center soon moved from Ruffner Hall to larger quarters in Lambeth House. In 1998 the Curry School received the first annual American Association of Colleges for Teacher Education (AACTE) Best Practice Award. The award recognized more than twenty years of work by many faculty at the Curry School, dedicated to uniting in the goal of enabling students to use instructional technologies in their teaching and to serve as leaders for technological change. Currently the Center for Technology and Teacher Education has joined nine other institutions in a project that will follow a group of teacher candidates from their last year of education school through their initial years of teaching, observing the ways they integrate technology into their teaching.[4] The center continues to receive national and international attention; faculty and graduate students enhance the introduction of technology in all the school's courses.

The use of technology in teaching has broadened significantly in the past ten years. Today an Educational Technologies Office (ETO), headed first by John Lloyd and now by Luke Kelly, oversees the issues related to technology use in the school. Under the leadership of David Drucker, an Educational Technology Center offers technical support for faculty and students.[5] All Ruffner Hall classrooms have been retrofitted with electronic equipment.

Many Curry faculty members have made inroads in the use of technology in teaching. The work of Mable Kinzie received national attention in 1994 when *Newsweek* ran an article about Net-Frog, an online interactive frog dissection tutorial that she and two colleagues, Richard Strauss and Jean Foss, created for high school use.[6] Other faculty members have developed courses on the use of computers for analyzing qualitative data, have expanded opportunities for videoconferencing and distance supervision, and have developed courses for distance-learning instruction. Developed by Zarl Schoney, the Virginia Initiative for Technology and Administrative Leadership (VITAL) helps familiarize school administrators with management and policy issues raised by computers in the classroom.

Three principles guide technology programs at the Curry School: a commitment to teaching with technology rather than teaching about technology; an emphasis on creating partnerships with local school divisions and state policy makers; and an awareness that the best uses of technology are often specific to particular subjects and content areas.

Bill Clinton, governor of Arkansas, and President George H. W. Bush during the National Governors' Education Summit at the University of Virginia, 1989

district administrator. This message of confidence conveyed the seriousness of purpose shared throughout the Curry School and the University of Virginia about its new teacher education program.[11] The message also brought a new level of national attention to the school.

In 1987 the Curry School of Education was nominated as one of seven Commonwealth Centers in the State of Virginia for teacher education. The center was a collaborative effort with James Madison University and was directed by Professor Robert McNergney. During the five years of its existence, the center in Charlottesville provided a variety of services to teachers and school personnel in the state. From the work of the center, a new method emerged as a way to examine critical issues in teaching. Following the technique already used in law and business education, center faculty developed case studies to be used as instructional aids for teachers, administrators, and other educators. The center hosted three conferences and held case competitions at them, encouraging teachers around the state to interact with the realities of education practice.[12] In 2001 a for-profit company, CaseNEX, was formed as a spin-off from research on the use of cases in education. CaseNEX commercially distributes web-assisted, case-study method curricular units for in-service and pre-service teacher training and professional development.

National Prominence

The Curry School moved into the national spotlight in 1989, when President George H. W. Bush convened a national education summit at the University of Virginia. The legacy of Thomas Jefferson's educational ideals and philosophy drew the meeting to Charlottesville, and its presence brought attention to the work and accomplishments of the Curry School of Education. State governors, the president and his cabinet, national leaders in education, and educational policy makers attended. The summit convened in order to identify major goals for improving American education. In the end, these included improving teacher education; ensuring that all children started school ready to learn; reducing high school drop-out rates; securing safe, drug-free schools; increasing adult literacy; training capable workers for high-tech industry; and improving student performance on assessments resulting in ratings internationally.[13]

Soon after, writing a memo to President O'Neil in January 1990, Dean Cooper used the key points of the summit as benchmarks for the development of Curry School programs. Many programs already in place reflected the conclusions of the summit, he noted: the five-year teacher education program, the Bureau of Educational Research, the Beginning Teachers Assistance Program, the Virginia School-University Partnership, Teacher-LINK, the Virginia School Boards Association and Virginia Association of School Superintendents, the Virginia Educational Policy Analysis Center, the four-year-old at-risk program, the Learning Needs Center, the McGuffey Reading Center, the Speech and Hearing Center, and the Institute for Substance Abuse.[14]

Once the five-year teacher education program was established, Cooper focused on other aspects of the Curry School. He encouraged significant new outreach programs such as Professor Lynn Canady's developing research on the block system of scheduling in secondary schools.[15] Cooper helped the Curry School Foundation celebrate fifteen years of work, noting that private gifts to the School rose by more 200 percent. The number of endowed professorships increased from one to five. Cooper stayed actively involved in state and national organizations, addressing issues of teacher education and the use of technology in teaching, among other concerns. With the success of many of its programs, including the teacher education program, in April 1995 *U.S.News & World Report* ranked the Curry School of Education one of the top twenty schools of education in the United States.

Many changes made under James Cooper's leadership solidified the direction of the Curry School of Education. Securing teacher education, supporting developments in technology and other research endeavors, establishing a strong financial base, and continuing to value professional links within the state and the nation—these four efforts represented the critical aspects of his deanship. The five-year program required active collaboration with the College of Arts and Sciences. Five of the Curry School's graduate programs gained rankings among the top twenty-five in the country. Strong links with Continuing Education were reestablished.[16]

In addition to his distinguished academic contributions, Jim Cooper left another legacy at the Curry School: a symbol of the spirit of his deanship, arising out of a distinctive proficiency all his own. From his first days as dean, Cooper involved himself with student activities—fundraising phonathons, student organizations, and student-run talent shows, at which he displayed his champion abilities with the yo-yo. Students knew the dean was at work in Ruffner Hall when they saw his car with the license plate "Dr. Yo Yo" parked beside the building.

Dean Cooper and his famous yo-yo

Curry School student teachers at Venable School,
Charlottesville, 2005

CHAPTER 10

Spires of Excellence

David W. Breneman, 1995–

Our goal is to make Curry stronger, more intellectually exciting, more productive, and more socially useful than it already is. . . . We will emphasize a team approach, with strong associate deans and department chairs and reduce the programmatic balkanization of the Curry School. [1]

— David W. Breneman, 2000

Once James Cooper announced that he planned to step down in the fall of 1993, a national search began for his replacement. University Provost Thomas Jackson issued the charge to a search committee, summarizing the dean's responsibilities as academic leadership, external constituent relations, and administrative oversight and direction.[2] Robert Pate, chair of the Department of Human Services, was appointed interim dean in July 1994 after an initially unsuccessful search for Cooper's replacement.

Under Pate's leadership, a faculty retreat in September 1994 addressed concerns arising from a University-wide self-study: the need for increased interdepartmental collaboration, curriculum review with student needs in mind, and ways to integrate public service activities. Faculty also discussed ways to diversify the Curry School's faculty and student populations and the need to develop an overall sense of community in the school. Several resolutions resulting from these conversations remained formative in the upcoming administration, including increased collaboration among Curry departments and with other schools in the University, renewed efforts to create a welcoming climate in the School, and a focus on fundraising, to increase private giving to the school.

David W. Breneman was named to head the Curry School of Education in the spring of 1995. He brought to the position a background in the economics of education, especially higher education, as well as experience gained as president of Kalamazoo College, a small liberal arts school in Michigan, from 1983 to 1989. Breneman had also been a fellow in the Economic Studies Program at the Washington, D.C., Brookings Institution and had spent five years as a visiting

Venable School students joking with their teacher, a Curry graduate, 2002

professor at Harvard University's Graduate School of Education. His expertise in educational policy matters proved key in building Curry School leadership in the state and nationally, and his background in fundraising for Kalamazoo College made him well aware of the importance of developing a base of private giving for the Curry School.

Dean Breneman has said many times that he felt he inherited an education school of high quality in sound physical and financial shape—"not beset with crisis." The only charge he received from University President John T. Casteen III was to work closely with others in the University on any new programs. Breneman began by building on existing strengths in the school—the teacher education programs, the instructional technology programs—and by further developing the program in policy studies. During much of his first year his efforts went to becoming acquainted with the faculty and students. His role as dean, he said, was not unlike that of president of a small college.

Early on in Breneman's administration, the Departments of Educational Leadership and Policy Studies merged with the Department of Educational Studies, a move taken when the chairs of both departments elected to step down in the spring of 1996. Faculty in both departments approved the consolidation, which allowed broader teaching opportunities and resulted in a department equivalent in size to the two others. Appointed chair of the new department, Harold Burbach considered the consolidation a "great way of getting all our creative juices flowing . . . we think faculty members will collaborate in new ways and forge productive new alignments."[3]

Breneman's Goals

During a faculty retreat in September 1996, Dean Breneman shared his vision of issues to be faced in the coming decade. He highlighted the necessity for a strong private financial base, encouraged faculty to work closely with practitioners, and resolved to invest more decision-making power in the associate deans and department chairs. He charged the academic affairs committee to articulate priorities as a guide to future decisions and resource allocations. Breneman emphasized that as a professional school with "obligations to the field of education at all levels" and as "part of a research university, the research of Curry School faculty "is (and should be) grounded in the practice and problems of education."[4]

Saying that he did not wish to see one at the Curry School, Breneman defined an "inertial model" of institutional change: one in which a department continues with business as usual, replacing retiring faculty members with more with the same qualifications. "The problem with this process is that, in a world with a limited opportunity for growth, the Curry School would look just like itself ten years from now if this replacement model continues to operate," Breneman argued. In this spirit, faculty hired in 2004 and 2005 filled positions that in many cases crossed disciplines and departments. He urged faculty to rethink the school's curricular and professional needs and specified several criteria to guide this process: the need to connect teaching and scholarship to education in logical and useful ways; the importance of connecting through teaching and research with colleagues across departmental lines and in the other parts of the University; and the principle of viewing applied research as equal in value to theoretical work. The Virginia Center for Educational Policy was established as one way to share the resources of the Curry School, as well as of the broader University faculty, with state and national policy makers in education.

These premises have to a large extent guided the direction of the Curry School of Education to the present. David Breneman has increased the focus on fundraising, has maintained a national and international presence for the school, and has delegated instructional responsibilities to administrators working with him. Late in 2003 the faculty adopted a governance procedure that creates avenues for all faculty to participate in discussions about the school's decision-making process and to provide feedback about policies developed for the school.

In December 2000 Dean Breneman stated his goals for the next five years. They included reducing the programmatic "Balkanization" of the school; increasing diversity among students, staff, and faculty, to mirror changes in the broader society; and securing a $10 million gift for a new building adjacent to Ruffner Hall.[5] The school is meeting these goals in a variety of ways; a description of its current organization reflects recent progress.

Curry School staff: Becky Burbach (above); from left, Sheila Sprouse, Helen Clark, Peggy Blinco, Linda Berry

As the Curry School celebrates its centennial year, it is organized into three academic departments: Human Services; Curriculum, Instruction, and Special Education; and Leadership, Foundations, and Policy. There are eighty-six full-time tenured and tenure-track faculty, thirty-three full-time general and research faculty, and twenty-eight part-time faculty members. Curry School programs lead to six degrees: bachelor of science in education, master of teaching, master of education, education specialist, doctor of education, and doctor of philosophy. In Fall 2005, the Curry School of Education enrolled 331 second-, third-, and fourth-year B.A./M.T. students, 79 B.S.Ed. students, 79 professional development students, 188 M.T. students, and 586 students in other graduate programs: a total of 1,263 students.[6]

Reading tutorial

The Department of Human Services, chaired by Ronald Reeve, offers programs in Clinical and School Psychology, Communications Disorders, Counselor Education, Kinesiology, and Risk and Prevention in Education Sciences—all designed to educate and train professionals for careers in areas related to human development.

The Department of Curriculum, Instruction and Special Education, chaired by Daniel Hallahan, oversees the Teacher Education program and nine others: Curriculum and Instruction; Elementary Education; English Education; Foreign Language Education; Mathematics Education; Reading Education; Science Education; Social Studies Education; and Special Education. All are designed primarily to prepare students for the teaching profession. Faculty in this department also lead the Central Virginia Writing Project (CVWP), part of a state and national effort to improve the written skills of students. Together with professional development courses during the year, the CVWP also sponsors summer institutes to train teachers to become change agents in their schools and districts by improving strategies for teaching writing.

The Department of Leadership, Foundations, and Policy, chaired by Carolyn Callahan, includes programs in Educational Psychology, Educational Research, Higher Education, Instructional Technology, Administration and Supervision, Psychology and Education of the Gifted, Social Foundations, and Research, Statistics, and Evaluation. These are all designed to meet the need for educational leaders with backgrounds in administrative leadership and foundations in education and educational policy. Dean Breneman is assisted by three deans: Robert Pate, senior associate dean for administrative services; Rebecca Kneedler, associate dean for academic affairs; and Joanne McNergney, assistant dean for admissions and student affairs.

The Curry School of 2005 is also home to a variety of centers and related programs, including the Center for Technology and Teacher Education, the National Research Center/Gifted and Talented, the Virginia Association of School Superintendents, the UCEA Center for the Study of Leadership and Ethics, the Virginia Center for Educational Policy Studies, the Virginia

U.S. Secretary of Education Richard Riley visits Johnson School, Charlottesville, 1999

School-University Partnership, the Emerging Pathways Project, the Virginia Youth Violence Project, the Women Education Leaders of Virginia, the Young Women Leaders Program, the Darden/Curry Partnership for Leaders in Education, and the Center for Advanced Teaching and Learning. The school offers programs in six off-Grounds centers: in Northern Virginia, Hampton Roads, Richmond, Roanoke, Southwest Virginia, and Charlottesville, at the University Center.

Strategic Planning: Spires of Excellence

On several occasions, Dean Breneman publicly stated his concerns with streamlining the operations of the school. After he made one such comment in the spring of 2001, an alumnus of the University of Virginia's Darden Graduate School of Business Administration asked, "Is Curry a school of education or a holding company with many different parts?" The comment highlighted the difficulties of promoting the various strengths and accomplishments of the school and led to a strategic planning retreat in January 2002. The purpose of the retreat was to develop a sharper sense of direction for the school, expressed specifically through explicit criteria for internal resource allocation and a set of transformational concepts to guide the search for potential large gifts to the school.

A primary outcome of those discussions was the Curry School's "Statement of Strategic Intent": "We will be a model of excellence for Schools of Education by developing educational leaders throughout the Commonwealth and nation, by enhancing the quantity and quality of our scholarly work, and by increasing our influence in the shaping of educational policy."[7] This statement has become the guiding principle for the school's operations today.

During the strategic planning retreat, the dean and faculty identified key "spires of excellence"—focus areas whose identification could guide programmatic development in the school: educational technology, teacher education, and at-risk educational programs. By

Daniel Meyers with nieces and nephews, 2004 (top)

Dean Breneman, Daniel Meyers, and President Casteen, 2004

Foundation for a New Building

By the time the Curry School moved into Ruffner Hall in the winter of 1973, its programs exceeded the capacity of the building. Newer programs have had to move into offices and buildings away from Ruffner Hall. Physical improvements have been needed for years, but it was hard to address them without funds allocated for the purpose.

Now, through the generosity of Daniel Meyers, a Boston businessman and longtime friend of Dean David Breneman, there is a way to meet this challenge. In September 2004 Meyers pledged $22 million, thereby launching a new building campaign for the Curry School. Associated with the Curry School for ten years, Meyers served on the campaign committee in the late 1990s and became chair of the board for the Curry School Foundation. He made his first major gift to Curry in 1998, honoring his parents by funding the Newton and Rita Meyers Professorship in the Economics of Higher Education. His 2004 gift of $22 million is the largest in school history and the second largest gift to any American school of education.

Meyers first met Breneman in 1990 when he was interested in developing a company to fund private higher education loans at competitive interest rates. Breneman, then visiting professor at Harvard, taught a course on the economics of higher education. Seeing the potential in Meyers's ideas, he encouraged him to go further. In 1991 Meyers and Stephen Anbinder founded First Marblehead Corporation, a private company formed to raise money on Wall Street to offer individual colleges supplementary sources of loan money. In 2000, First Marblehead purchased a company to process and service student loans. After that, the company's customer base expanded to include banks and went public in 2003. In its first year as a publicly traded corporation, First Marblehead facilitated disbursement of more than one billion dollars in loans to students at more than three thousand schools.[1]

Speaking of his personal commitment to higher education, Meyers cites the example set by his parents and especially his mother when, as a young widow and teacher, she supported Meyers and his three siblings through college. Meyers's gift also memorializes Anthony D. "Wally" Bavaro, a Bostonian who played football for the San Francisco 49ers, then, after a knee injury, coached and taught history for forty years in the public schools of Malden and Chelsea, Massachusetts.[2] Bavaro died in 2002, and Meyers chose to honor him as an exemplar of dedicated teaching, a man so committed to inner-city schoolchildren that he turned down administrative promotions because he knew he was really needed in the classroom. Daniel Meyers's heartfelt and generous gift laid a foundation for the long-needed expansion of the Curry School's facilities. The plans for Bavaro Hall are well under way. After a national competition, in May 2005 the New York architectural firm of Robert A.M. Stern was selected to design Bavaro Hall.

identifying these areas, Curry faculty become more aware of reciprocal programs, research projects, and strengths they might tap into, an important step toward breaking down the conventional barriers between departments. Technology is integrated throughout the school. Led by a chief technology officer and with support from the Educational Technology Office, faculty, staff, and students make the most of integrated technology systems in their work. Teacher education has been, and continues to be, the central mission of the school in many aspects. The urge to design program structure with schoolwide themes in mind is a continuing challenge that guides change within the school. The At-Risk program has developed rapidly to span across departmental areas and now also includes other departments in the University.

A program already in place at the time of the planning initiative was the Thomas Jefferson Center for Educational Design, established in 1996 and headed by faculty member Daniel Duke. The center's goal is to change the model of leadership in education circles from problem solver to creative thinker and designer of learning environments. Center staff work closely with school personnel and other professionals to propose new learning environments and encourage educators to think in new ways about schools. Duke is also partnering in the Virginia School Turnaround Specialist Program, which offers new strategies to school administrators working to improve student achievement.

Curry faculty members Alton Taylor and Linda Bunker (top)

Curry faculty member Henry Allen and student award winner Cortnee Slocum, 2003

In 2004, for the eighth year in a row, the Curry School ranked among the top twenty-five education schools in the United States. Seven programs ranked in the top twenty-five nationally as well: Administration and Supervision, Counseling and Personnel Services, Higher Education, Curriculum and Instruction, Elementary Education, Secondary Education, and Special Education. A snapshot of faculty accomplishments in 2003–2004 showed the publication of 165 journal articles and more than twenty books and book chapters. In that year Curry faculty gave 483 presentations and speeches at international, national, regional, and state conferences and gatherings. They worked as editors for twenty-seven journals and as guest editors for twelve others; they served on seventy-one editorial boards and as reviewers for 177 articles and grant competitions. In one decade, grant funding coming into the Curry School increased dramatically, from twenty-eight awards totaling under $2 million in 1995 to forty awards totaling nearly $9 million.[8] The Curry School Foundation has greatly expanded the school's financial base of private giving and, thanks to the generous pledge of Daniel Meyers, new facilities will be constructed over the next five years. Several years after their arrival at the University, David Breneman and his wife, Donna Plasket, moved into Pavilion I. Their Lawn residence signifies the Curry School's place among all the schools of the University, and they have done much to create a presence for the school by hosting many events in their home.

Teachers for a New Era

Early in 2002, the University of Virginia was selected by the Carnegie Foundation of New York to be one of the first four schools in the nation to receive a $5 million grant over five years to strengthen the preparation of future teachers.

At-Risk Programs

Student teaching, ca. 2000

Spurred on by strategic planning discussions that took place in 2002, Curry School faculty members began an at-risk initiative that has turned out to have a long-lasting impact on student performance across Virginia and to provide a thematic structure joining varied programs within the school. Robert Pianta—a faculty member in the Department of Human Services with a background in psychology and an interest in the ways schools influence personal development—headed efforts to conceptualize the direction this initiative might take. His group identified three guiding principles: dedication to interdisciplinary perspectives; focus on prevention—that is, early interventions rather than observation of failures; and recognition that complex challenges require complex ideas.[1]

The at-risk group established a monthly lecture series, bringing together experts from many fields to share research on work with groups needing particular services. A faculty team including Robert Pianta, Sara Rimm-Kaufman, Laura Justice, and members of several college departments designed Risk and Prevention in Education Sciences (RPES), a research-intensive interdisciplinary doctoral program in the Curry School. Focusing on risk and prevention, the program draws in faculty from across the University. RPES received a training grant from the U.S. Department of Education's Institute of Education Sciences in 2004 and is currently staffed by core faculty members from education, psychology, economics, and sociology.

Paige Pullen, a special education faculty member, has developed Early Childhood and Developmental Risk (ECDR), a teacher education program with an interdisciplinary approach, integrating psychology, early childhood education, and early childhood special education. Along similar lines, the Curry School recently received a $1.5 million grant from the Department of Education for a graduate-level early childhood education program. Combining developmental psychology, early childhood education, and special education, the program prepares graduates to work with children from birth through age eight who suffer from a range of disabling conditions. Associated with these programs, faculty member Laura Justice is conducting several large-scale studies on language and literacy in early childhood development.

Also under way as part of the At-Risk initiative is My Teaching Partner (MTP), a federally funded project to research how the quality of training and support offered preschool teachers affects their students' later success in school. A $5 million project, it is one of eight in the nation supported the U.S. Departments of Health and Human Services and of Education. The national effort grew out of the 2001 White House Summit on Early Childhood Cognitive Development, which highlighted the need for better ways to help parents, teachers, and caregivers provide the intellectual and social skills young children need to succeed.

Led by Pianta, the Curry School's MTP project currently involves 300 pre-kindergarten teachers from forty school districts in Virginia. It provides teachers with web-based materials including curriculum plans, video-based teaching tips, self-evaluation directions, and ongoing web-based consultations with Curry School faculty. At three stages—four-year-old pre-kindergarten, kindergarten, and first grade—children in the classrooms of these teachers will be evaluated for their progress in language, literacy, and social relationships, testing the value of the online support and consultations.[2] In the spring of 2005, Pianta's research projects were incorporated into the newly formed Center for the Advanced Study of Teaching and Learning.

Together with the Annenberg and Ford Foundations, Carnegie launched Teachers for a New Era (TNE) after several large-scale studies showed that the quality of the classroom teacher is the most important determinant of pupil achievement. Introducing this initiative, Vartan Gregorian, president of Carnegie, stated: "If we really want to improve student achievement, we have no choice but to improve teaching. As the nineteenth-century French philosopher, Victor Cousin, has said, 'As is the teacher, so is the school.'"[9]

The TNE project, a collaborative effort between the College of Arts and Sciences and the Curry School, is headed by Victor Luftig, a member of the English department and director of the University's Center for the Liberal Arts. TNE has two overarching missions: to build a university community that supports teacher education through mentoring, partnership-building, and professional support for novice and master teachers; and to collect evidence-based assessments of the teacher education program in the Curry School. In the first two years of TNE, the College of Arts and Sciences developed several interdisciplinary, or "common," courses to synthesize information across traditional boundaries as well as "counterpoint seminars" designed for pre-service students to introduce ways to integrate information from large-scale Arts and Sciences classes in their teaching.

Among Curry participants of TNE, research projects have been designed to examine the effect of pre-service students and Curry graduates on pupil learning. Under the leadership of Scott Imig, Curry faculty and students are designing studies to fulfill the assessment goals of TNE, seeking ways to gauge the effectiveness of Curry teacher preparation programs in yielding strong pupil gains, greater teacher satisfaction, and other measures of success. The focus on assessment is already influencing faculty work with pre-service students, encouraging them to develop ways to assess student learning in their early field placements. The TNE project has also developed a new teacher mentoring program. Now in its second year, the program is designed to involve experienced teachers and University faculty in programs to support all first- and second-year teachers in Charlottesville and Albemarle County.

Another piece of the Curry commitment to the TNE project includes recruitment of teacher education students from traditionally underrepresented groups, including people of color; men, especially in elementary education; those wanting to teach science and math; and those wanting to teach in rural areas. Courses have been developed in these areas as well as courses designed to introduce "late deciders"—fourth-year students—to issues in teaching.

All in all, Teachers for a New Era supports University efforts to integrate teacher education with the liberal arts, a goal that has been a part of the Curry School vision since its earliest days. Furthermore, in the current educational climate of local, state, and national emphasis on standardized testing and teacher accountability, the project confirms assessment skills as a critical component of the pre-service experience with the Curry School's teacher education program.

The last ten years in Curry School history have seen a coalescing of many program initiatives that have evolved over the hundred years since the founding of the school. The school has maintained a perennial focus on educating professionals for service in schools and colleges, on developing a strong research base and regarding it as essential to sound educational practices, on providing public service and outreach programs for Virginia, and on key involvement, often leadership, in professional educational associations.

Curry School student working with Charlottesville elementary school student

AFTERWORD

The Curry School in the 21st Century

There were rumors around Charlottesville that Mr. Jefferson's Ghost had been seen walking on several nights around his home, Monticello, which stands on the hill overlooking the University. The Ghost appearances became so frequent that they were disturbing to the citizenry. Consequently, the President of The University was asked to investigate.

As President Darden approached the hill top at midnight, he saw Mr. Jefferson looking through his telescope in the direction of The University. "Mr. Jefferson," the President inquired, "What causes you unrest? What do you search for through your scope?"

In a frail voice the answer came, "Mr. President, I am looking for that great State University I envisioned when we opened its doors in 1825."

"Do you not see the beautiful grounds you laid out, the Rotunda, the Lawn, the Pavilions?" Mr. Darden inquired.

"Yes, yes, and the serpentine walls still stand as I designed them—one brick wide. But I see no State University, no school of the people."

President Darden said, "Mr. Jefferson, train your telescope on Peabody Hall, which houses the School of Education. The State University of your dreams is being formed there as we speak."

"Good," replied Mr. Jefferson's Ghost. "I can now rest in peace."

— Lindley J. Stiles, 2001

In December 2001 the five living deans of the Curry School of Education—Lindley Stiles, Frederick Cyphert (via teleconferencing technology), Richard Brandt, James Cooper, and David Breneman—gathered in Ruffner Hall to share experiences and discuss key issues they had faced during their administrations. Their memories represented more than half the school's history, from 1949 to the present, and provided a lively picture of the issues and events of their times of leadership. The admittedly apocryphal story above was shared by Lindley Stiles during this gathering.[1] He had told the same story to audiences throughout the Commonwealth in the 1950s as he worked to enhance the reputation of the Curry Memorial School of Education. It brought appreciative chuckles from the group, as it must have to his listeners half a century ago.

In many ways, the stories told by the deans echoed one another. All but one of them, Dick Brandt, had come to the school as an outsider, a situation that posed challenges as they became familiar with the school, the University, and the state. Nearly thirty years ago, Ralph Cherry said in an interview that the University of Virginia was an institution "unlike any other I have been associated with," and the others might well concur with that observation. As the dean of an education school within a major state university, all men faced the challenges that come in

Venable School library, Charlottesville, 2002

the administration of a semi-autonomous unit within a larger administrative structure. For many years, access to the chief financial officers of the University ensured faculty and programmatic developments. Other administrators at times cast a critical eye on the school and its offerings, and University presidents were essential to its survival time and time again.

All five deans faced the challenges of financing student support, critical to the survival of any school. They all stayed attuned to educational developments at the state and national level, responding to calls for reform in key programs at times that ensured the school's continuance. They strongly encouraged their faculties to maintain professional relationships with state, national, and international organizations as a form of educational service. All the deans valued educational research and encouraged faculty to develop external funding for their programs, so many of which continue at the heart of the Curry School today.

The deans felt teacher education was a critical part of their mission. All agreed that education school offerings should integrate closely with those of the College of Arts and Sciences, although it wasn't until the 1980s, with the five-year teacher education program, that true programmatic integration occurred. Throughout the history of the school, committees of faculty members from both the College of Arts and Sciences and the Curry School have met to evaluate and shape the University's teacher education programs. In many ways, the fortunes of the school ebbed and flowed over these fifty years with the direction and success of the teacher education programs. Courses for those wanting to be secondary education teachers were offered from the beginning. Throughout Manahan's deanship, collaborations with local schools allowed the practical training of teachers. During the last years of Manahan's tenure, elementary teacher education programs were developed. Stiles raised the requirements for admission into teacher education programs while developing a graduate program of study in education. Cherry oversaw the first national accreditation of Curry's teacher education program as it was dividing into particular areas of certification and steered the school into a departmental structure. Cyphert's own interest lay in educational research, but with his ability to hire new faculty members, he formed a solid base for instruction in all areas of teacher education. Brandt faced the most serious challenges to the school, with criticism leveled at the perceived lack of standards in the teacher education program. Cooper helped reestablish the teacher education program as an integral part of the University as well as a graduate program, earning it national recognition. Curry teacher education programs under Breneman have continued to be highly regarded. Recently the school became first in the country to be accredited by two national associations for teacher education.

Each dean left a strong impression during his era in office. Mileposts associated with each can illustrate the Curry School's past one hundred years. Under John Manahan's leadership, the Department of Education established strong ties with the state's school administrators and initiated many programs that continue today, including the McGuffey Reading Clinic and the Speech and Hearing program. Lindley Stiles oversaw the transition from a department of education to a school of education, with authority to grant its own degrees. Ralph Cherry managed the growth of many programs and oversaw the departmental organization of the school.

For Ted Cyphert, the challenge was to energize students and encourage faculty to become more involved in research. The faculty nearly tripled during his deanship; many of those he hired have had significant impact on Curry School programs ever since. Dick Brandt established a foundation for private giving, thus providing the framework for financial contributions to the school to grow. Jim Cooper reorganized the school's departments and created the five-year teacher education program, increasing interaction with the College of Arts and Sciences and responding to national calls for reform in teacher education. David Breneman's leadership has thus far seen significant fundraising efforts promising a new building at a time when state support is diminishing significantly, as well as the development of new areas of scholarly activity.

There have been times of growth and times of stagnation, yet the Curry School today continues to reflect the aspirations of Edwin Anderson Alderman a century ago. The mission continues to be, as it was in Alderman's vision in 1905, to prepare students for positions of educational leadership. One needs only substitute the current term "Curry School of Education" for his "Department of Education" to turn an early catalog description into a summary of the hundred-year history chronicled here:

> It is the main purpose of the Department of Education to provide opportunity for [the] professional training of those who expect to teach or administer school affairs. Since education is of great importance as an agency of Democracy and as an aspect of civilization, the [Curry School] also aims to provide courses of cultural value for citizens generally. In addition to affording opportunities for study and training, the [School], as part of the State University, offers its services to school authorities throughout Virginia, with a desire to cooperate in the solution of practical educational problems and in the furtherance of public education.[2]

Through its first century, the Curry School has stayed true to the vision of its original founder, the first president of the University of Virginia and a legendary educator in the South, Edwin Anderson Alderman, while reinterpreting his intentions in ever new ways, responding to changing times in the Commonwealth, the nation, and the world. Today, in 2005, the Curry School ranks as one of the outstanding schools of education in the United States of America. Its success stands as a tribute to those who have come before and a promise of hope for the teachers and the children of the future.

Five Curry School deans in 2001. From left: Stiles, Brandt, Cyphert (on TV monitor), Cooper, Breneman

Acknowledgments

As I began this project, I certainly was unaware of the many threads of the University's history that begin with the Curry School. Untangling these threads and providing the context for developments influencing the school today has been a challenging and enlightening task. The documents used for this history include the resources contained in the Alfred and Shirley Small Special Collections Library at the University of Virginia: from the papers of the University presidents, Boards of Visitors, and provosts to files related to the School of Education, the Summer School, and the Extension Programs (today's School of Continuing and Professional Studies). Many faculty members, past and present, have contributed generously of their time, patiently answering my questions and clarifying the sequence of events occurring in their respective programs. I hope that in the final event I have provided a faithful and accurate record of our history.

From the outset of this project, David W. Breneman has been generous with his support, providing me with the release time essential to completing the history. Along with Deans Lindley Stiles, Ted Cyphert, Dick Brandt, and Jim Cooper, he has provided access to information and contributed insights concerning issues central to his time in office. All five deans generously shared documentation of events during their deanship; the story of the Curry School is greatly enriched by their contributions. The deans' lively discussions at a gathering in December 2001 highlighted their personal goals for the school and their respective identification of many key issues central to leading the school.

Barbara Brodie, author of *Mr. Jefferson's Nurses*, has been unfailingly supportive of this project, encouraging me many times as I faced the challenges of bringing together information from many sources to create a cohesive story. Her question to me—"Why a school of education at the University at a time when normal schools were well established in Virginia?"—provided a useful framework for this history.

Former students Elsie Babbit, Kathleen Coyle, Kate Dabney, Cara Johnson, Kris Kishore, Diana Smith, and Abbie Wilson gathered data related to this history, as did Linda Price and Tina Longacker.

The staff of the Small Special Collections Library, headed by Michael Plunkett, was most helpful in ferreting out information and elusive photographs related to the education school. Regina Rush, Margaret Hrabe, Heather Riser, Jeanne Pardee, Bradley Daigle, Ervin Jordan, Eva Chandler, Gayle Cooper, Ed Gaynor, and Daisy Wright were always ready to answer the smallest inquiry and helped unearth much useful information previously not used, as did the staff in the Heck Memorial Library of the Curry School: Betsy Anthony, Kay Buchanan, and Carole Lohman. Margaret O'Bryant of the Albemarle Historical Society was similarly enthusiastic and helpful.

I am indebted to the work of many people who generously shared information and their prior research with me. Richard Jenkins began research on the Curry School's history in the 1990s and gave me his files related to the early years of the school. Professor Greg Michel at the University of Texas provided useful information related to the Deseg Center as did Hank Allen, Jim Bash, and John Mesinger; Jennings Wagoner contributed information based on his history of the Center for Higher Education; Phyllis Leffler supplied information related to women at the University, as did Mary Whitney; Frank Barham clarified aspects of the complex history of state professional organizations' relationship to the school of education; Linda Bunker described events related to the history of physical education programs, as did Joe Gieck; Mike Caldwell found the informal history of the Bureau of Educational Research written by Edith Mosher; Sondra Stallard clarified the historical events related to the School of Continuing and Professional Studies; Al Taylor and Dudley Doane made available information related to the University's Summer School; and Ralph Stoudt shared with me his history of the Communications Disorders programs. George Stovall and the Office of Institutional Records and Assessment were extremely helpful in making available data related to the school.

Many other Curry faculty and staff provided useful feedback and clarification about events occurring in the school in response to my seemingly endless questions, including Jerry Moore, Glen Bull, Jim Kauffman, Dan Hallahan, Carolyn Callahan, Annette Gibbs, Bob Pate, Mary Abouzeid, Marcia Invernizzi, Tom Estes, Ron Reeve, Dick Abidin, Cheryl Henig, Jim Esposito, Andy Stamp, Scott Imig, Al Butler, Carol Dudding, John Bunch, Rebecca Kneedler, Dave Drucker, and Bob Pianta, in addition to those I cornered in the halls of Ruffner whenever I could. I owe a special debt of gratitude to Becky Burbach, whose ability to answer questions about details related to this project was amazing: through her detective work, many issues were clarified. Jay Jackson has endured my almost daily interruptions as this project has neared completion and has been most supportive throughout this process.

Former alumni have shared their stories with me about their times in the school of education; their contributions give a personal view to the sometimes dry stories of events unfolding over time. Two special photographs are included here as a result of the generosity of family members: Ralph Rush found the picture of his aunt Mary, and Pamela Booth tracked down the picture taken of her grandfather Ed Alvey with other Curry faculty members on the steps of Peabody Hall in 1931. Elizabeth Smith provided pictures of her days in the education school as did Athena Angelus, who found documentation of her role as the first woman president of the SVEA. Robin Lee donated the picture of the 1947 Venable Elementary School band.

Jennings Wagoner read early drafts of the manuscript, and I am indebted to him for much of the original research on the early days of the Curry School. Jennifer de Forest provided useful feedback, and Sandy Gilliam read a draft with an eye on University-wide developments. Kenny Marotta edited the first draft of the manuscript, helping to organize the many parts of the story into a more readable format. Susan Tyler Hitchcock has been the perfect editor, shaping the manuscript into its present form and tolerating many suggestions on my part. Nic Siler was flexible and resourceful with the seemingly endless task of procuring illustrations. Charlotte Barber and Garth Anderson helped us find key images. Laura Holian designed the tables and charts illustrating enrollment patterns and degrees awarded over time, providing the reader with a useful overview of these aspects of the school's history. Diane Nelson crafted an elegant design, pulling all the elements together into a graceful volume.

Friends and colleagues, too many to name, have listened to my many tales of the school's history, frequently hearing far more than they wanted to know. Kristina Wilson, David Geist, and Abigail Wilson have been unfailingly interested in this project, as has my husband, Richard. Without his support, this history of the Curry School of Education would not be what it is, and for that I am unfailingly grateful.

ELEANOR VERNON WILSON

Major Sources

Much information and many quotations in this book come from documents in the University Archives of the University of Virginia's Small Special Collections Library. These include the papers of the presidents, provosts, and Boards of Visitors, along with faculty minutes and other administrative records from the Curry Department and School of Education. All such sources are cited by author, date (if known), and archival record group number. Student, alumni, and registration publications were also important sources. Statistical information from the University of Virginia's Office of Institutional Assessment and Studies is simply listed as such.

Alderman, Edwin Anderson. *The Function and Needs of Schools of Education in Universities and Colleges.* New York: The General Education Board, 1917.

Alderman, Edwin Anderson. "Inaugural Address." *Alumni Bulletin of the University of Virginia*, April 1905.

Alderman, Edwin Anderson, and Armistead Churchill Gordon. *J. L. M. Curry: A Biography.* New York: The Macmillan Company, 1911.

Allison, Clinton B. *Teachers for the South: Pedagogy and Educationists in the University of Tennessee, 1844-1995.* New York: Peter Lang, 1998.

Alvey, Edward, Jr. *Along Life's Way: Reminiscences of a Journey.* Fredericksburg, Virginia: Mary Washington College Foundation, 1996.

Barham, Frank. "Institutional Self-Study of Graduate Programs in Education: The Department of Administration and Supervision." Charlottesville: Curry Memorial School of Education, July 3, 1985.

Bash, James H. *Effective Teaching in the Desegregated School: A Guide Book.* Bloomington, Indiana: Phi Delta Kappa, 1966.

Bestor, Arthur Eugene. *Education Wastelands: The Retreat from Learning in Our Public Schools.* Urbana: University of Illinois Press, 1953.

Brandt, Richard M. *Public Education Under Scrutiny.* Washington, D.C.: University Press of America, 1981.

Brodie, Barbara M. *Mr. Jefferson's Nurses: University of Virginia School of Nursing, 1901-2001.* Charlottesville: Rector and Visitors of the University of Virginia, 2001.

Brown, Phyllis G. "Historical Sketch of Your Professional Organization through the Century," *Virginia Journal of Education: Centennial Issue*, vol. 57, September 1963–May 1964, 6–25.

Bruce, Philip Alexander. *History of the University of Virginia*, 5 vols. New York: Macmillan, 1921–1922.

Canady, R. Lynn, and Michael Rettig. *Block Scheduling: A Catalyst for Change in High Schools.* Larchmont, N.J.: Eye on Education, 1995.

The Carnegie Forum on Education and the Economy. *A Nation Prepared: Teachers for the 21st Century: The Report of the Task Force on Teaching as a Profession.* New York: Carnegie Foundation, 1986.

Chernow, Ron. *Titan: The Life of John E. Rockefeller, Sr.* New York: Vintage Books, 1999.

Clifford, Geraldine, and James Guthrie. *EdSchool: A Brief for Professional Education.* Chicago: University of Chicago Press, 1988.

Conant, James Bryant. *The Education of American Teachers.* New York: McGraw-Hill, 1963.

Conkin, Paul Keith. *Peabody College: From a Frontier Academy to the Frontiers of Teaching and Learning.* Nashville, Tennessee: Vanderbilt University Press, 2002.

Cremin, Lawrence, and Merle L. Borrowman. *Public Schools in Our Democracy.* New York: Macmillan, 1956.

Cyphert, Frederick R., and Walter L. Grant. "The Delphi Technique: A Tool for Collecting Opinions in Teacher Education." *The Journal of Teacher Education*, vol. XXI, no. 3 (Fall 1969), 417–425.

Dabney, Charles W. *Universal Education in the South*, vols. 1 and 2. New York: Arno Press, 1969.

Dabney, Virginius. *Mr. Jefferson's University: A History.* Charlottesville: University Press of Virginia, 1981.

DePorry, Andre C., ed. *For the Commonwealth: Extension and Continuing Education by the University of Virginia, 1912–1973.* Charlottesville: School of Continuing Education, 1974.

Dorn, Sherman. *A Brief History of Peabody College.* Nashville, Tennessee: Peabody College of Vanderbilt University, 1996.

Education Review, vols 1–12. Charlottesville: Curry School of Education, 1963–75.

Edwards, Elizabeth. *Women in Teacher Training Colleges, 1900-1960: A Culture of Femininity.* London: Routledge, 2001.

Fife, R. H. "School of Methods." *University of Virginia Bulletin*, October 1903.

Heatwole, Cornelius J. *A History of Education in Virginia.* New York: Macmillan Company, 1916.

Herbst, Jurgen. *And Sadly Teach: Teacher Education and Professionalization in American Culture.* Madison, Wisconsin: University of Wisconsin Press, 1991.

The Holmes Group. *Tomorrow's Teachers.* East Lansing, Michigan: The Holmes Group, 1986.

Howsam, Robert B., Dean C. Corrigan. George W. Denemark, and Robert J. Nash. *Educating a Profession.* Washington, D.C.: American Asociation for Colleges of Education, 1985.

Hylton, Vallie Wendell. "A Historical Review of the Technical Assistance and Services of the Consultative Resource Center on School Integration (Title IV, Civil Rights Act 1964, Public Law 88-352, Sections 403 and 404), School of Education, University of Virginia, from March 1967 to February 1972." Unpublished dissertation. Charlottesville: University of Virginia, 1973.

Jefferson, Thomas. Letter to Joseph Priestly, January 18, 1800. In Merrill D. Peterson, ed., *Thomas Jefferson Writings.* New York: Library of America, 1984.

Jefferson, Thomas. *Rockfish Gap Report* (1824). In Roy J. Honeywell, *The Educational Work of Thomas Jefferson.* Cambridge: Harvard University Press, 1931.

Kauffman, J. M. "Introduction: Historical trends and contemporary issues in special education in the United States." In J. M. Kauffman and D. P. Hallahan, eds., *Handbook of Special Education.* Englewood Cliffs, New Jersey: Prentice-Hall, 1981.

Koerner, James D. *The Miseducation of American Teachers.* Boston: Houghton Mifflin Company, 1963.

Labaree, David F. *The Trouble with Ed Schools.* New Haven: Yale University Press, 2004.

Lagemann, Ellen Condliffe. *An Elusive Science: The Troubling History of Education Research.* Chicago: University of Chicago Press, 2000.

Leffler, Phyllis. "Women in Education at the University of Virginia," unpublished paper, 2002.

Lewis, Ivey. "William Harry Heck, 1879-1919." *Alumni Bulletin of the University of Virginia*, October 1919.

Maiden, Marvin G. "The History of the Professional Training of Teachers in Virginia." Unpublished dissertation. Charlottesville: University of Virginia, 1927.

Malone, Dumas. *Edwin A. Alderman: A Biography.* New York: Doubleday, Doran & Company, 1940.

Matthews, Sarah S. *The University of Virginia Hospital: Its First Fifty Years.* Unpublished paper, [1960].

Michel, Greg L. "Fellowship Report." Unpublished document prepared for the Carter G. Woodson Center, University of Virginia, 2000.

Moran, Charles E. "Oral History Interview of Ralph Cherry." February 3, 1976.

Moran, Charles E. "Oral History Interview of Francis G. Lankford, Jr." September 22, 1976.

Myers, Richard. "Edwin Anderson Alderman: Public School Missionary and University President." Unpublished paper, 1993.

Ogden, Jean, and Jesse Ogden. *These Things We Tried: A Five-Year Experiment in Community Development.* Charlottesville: University of Virginia Extension Division, 1947.

Payne, W. H. *The Education of Teachers.* Richmond, Virginia: B. F. Johnson Publishing Co., 1901.

Peaslee, Catherine. "Summer School, the Incubator for Women's Reforms." *Magazine of Albemarle County History*, vol. 55, 1997, 1–15.

Powell, Arthur G. *The Uncertain Profession: Harvard and the Search for Educational Authority.* Cambridge, Massachusetts: Harvard University Press, 1980.

Quantz, Richard A. "Edwin Alderman and the Founding of the University of Virginia School of Education." Occasional Paper no. 3, Department of Foundations of Education, School of Education, University of Virginia, 1979.

Rice, Jessie Pearl. *J. L. M. Curry: Southern Statesman and Educator.* New York: Columbia University King's Crown Press, 1949.

Richards, Herbert C., Nathan Johnson, and James Bash. *The Evaluation of Racial Attitudes and Attitude Change.* Monograph 3. Charlottesville: ED Publications, Curry School of Education, June 1972.

Seawell, William H., and Harold Ramsey. "The Superintendency in Virginia: A Century of Public Service to Virginia." *Virginia Journal of Education*, vol. 58, no 1 (September 1964), 18-28.

Shenkir, William G., and William R. Wilkerson. *The University of Virginia's McIntire School of Commerce: The First Seventy-Five Years, 1921-1996.* Charlottesville: The McIntire School of Commerce Foundation, 1996.

Smithey, William Royall, ed. *Secondary Education in Virginia*, nos. 1–32. University of Virginia Record: Extension Division. 1927–1948.

Stiles, Lindley. *Cowboy in the Classroom: A Trilogy of Reflections on a Teaching Career.* Evanston, Illinois: Northwestern University (private printing), 1979.

Stiles, Lindley J. *Moods and Moments.* Private printing, n.d. [1952].

Stiles, Lindley J. *The Present State of Neglect: A National survey of graduate school programs in the field of educational public information conducted for Project Public Information.* Madison, Wisconsin. November 1967.

Sublette, William. "Hearing Things and Talking Back: For Fifty Years a U.Va. Program has helped Children and Adults do both." *University of Virginia Alumni News*, March 1992.

Thorton, Martha. "The Department of Education and the Struggle for Coeducation at the University of Virginia." Unpublished paper, October 1999.

United States. National Commission for Excellence in Teacher Education. *A Call for Change in Teacher Education.* Washington, D.C.: American Association of Colleges for Teacher Education, 1985.

Urban, Wayne, and Jennings L. Wagoner, Jr. *American Education: A History*, 2nd ed. Boston: McGraw Hill, 2000.

Wagoner, Jennings L., Jr. *Jefferson and Education.* Chapel Hill, North Carolina: University of North Carolina Press, 2004.

Wagoner, Jennings L., Jr., and Richard Quantz. "Public Education, The University of Virginia and the Curry School of Education: The Beginnings of a Tradition." In *Three More Schools of Education.* Tampa, Florida: SPE Monograph Series, 1985–1986.

Warren, Donald, ed. *American Teachers: Histories of a Profession at Work.* New York: MacMillan, 1989.

Whitney, Mary E. *Women and the University.* Charlottesville, Va: University of Virginia, 1969.

Wilson, Richard Guy, and Sara A. Butler. *University of Virginia: An Architectural Tour.* New York: Princeton Architectural Press, 1999.

CHAPTER 1

The Study of Education in the Nineteenth Century

[1] Thomas Jefferson, *Rockfish Gap Report*, 1818

[2] Jefferson to Joseph Priestley, January 18, 1800

[3] V. Dabney, 6

[4] Ibid., 41

[5] Wagoner and Quantz, 2

[6] "Breaking and Making Tradition," University of Virginia Libraries Exhibition archived at http://www.lib.virginia.edu/small/exhibits/women

[7] Wagoner and Quantz, 4

[8] Bruce, vol. 4, 235

[9] University of Virginia Annual Announcements, 1886, 38–39

[10] Wagoner and Quantz, 6

[11] Ibid., 7, citing R. H. Fife Jr., "School of Methods," *University of Virginia Alumni Bulletin* (hereafter cited as *Alumni Bulletin*), October 1903, 189

[12] Bruce, vol. 4, 236

[13] *Virginia Journal of Education*, 1963, 44

CHAPTER 2

Founding the Curry Memorial School of Education: The Vision of Edwin Alderman, 1905–1920

[1] Alderman, "Inaugural Address," 1905

[2] Wagoner and Quantz, 13

[3] *Charlottesville Daily Progress*, June 28, 1904

[4] Malone, 96

[5] Wagoner and Quantz, 13

[6] Alderman to Charles Fenner, January 21, 1905, RG 2/1/2.472 Box 10

[7] This is noteworthy given the fact that several education deans, beginning with Manahan, expressed interest in a model, practice, "laboratory," or professional development school as part of the education school's operations but never succeeded in establishing one.

[8] Frederick Gates served as Rockefeller's chief philanthropic officer for twenty years, between 1891 and 1912. He enjoyed Rockefeller's trust, although he never had complete freedom to draw up programs: "His power, if vast, was circumscribed." Rockefeller said of Gates in 1917 that "he combines business skill and philanthropic aptitude to a higher degree than any man I have ever known." Chernow, 367–370

[9] Alderman and Gordon. Curry served the Peabody Fund from 1881 to 1885 and from 1889 until his death in 1903.

[10] Ibid., 8

[11] Harry Heck graduated from Wake Forest College at the age of seventeen with a 98.25 record. He received a master's degree from Wake Forest as well, then attended Columbia University for three years as a postgraduate fellow. In 1902 Heck became assistant secretary of the General Education Board. In that role, he investigated and reported on public education in each state. *College Topics*, November 1, 1905

[12] Wagoner and Quantz, 16

[13] Ibid., 18

[14] Hopes for the role of the "department of Secondary Education" in the state were described in the *Alumni Bulletin*: "With a knowledge of the actual conditions of secondary school work . . . the instruction given in Secondary Education at the University should in the future possess a directness of force which will render a distinct service to the new and powerful movement now being generated all over the South for a complete system of education organically related and open to all, from the kindergarten to the university." March 1906, 271

[15] Payne to Alderman, October 18, 1905, RG 2/1/2.472 Box 17

[16] RG 2/1/2.472 Box 8

[17] Ibid.

[18] Myers, "Edwin Anderson Alderman"

[19] Payne, "Five Years of High School Progress in Virginia," *Alumni Bulletin,* April 1910, 130–141

[20] Ibid.

[21] Payne to Alderman, May 6, 1911, RG 2/1/2.472 Box 22

[22] RG 2/1/2.472 Box 9

[23] Bruce, vol. 5, 209

[24] Bruce, vol. 5, 203. While some felt this was a blow to the University, Payne's work in establishing public secondary education in Virginia had lasting effects for the state.

[25] Bruce, vol. 5, 210–211: "The 91 graduates admitted represented one-third of all male graduates of the accredited public high schools in Virginia. Twelve years before, there had been to all intents none."

[26] Unpublished document, U.Va. Summer School Office

[27] Eggleston (Superintendent of Public Instruction) to Alderman, April 16, 1906, RG 2/1/2.472 Box 9

[28] Lindley Stiles, "University of Virginia—Summer Session: Historical Sketch," RG 2/1/2.591 Box 28

[29] Annual Report, October 9, 1911: "The University Summer School has grown into an institution of real power and usefulness . . . 1263 students were enrolled in it last year . . . I feel that through the means of the Summer School it is reaching out and touching helpfully the life of our people in ways that it could not hope to do if its activities were confined to the work of a regular term." RG 2/1/2.472 Box 4

[30] All of this was not accomplished without a fair amount of stress on the part of Payne. He wrote to Alderman, August 21, 1908: "I have had several attacks of nervous disorders brought on by the extra incidental to the opening [of summer school], about 3 times as much as I have ever had before." RG 2/1/2.472 Box 21

[31] Annual Report, RG 2/1/2.472 Box 4

[32] Bruce, vol. 5, 212

[33] Ibid., 214. According to Bruce, Eggleston did not wish to discontinue "the old work of equipping teachers for the elementary schools," but through the "employment of the University's professors, in cooperation with other distinguished educators, the ripest instruction could be rendered practicable for men and women who were already engaged as teachers, principals, or superintendents of high schools or colleges."

[34] Ibid.

[35] Maphis, "Rural Life Conference," 1–2, RG 2/1/2.472 Box 20

[36] *University of Virginia Record 1913–14*, 38–44. The catalogue also reported that "A very important and helpful feature of the work in elementary education this year will be a regular vacation school for observation purposes. The city of Charlottesville will conduct a vacation school for work in all the grades, which will be in charge of trained expert teachers and under the general supervision of the instructors in elementary education in the Summer School. Arrangements have been made for daily observation work and some practice teaching" (42)

[37] *College Topics*, September 20, 1905

[38] Lewis, "William Harry Heck," *Alumni Bulletin,* October 1919

[39] Bruce, vol. 5, 208

[40] Heck to Alderman, July 18, 1907, RG 2/1/2.472 Box 13

[41] Stone to Alderman, July 17, 1907, RG 2/1/2.472 Box 18

[42] Writing in April 1912, Alderman said, "We are about to inaugurate a real Department of Education here with a moderate income to be sure of about $10,000.00 which will provide for one Professor of Education and one Professor of Secondary Education, another professor of Education with Psychology and later a psychologist pure. There may one day be a coordinate college for women in our vicinity, but that is not at all certain. I believe there is a field for such a Department. This needs a man of real personality and dignity of character and attainments at the head of it all." RG 2/1/2.472 Box 9

[43] In an announcement of extension services organized in 1913–1914, Alderman wrote: "The ultimate mission of the State university in America [is to provide educated leadership] to all people who constitute the life of the State. Universities must, therefore . . . draw near to the people, young and old, in helpfulness and service . . . The University of Virginia, founded by the greatest individual and democrat of the age, would be strangely false to its origin and genius if it did not seek to illustrate this idea." *University of Virginia Record: Extension Series* 1915, 5

[44] *College Topics,* April 13, 1891: "A system of education known as university extension was discussed by leading professors and learned men. This system is the extension of the University system of education to the masses by courses of lectures. In short, it is education by lectures." Senate Document No. 3 (1912): "The University of Virginia should inaugurate and carry on a system of University Extension which should carry knowledge to the people of the State who cannot take courses in residence there, thus drawing near to the people and cultivating and strengthening the common life." RG 2/1/2.472 Box 11

[45] De Porry, 4–6

[46] Alderman, Annual Report to Armistead Gordon, Rector, October 28, 1912, 5–6. Alderman closes the report by saying a "helpful and increasing tendency, in which this University is rapidly taking its part, is the tendency to consider the whole of society as the field of a university and to count it an opportunity and a privilege to render service wherever service makes for the development of a larger and fuller life for the whole people." RG 2/1/2.472 Box 18; Bruce, vol. 5, 209; V. Dabney, 44

[47] Peabody Fund 1909–1912; Peabody Fund to Alderman, September 25, 1911, RG 2/1/2.472 Box 9

[48] July 8, 1912, RG 2636 Box 9

[49] Wilson and Butler, 68

[50] Alderman to Payne, December 4, 1926, RG 2/1/2.472 Box 7

[51] *College Topics*, April 18, 1914

[52] Ibid.

[53] Wilson and Butler, 69

[54] "Announcement of the Curry School of Education" [1914], RG 10/7/1.851 Box 1

[55] Maphis to Alderman, October 19, 1914, RG 2/1/2.472 Box 20

[56] *University of Virginia Record* 1911–12, 2, 161. It is sometimes difficult to establish the exact dates of proposed changes because the *Record* was published several times a year.

[57] *University of Virginia Record* 1913–14, 7, 151

[58] *University of Virginia Record* 1915–16, new series vol. 2, no. 3, 139

[59] *University of Virginia Record: Extension Services,* "Announcement of the Curry Memorial School of Education," vol. 1, no. 6 (May 1916), 194

[60] *University of Virginia Record,* February 1917, 131

[61] School of Education Faculty Minutes, 1917–1972, 1, RG 2/1/2.472 Box 3. Handwritten versions of the minutes of the education faculty for the first several years also exist.

[62] There was some confusion about Manahan's appointment. Manahan contacted Alderman in the spring of 1915, but Alderman was not able to work out the details of his appointment until early in 1916. In the meantime, Maphis had apparently approached a Mr. Jocelyn of Lawrence, Kansas, about the position. Alderman retracted the offer to Jocelyn, apologizing and explaining about his earlier commitment to Manahan in a letter dated March 27, 1916. Manahan accepted the offer on March 28, 1916. RG 2/1/2.472 Box 3

[63] Hanus to Alderman, Feb. 11, 1916, RG 2/1/2.472 Box 2

[64] *University of Virginia Record*, 1919–20, 9

[65] Affixed to the photocopy in the President's Papers is a handwritten note from Manahan to Maphis, urging him to seek approval.

[66] Manahan to Newcomb, January 7, 1935, RG 2/1/2.491 Box 10. The scholarship aid was reinstituted late in the twentieth century, with similar conditions.

[67] RG 10/7/1.851 Box 1

[68] Office of Institutional Assessment and Studies

[69] Alderman, *The Function and Needs of Schools of Education in Universities and Colleges*, published by the General Education Board (GEB), 1917. The GEB was established in 1903 as a philanthropic foundation that had as its focus the improvement of education (and social and economic) conditions in the South. Initially funded with a gift of more than $1 million from John D. Rockefeller, Sr., the organization assisted the Southern Education Board and absorbed the functions of the Peabody and Slater Funds, earlier philanthropic organizations that focused on Southern educational uplift. Through the GEB, Northern capitalists and Southern "progressives" pushed reforms that improved education without challenging the "separate but [un]equal" racial caste system of the Southern social order. The board was especially active before 1940; after this, many programs were brought to a close. The last appropriations were made in 1964. See also Chernow, 483ff.

[70] RG 2/1/2.472 Box 3

[71] Alderman, *Function and Needs*, 10

[72] V. Dabney, 135–136. After Alderman was diagnosed with tuberculosis in 1912, he spent only part of each day in his office, resting in the early afternoons, seldom going out in the evenings, and taking long and frequent vacations. John Lloyd Newcomb, who would become president after Alderman's death, was primarily responsible for keeping the University administration operating during the latter part of Alderman's presidency (Malone, 280–297).

Summer School

[1] V. Dabney, 103

[2] President's Papers, 1920–1925: Summer School, RG 2/1/2.472 Box 6

[3] V. Dabney, 104. A total of 1,816 students were enrolled in both terms in the summer of 1920, and 2,713 in 1921; 2,004 women and 709 men representing 28 states and 3 foreign countries. Three-quarters of the students were women. The 1923 enrollment was 2,523, considerably larger than that of the regular session.

[4] Wilson Gee (Professor of Rural Economics and Rural Sociology, University of Virginia), *The Manufacturers Record,* January 22, 1925, 58

[5] RG 2/1/2.472 Box 22

[6] Alton Taylor, interview, November 2004; *Curry School Newsletter,* Fall 2003, 8

[7] Darden to Stiles, memo on Maphis's resignation, abolishing title of "Dean of Summer School," and transfering summer school activities to the education school, October 17, 1951, RG 2/1/2.581 Box 12. Also see Stiles, interview, 2001. Concerned with establishing oversight of course offerings, Stiles felt his association with the summer quarter would separate it from the Extension Division, providing programs that would contribute more specifically to the needs of teachers.

[8] Faculty minutes, March 19, 1974, 75–77

[9] Office of Summer Session, unpublished document [2002]

[10] http://www.virginia.edu/summer

[11] Dudley Doane, interview, 2004

The Bureau of Appointments

[1] *University of Virginia Record* 1911–12, 161

[2] President's Papers: Annual Reports, September 11, 1934, RG 10/1/6.851 Box 1

[3] Gigi Davis-White, memo, March 2005

CHAPTER 3

Establishing the Curry Memorial Department of Education, 1920–1930

[1] Manahan to Alderman, accepting an appointment as professor of educational administration, June 24, 1916. RG 2/1/2.472 Box 3

[2] Alderman's concern with appointing leadership for the department is reflected in his correspondence. Writing to Manahan with copies to Maphis and Ferguson on July 4, 1919, he speaks of the "present great need" of the department for "earnest, thoughtful, unselfish cooperation of strong and capable men looking towards planning a foundation here so well based that it will grow and become one of the striking activities of the University's life." Alderman indicated he was still consulting others about the dean and explains to Manahan that he is not ready to complete the organization of the department without a dean and did not wish to "make a serious mistake." Alderman asks Manahan to be secretary of the faculty and that the faculty elect their own chairman. Writing to Alderman on October 14, 1919, Ferguson and Maphis ask Alderman not to appoint a dean at this time, citing "an increasingly intimate experience with the various factors involved, and a constant consideration of them" and requesting the communication be confidential "out of courtesy" to Manahan. RG 2/1/2.472 Box 3

[3] V. Dabney, 407

[4] Manahan to Alderman, September 19, 1920, RG 10/1/1.711 Box 4

[5] RG 10/1/1.771 Box 7

[6] Manahan wrote Alderman on October 12, 1920: "The establishment of this library will mean much to the Department of Education because it provides an opportunity for real study." RG 10/1/1.711 Box 4. See also Lewis, 357–392. Among elegies honoring Heck, it was said of him that he was a "pioneer" in developing an introductory education course: "Its method and content was duplicated in no other university in the United States . . . All he asked of his students was that they think and reason for themselves" (368).

[7] RG 10/1/1.771 Box 4

[8] Manahan wrote Alderman on October 29, 1920: "It might be in order for me to state here one of the chief criticisms . . . from various sections of the state, is that when communications are addressed to various members of the faculty, their replies are so long delayed, if any replies are to be made, as to be of little value. I have aimed to answer promptly the many communications that are constantly coming. As one might suppose, these communications have greatly increased in number since my appointment as Dean of the Department." RG 10/1/1.771 Box 4

[9] RG 10/1/1.711 Box 5

[10] This vote was so important to Manahan that his handwritten notes of faculty voting pro/con exist in his personal files. Also, there is a lengthy "Minority Report on the Recommendation of the Academic Faculty to the General Faculty Touching on the Granting of the Degree of Bachelor of Arts to Students in the Department of Education." RG 2/1/2.562 Box 10

[11] RG 10/7/1.851 Box 1

[12] Whitney, 39ff.

[13] Peaslee, 1–15

[14] RG 2/1/2.472 Box 22

[15] RG 10/7/1.851 Box 1

[16] http://www.lib.virginia.edu/small/exhibits/women/grad

[17] V. Dabney, 67

[18] Edith Rudy, B.S. 1940, and Joyce Mao Cofer, B.S. 1953. Rudy cites Gwathmey's philosophy as one of encouraging women to "fade into the background"—a philosophy accepted by most of the women with whom she dealt. http://www.lib.virginia.edu/Small/exhibits/women/grad

[19] Phyllis K. Leffler, "Education," unpublished manuscript. Madeline Whitemore, who received a B.S. in 1928, described her classroom experiences as "interesting and agreeable, though unnaturally reserved. I did not answer questions voluntarily as the students would stamp" (http://www.lib.virginia.edu/Small/exhibits/women/grad). See also V. Dabney, 67

[20] RG 10/1/6.851 Box 1. See also Thornton, "The Department of Education"

[21] RG 10/1/6.851 Box 1

[22] There is little documentation of the activities of the Bureau of Tests and Measurements in annual reports or faculty minutes, but the office is listed in the *Record* through 1953.

[23] Office of Institutional Assessment and Studies

[24] Annual report for the Department of Education, January 25, 1927, RG 10/1/6.851 Box 1

[25] *University of Virginia Record—Curry Memorial Department of Education 1923–24*, 4

[26] Drafts of both proposals in Manahan's hand, RG 10/1/1.711 Box 5

[27] Education minutes, 1921–1954, 15–17, RG 10/7/1.851 Box 1

[28] Kimball to Manahan, May 12, 1922, RG 10/1/1.711 Box 7

[29] Manahan [June 1922], RG 10/1/1.711 Box 7

[30] Manahan to Miss Amelia McLester, Fairmont, W. Va., October 27, 1922, RG 10/1/1.77 Box 7

[31] Manahan to McLester, January 5, 1923. He goes on to say, "I regret exceedingly that things have turned out as they have because I was tremendously interested and exceedingly hopeful regarding the future of such a school. I cannot give you at this time the reasons for this decision, but shall be glad to do so when I see you." RG 10/1/1.77 Box 7

[32] RG 10/7/1.851 Box 1

[33] Manahan to Alderman, April 16, 1925, RG 2/1/2.472 Box 10

[34] RG 10/7/1.851

[35] In July 1925 Luther Gilbert of Meridien, Mississippi, was appointed to be in charge of directed teaching and supervision, receiving a salary of $2,500, of which $1,500 was to be paid by the University and $1,000 by the Charlottesville School Board. RG 10/7/1.851

[36] RG 10/7/1.851 Box 1

[37] Manahan to Alderman, February 15, 1929 RG 2/1/2 Box 7

[38] Alderman to Manahan, May 29, 1928, RG 2/1/2.472 Box 7

[39] *University of Virginia Record—Curry Memorial School of Education 1950–51*, iii. "In 1928 plans were matured to provide more adequate facilities for observation, practice teaching, and experimental studies. The school authorities joined with the University of Virginia in establishing a program of experimental education and teacher-training. After the preliminary program of organization had been approved, the General Education Board of New York City gave the University a two-year grant; with this grant, supplemented by an appropriation from the Rector and Visitors, the cooperative program was successfully initiated and has been continued and expanded in subsequent sessions."

[40] Edward Alvey, interview, January 1996; personal memoir, n.d. "I began my work in 1928 as an instructor in the School of Education . . . My duties involved offering a course in the teaching of English; supervising student teachers in high school English in the Charlottesville City and Albemarle County Public Schools; and serving as head of curriculum development and instruction in English in the city and county high schools. A large order . . . It involved having actual charge of two classes in English daily in the city schools, in which student teachers observed and then taught under my supervision; two in each class each semester; weekly seminars for the entire group of high

school student teachers; serving as department head for English instruction (both the city and the seven county schools); and preparing professional articles and reports on the new program of experimental education and teacher training, financed by a two-year grant from the General Education Board." Alvey's memoirs are corroborated by the May 4, 1929, agreement signed by the University and the Charlottesville School Board, specifying that critic teachers would teach two regular high school classes, supervise student teachers, and conduct "such experimental studies . . . as deemed advisable for the improvement of the school." For the school year 1929–1930, five teachers were appointed, one-third of their salary paid by the city and two-thirds by the University. RG 2/1/2 Box 7

[41] RG 2/1/2.531 Box 5

[42] Francis Lankford, interview, September 1976. Lankford described his experiences with this collaboration much as did Alvey: "We worked on our research, developing units of instruction in 4 subjects, math, social studies, English and Science, in the mornings and then went to Lane High School and taught two classes in the afternoon in which we also supervised student teachers … and also taught methods courses in all subject areas." At this time, enrollment was less than 300 students in the education department and there were always three to five student teachers in each of the high school classes where the faculty taught. RG 26/81

[43] Annual Report of the School of Education, January 19, 1953, 12. RG 10/1/6.851 Box 1

[44] RG 2/1/2.491 Box 8

[45] Zehmer stated that as of 1922 there were between 600 and 700 students enrolled, courses in at least ten subjects were given in ten locations, and the same degree requirements were awarded as were available to full-time students. V. Dabney, 104; *University of Virginia Record,* 1915 through 1956.

[46] V. Dabney, 7

[47] Writing Alderman on January 5, 1925, Manahan requested that Zehmer be appointed a member of the faculty of education. RG 10/1/1.711 Box 4

[48] Unpublished notes, SCPS, circa 1990.

[49] RG 2/1/2.472 Box 5

[50] Memo from George Zehmer to Academic Faculty, December 11, 1934. Zehmer reported a high quality of achievement. RG 10/1/6.851 Box 1

[51] In his 1951 Annual Report, Stiles adds: "Faculty members of the Department are more and more calling upon the services of the Bureau in efforts to vitalize the work for prospective teachers." He saw the new office as having potential "to be of real assistance to the faculty of the University in improving instruction" and as a means "to make its assistance to public schools increasingly more valuable." RG 10/1/6.851 Box 1

[52] De Porry, 20–21

[53] Memo from Dean Robertson concerning the move of the Bureau from Ruffner Hall to Zehmer Hall [1980], RG 2/1/2.831 Box 8

[54] Sondra Stallard to John Casteen, memo, January 22, 2000

[55] Faculty minutes, January 16, 1962, RG 10/7/1.851. It is difficult to determine the exact policies governing education faculty teaching loads over time and the extent to which faculty were paid additional funds for teaching these courses.

[56] Emily White, unpublished document, 1973. Writing in this informal history of the changes that had taken place over thirty years, White noted little similarity between the facilities of the Extension Division in 1935 and the new school in 1973. She described the cooperative spirit that existed among extension employees, attributing this to the strong leadership of Zehmer: "It was impossible to be associated with him without being influenced by his dedication to his work. His staff almost unconsciously absorbed his enthusiasm and worked willingly and diligently to complete any project which he planned" (3–4).

[57] RG 2/1/2.751 Box 17

[58] Jerry M. Moore, personal correspondence, October 2004. Programs were located in Wise County, Grundy, Claypool Hill, Henry County, Pittsylvania, Roanoke, and Fredericksburg.

[59] "Degree Program a Big Success: UVa sets new two-year project," *Danville Bee,* August 1977. RG 2/1/2.80 Box 7

[60] Resolution, Roanoke City Council, October 9, 1987, RG 2/1/2.901 Box 17

[61] James Esposito, memo, April 5, 2005. Between 1995 and 2005, the program served more than 300 students including more than seventy doctoral students.

[62] RG 3/1/2.881 Box 3

[63] Bruce Nelson, Dean and Assistant Provost of Continuing Education, to David Shannon, Vice President and Provost, July 7, 1976, RG 10/1/1.861 Box 31. In 1977 correspondence with Shannon, Brandt urges consideration of the school's issues: "For almost three years we have tried to work cooperatively with the School of Continuing Education to improve our off-grounds activities . . . We shall have to cooperate fully with the School of Continuing Education and depend on its administrative expertise. I do not believe that the cooperative attempts will succeed fully, however, unless the locus of final judgment regarding instructional decisions is clearly identified as ours." RG 2/1/2.791 Box 13. Also Richard Brandt, interview, February 2001.

[64] Sondra Stallard to John Casteen, memo, January 22, 2000. Stallard notes that many applicants to the division believe that Continuing Education is a division of the Curry School of Education and that a School of Continuing and Professional Studies will "distinguish us from the Curry School and emphasize our commitment to professional development."

[65] Sondra Stallard, letter to students, faculty and friends announcing the establishment of the school, March 17, 2000

[66] School of Continuing and Professional Studies, http://www.scps.virginia.edu

[67] RG 2/1/2.472 Box 8

[68] Office of Institutional Assessment and Studies; RG 2/1/2.491 Box 8

[69] V. Dabney, 132. As Alderman's time away from the University increased, Newcomb assumed more and more responsibility for managing daily operations.

[70] Ibid., 141

[71] William B. Smithey, Chair, Report of the Special Committee on University and High School Relations, December 16, 1937. RG 21/54.801 Box 5

[72] "The University of Virginia Extension Department: Nine Lectures on Child Study." RG 2/1/2.491 Box 20

[73] *University of Virginia Record—Curry Memorial Department of Education 1931–32*, 15. With Smithey as editor, the journal was "devoted to the encouragement of research in Virginia secondary school problems and to the reporting of research through its columns."

[74] *Secondary Education in Virginia*, vol. 21, no. 5, November 1936

[75] Francis Lankford, interview, 1976. In this interview, Lankford reminisced about the journal's publications, saying it was a place where samples of faculty work could be published, units developed, and the like. While perhaps not very sophisticated research at the time, it "attracted a lot of attention around the state," he said. He added that the summer conferences provided ways for faculty to read papers and discuss ideas with attendees from around the state. RG 26/81

[76] Seawell and Ramsey, 24–28

[77] Barham, 4–5

[78] John C. Metcalf, memo to John L. Newcomb, September 18, 1934. RG 10/1/6 Box 1. As Manahan continued these classes, they came under scrutiny from President Newcomb. A 1934 memo notes that class participants had not registered with the graduate department or paid a fee, had enrolled in degree programs, and yet were seemingly "padding the rolls" of the graduate department, an "irregular procedure."

[79] RG 2/1/2.491 Box 8. Manahan wrote President Alderman, inviting him to join these meetings and thanking him for the opportunity to meet with the students at the University "without cost." The course met with an "unusual response," as it provided useful support for the twenty superintendents representing twenty-three counties who participated in these first meetings, held for three hours on Monday afternoons.

[80] Manahan to Alderman, Annual Report, January 10, 1931, 5, RG 10/1/6.851 Box 1

[81] Barham, 5

[82] *Curry School Newsletter,* Spring 1986, 5. At this time, VASA was described as a professional organization open to division superintendents, assistant superintendents, administrative assistants, and state superintendents as well as to professors of administration and principals who qualified to be superintendents. "Promoting high and ethical standards among those in the teaching profession is the main purpose" of the organization, the article stated. The organization met in October to discuss legislative issues affecting education.

[83] Albert S. Armentrout, "A History of the Virginia Association of School Administrators (VASA)," unpublished paper presented to the VASA membership in celebration of the organization's centennial anniversary, June 1985

[84] Frank Barham, personal memo, February 5, 2005, 28

[85] Pamphlet, *The Virginia Association of School Superintendents.* [2002]; see also http://curry.edschool.virginia.edu/centers/vass/

[86] *Curry School Newsletter,* Spring 1986, 1

[87] *Curry School Newsletter,* Fall 1994, 4

[88] *Curry School Newsletter,* Fall 2002, 5

[89] *Curry School Newsletter,* Fall 2003, 2–4

[90] *Inside UVA,* vol. 34, no. 17 (October 1, 2004), 1; *Curry School Newsletter,* Fall 2004, 16

[91] There were many attempts to organize educational professionals in the late nineteenth century. As mentioned previously, the National Education Association, of which the VEA would become a part, was founded in 1865 as a result of the National Association of School Superintendents joining with the National Teachers Association and the American Normal School Association. The Virginia Association of School Administrators traces its origin to 1885.

[92] Lindley Stiles, interview, March 2001. B. J. Chandler, "Cooperative Program in Educational Administration: Division Superintendents Program," Annual Report of the Dean 1952. RG 10/1/6.851 Box 1

[93] Lindley Stiles, Annual Report for the Year 1954, December 14, 1954. RG 10/1/6.851 Box 2

[94] Frank Barham, interview, June 2004

[95] Moran, interview with Ralph Cherry, 1976: "This has been a very useful relationship as it gave us insights into their policy making functions" (RG 26/56). Deans following Cherry continued to support these connections.

[96] Herbert Phillips, president of VASSP to University President Frank Hereford on July 16, 1982. Citing the twenty-year relationship of VASSP with the Curry School, he expressed regret for leaving the support of the school but the necessity of establishing offices in Richmond near the State Department of Education. RG 3/1/2.871 Box 20

[97] Andy Stamp, interview, June 2004

[98] Pamphlet, "Virginia School-University Partnership" [2003]. See also http://curry.edschool.virginia.edu/centers/partnership/

[99] Cheryl Henig, memo, April 2005

Nursing Education

[1] Brodie, 24

[2] Ibid., 47–48. The desire to create an autonomous school of nursing within the University was understandable. By 1953 there were three programs in nursing: a diploma program under the control of the hospital, the nursing baccalaureate program under the School of Medicine, and the baccalaureate nursing education program directed by the School of Education. RG 10/7/1.851 Box 1

[3] RG 2/1/2.491–I Box 8

[4] According to Brodie, the students, "by demonstrating their academic prowess and ability to articulate the role that professional nurses were playing in health care, helped pave the way for the University to re-think where nursing education should reside" (25).

[5] Office of Institutional Assessment and Studies

[6] RG 10/1/6 Box 1

Early Women in the Department of Education

[1] Office of Institutional Assessment and Studies

[2] Manahan to Darden, July 9, 1947, RG 2/1/2.551–II Box 13

[3] Office of Institutional Assessment and Studies. During this period, approximately 3,527 degrees were awarded to women; more than 1,900 M.Ed. degrees between 1950 and 1970. More than 7,300 degrees were awarded for all education degree programs.

[4] Anne Snead, B.S. 1940. "Looking back through my *Corks and Curls* I see there are no women in any of the University organizations," she added. Her comment and subsequent quoted comments, unless otherwise noted, appear online at http://www.lib.virginia.edu/Small/exhibits/women/grad

[5] Dorothy Eckford Wooster, B.S. 1946, personal correspondence, September 28, 2001

Physical Education

[1] V. Dabney, 265–266. Lambeth to Alderman, letter, November 24, 1925, RG 2/1/2.472 Box 7. In 1893, under Lambeth's guidance as project director, Fayerweather Gymnasium was designed and equipped with the latest "modern gymnastic applications that could be purchased" (Bruce, vol. 4, 151–152).

[2] December 7, 1937. RG 10/7/1.851 Box 1

[3] V. Dabney, 232. The "V" symbolized "Victory" for American forces during World War II.

[4] October 8, 1942. RG 2/1/2.531 Box 5. On October 13, Manahan wrote all students in the Department of Education, instructing them to enroll in these classes if they had not already done so.

[5] Faculty minutes, January 18, 1945, RG 10/7/1.851 Box 1

[6] Slaughter rode his "victory bicycle" to the University Grounds every day during the war. He was a friend of more University students than anyone else at the time, says V. Dabney. Respected across the University, he was called in to advise on many major projects, including the design of Newcomb Hall and University Hall.

[7] Office of Institutional Assessment and Studies

[8] Richard Meade to Darden, November 23, 1951, RG 2/1/2.581 Box 12

[9] Stiles to Darden, August 16, 1951: "I believe we have the way clear to assume leadership in the State of Virginia in developing the high type of physical education director and teacher." RG 2/1/2.581 Box 12

[10] Darden to Stiles, August 13, 1951. Physical education standards needed to relate to intercollegiate athletics, said Darden: "Nothing can more surely destroy your Department than the belief that it has become a haven for football players who have not the intellectual competence to do University work." RG 2/1/2.581 Box 12

[11] Shannon to Cherry, memo, September 5, 1967, RG 2/1/2.741 Box 18

[12] V. Dabney, 565–566

[13] Linda Bunker, memo, January 2003

[14] Richard M. Brandt, "School of Education: Highlights," unpublished document, RG 10/1/1.861 Box 9

Teachers Preventorium

[1] RG 2/1/2.472 Box 9

[2] RG 2/1/2.472 Box 5. In March 1928, when the building was almost ready for occupancy, 257 of the 600 teachers in the local district had not paid.

[3] *Virginia Journal of Education, Centennial Issue,* vol. 57, September 1963, 9. Also RG 10/1/1.711 Box 17. Teachers were urged to contribute to the campaign at the 1927 meeting of the Virginia Education Association, District J. As Fred Alexander, president of the Virginia Education Association, said, "I know of no other work that will contribute more to security and to professional and personal peace of mind than this one" *(University of Virginia Record: Extension,* "Conference of District J").

[4] Still on the wall in the Barringer Wing of University of Virginia Hospital.

[5] Barbara Brodie, personal correspondence, 2002. An indication of the teachers' appreciation of the preventorium was found in the papers of the McGuffey School in Charlottesville, Virginia, in a poem written by the teachers in the early 1930s as part of the campaign to raise funds. Titled "Our Preventorium," it reads in part:

Of our health, we're not sure
And we may need a cure
But now there's a way
How we'll not have to pay
A price so exorbitant and dear
Our private preventorium . . .

[6] September 1949, RG 2/1/2.561 Box 16; *Virginia Journal of Education*, March 1950, RG 2/1/2.562 Box 29

[7] January 8, 1963, faculty meeting notes report a request that all active members contribute three dollars and new members four dollars toward the fund "at a very early date." RG 10/7/1.851 Box 2

[8] "VEA Preventorium for Teachers At the University of Virginia Hospital, Charlottesville, Virginia." RG 2/1/2.681 Box 40. By the mid-1960s, the preventorium was one of many services the VEA provided for college teachers as well as public school teachers. It was noted when soliciting membership from college and university faculty members.

CHAPTER 4
Developing Education Programs:
John L. Manahan, 1931–1949

[1] C. E. Myers, Chairman, "The Effect of Educational Practices Upon Pupil Learning," The Commonwealth of Virginia, State Board of Education, Richmond, Virginia, 1931, RG 2/1/2.491 Box 8

[2] December 13, 1932; RG 10/1/6.851 Box 1

[3] William Knight, personal correspondence, June 23, 2001

[4] Annual Report of Manahan to Newcomb, January 18, 1934; RG 10/1/6.851 Box 1

[5] Office of Institutional Assessment and Studies; 332 B.S.Ed. degrees were awarded, 240 of these to women and 92 to men; 32 B.S.N.Ed. degrees were awarded; 35 M.S.Ed. degrees were awarded, all but one to men; and 102 M.A. degrees were awarded, 9 to women and the remainder to men. As in several other instances, the figures reported by the University Registrar and those cited in faculty reports do not always match precisely. See also RG 10/1/6.851 Box 1.

[6] Report of the Committee Appointed for the Purpose of Studying Ways of Extending and Improving the Usefulness of the Department of Education, December 19, 1935; RG 10/1/1.851 Box 1. The noted lack of scheduled faculty meetings was to recur during the rest of Manahan's tenure and often caused concern among faculty members.

[7] January 18, 1937, faculty minutes: Professor Acker noted that the "policy of the University in giving humiliating rank to certain members of the Department probably conveyed to the student body that the work of the Department was inferior to other University work" Pres. Newcomb was also focusing on this issue and looking for new leadership in the department (RG 10/7/1.851 Box 1).

[8] See Clifford and Guthrie.

[9] Faculty minutes, June 4, 1936, RG 10/7/1.851 Box 1

[10] "Educational Dep't Denied Representation As a Separate Group," *College Topics,* February 17, 1937, 1. The article also noted that "in the opinion of the Honor Committee and the Student Senate, the Department of Education has not yet attained sufficient stature to deserve separate representation."

[11] November 9, 1938, RG 10/7/1.851 Box 1

[12] Letter from McIntire School faculty member to Newcomb, September 23, 1938, saying, "What the University needs is an outstanding man of real quality. If we were to find such a man he would come to have influence and standing in the educational circles of the State in a relatively short time. The University needs just that sort of influence." Newcomb responded the next day: "We shall go forward rapidly with this . . . but I shall not make any hasty decisions which I may come to believe later to be unwise." RG 2/1/2.491 Box 5

[13] RG 10/1/6.851 Box 1

[14] September 11, 1934. The report also notes that records of the Summer School quarter show many elementary school teachers and prospective teachers "prefer the University to other State institutions," and that "other than at William and Mary College *men* who wish to enter the elementary field can find no opportunity in the State to get the necessary training." While Acker notes that it is "improbable" that any considerable number of men will be attracted to elementary school teaching positions, there is a "great need for them" in the upper grade levels and as "certification requirements are raised and as the salaries of elementary teachers are made commensurate with those offered high school teachers, it is reasonable to expect that men teachers will re-enter the elementary classrooms in such numbers as to justify training opportunities for them." RG 10/1/6.851 Box 1

[15] October 9, 1935, RG 10/7/1.851 Box 1

[16] As part of this departmental report, a committee on elementary education was formed. This group cited the need for the department to arrive at an "acceptable *point of view* with reference to several questions," including "What is the peculiar function of the University of Virginia as a State University that should differentiate its program of Education from that of other Teacher Training Institutions?" RG 2/1/2.491 Box 5

[17] Sidney Hall to Smithey, November 6, 1939, RG 2/1/54.801 Box 8; October 24, 1939, RG 2/1/2.491 Box 5

[18] February 1940, RG 21/54.801 Box 8

[19] William R. Dudenhausen, correspondence, July 30, 2001

[20] Newcomb to Manahan, memo, December 9, 1940 : "It has become necessary for the University of Virginia to give to the Navy Department the use of Peabody Hall for the duration of the war to care for some special training to enlisted men in the United States Navy. When the war is over and the University returns to normal life, this building will be returned as the home of the Department of Education." RG 10/1/6.851

[21] "Brief History of the Curry School of Education," 1976

[22] "University of Virginia School of Education Day 1976," 31–33

[23] January 18, 1945, RG 10/7/1.851 Box 1

[24] As one indication of the sharp decline in enrollment, the Summer Quarter, which frequently had enrollments of more than one hundred pupils, reported that 47 men and 135 women were registered for the first session in July 1944, as compared to 646 men and 263 women in 1943. RG 2/1/2 Sub Series I 1943–1944 Box 11

[25] Kauffman, 7–8. Professional organizations concerned with the care of exceptional children were founded in the 1920s, and training programs for teachers of the handicapped were begun in teachers' colleges and universities. "Between 1901 and 1950 special education became an identifiable . . . part of public education, at least in large cities," writes Kauffman. He describes the early research concerns of those working with handicapped children as early as the 1930s, including the debate that continues today on the best ways to provide education for these children and the longstanding discussion of inclusion versus segregation of children with special needs.

[26] Sidney Hall to Newcomb, May 11, 1939: "All teachers need first, to acquire mastery of the liberal arts and sciences, and secondly, to be well-trained in the techniques and procedures for the impartation of knowledge to the individuals to be taught," including those preparing to teach children with special needs. RG 2/1/2.491 Box 7

[27] Ralph Stoudt, interview, June 2004

[28] "Free Clinic for Speech Faults Opens: First in State," *College Topics,* January 31, 1941

[29] *University of Virginia Record—Curry Memorial Department of Education* 1946

[30] Annual Report 1945–1946, RG 10/1/6.851 Box 1

[31] In a letter to Darden requesting future support for the institute, February 27, 1948, Manahan noted that 95 people attended from public and private schools as well as 20 from the University, and that the conference concluded with a resolution for further conferences: "We have gained inspiration and information, we have learned techniques which we can and will put into practice in our classes, that we shall seek to disseminate into our school systems and communities the good ideas which we have learned here, that this conference has been a significant and important one for mathematics in Virginia's secondary schools." RG 2/1/2.532 Box 6. In another letter to Darden, April 27, 1946, Manahan pointed out that it is "time consuming to have the dean's secretary go to the placement office to tell the director that some one is on the telephone. It is often unsatisfactory to have to talk to some superintendent about a candidate in the presence of several students who may be in the Dean's office at the time." RG 10/1/6.851 Box 1

[32] "Preliminary Report on Ways to Expand and Improve the Work of the Department of Education" [1946], 1–3, RG 10/7/1.851 Box 1

[33] Manahan to Newcomb, January 27, 1947, RG 10/7/1.851 Box 1

[34] Office of Institutional Assessment and Studies

[35] "Report of the Virginia Education Commission: The Virginia Public School System. The Virginia Education Commission," 1944, 23–25, RG 2/1/2 Box 3. It also proposed industrial arts courses in state high schools and in teacher training programs, an initiative the Curry Department had already been considering.

[36] Manahan to Newcomb, October 11, 1944, RG 2/1/2 Box 3

[37] Professor Alex Rorer to Dr. A. G. A. Balz, Chairman, School Board of the City of Charlottesville, July 16, 1943. Balz wrote Rorer asking for suggestions about ways in which the schools might make changes to improve their instruction. Rorer replied that there were two things to address: a clear statement and definition of the curriculum of the public schools from the first grade through high school and, second, the need to provide guidance for high school pupils. RG 3795 Box 1

[38] Manahan to Newcomb, August 6, 1945, RG 2/1/2.541 Box 16

[39] Newcomb to Gee, October 16, 1944, RG 2/1/2.531 Box 3

[40] V. Dabney, 271

[41] "A Statement to the President of the University of Virginia From the Faculty of the Curry Memorial Department of Education," RG 10/7/1.851 Box 1

[42] *Corks and Curls* 1949, 61

[43] Marjorie Taite Austin, personal correspondence, October 5, 2001

[44] Manahan died on December 18, 1966, at the age of 79 and was honored at a December 21, 1966, service in the University Chapel. Dean Cherry, Francis Lankford, and Richard Meade served as three of the six pallbearers, and three ministers presided over the service. Broadside Box 1966 Folder J64

[45] V. Dabney, 105

McGuffey Reading Center

[1] November 16, 1936, RG 10/7/1.851 Box 1. The purpose of the clinic was "to provide facilities for students to become acquainted with effective methods and devices for
1. Determining readiness of children to learn to read, 2. Diagnosing reading difficulties, and 3. Determining remedial measures," *University of Virginia Record—Curry Memorial Department of Education 1937–38,* 25.

[2] Faculty minutes, June 1, 1948, RG 10/7/1.851 Box 1; Leavell to Lankford, July 10, 1946, RG 5677-c Box 10. Leavell, then at Peabody College in Nashville, came to the University of Virginia to collaborate with Professor Lankford in a Summer 1945 workshop focusing on reading strategies designed for superintendents and teachers. This conference was evidently so successful that afterward Leavell wrote Lankford, saying, "If you should sense any earth tremors in future days of matters faintly suggested by the Dean, I should be glad to hear from you."

[3] http://curry.edschool.virginia.edu/reading/projects/mcguffey. While at the University of Virginia, Professor McGuffey lived in Pavilion IX on the West Lawn, where the "McGuffey Ash" tree was planted in 1826. The tree became legendary for its height and width and survived until December 1989, when it had to be cut down. McGuffey is buried in the University Cemetery, and a wreath is laid at his grave every May in his honor.

[4] "Statement of Projected Program for the Reading Clinic in the Department of Education, University of Virginia," RG 10/1/6.851 Box 1. Manahan also sought funding for the reading program from the GEB, December 21, 1946, RG 2/1/2.551 Box 4

[5] "Report and Recommendation, McGuffey Reading Clinic, University of Virginia, January 1, 1949–December 31, 1949." RG 10/1/6.851 Box 1

[6] *Corks and Curls* 1948, 88. The heading reads, "Students teaching corrective reading, etc., etc. etc. (Just putting into practice some of those things learned in Education classes.)"

[7] Tom Estes, interview, February 2001

[8] Mary Abouzeid, interview, November 2004

[9] The Virginia State Department of Education awarded the Curry School a $13.2 million grant ($2.2 million per year over six years) to launch RFIV (*Curry School of Education Newsletter,* Fall 2003, 5).

Lankford and Meade

[1] *Charlottesville Daily Progress,* March 12, 1997. Among the texts he authored or coauthored were *Mathematics for the Consumer* (1953), *Basic Ideas of Mathematics* (1953), *Contemporary Algebra One* (1962), and *Contemporary Algebra Two* (1963).

[2] Moran, interview with Francis Lankford, 1976

[3] *Virginia English Bulletin,* vol. 33, no. 2 (Winter 1983), 3

[4] Ibid.

The Virginia Education Association

[1] *Virginia Journal of Education,* vol. 57 (September 1963–May 1964), 24–25. This journal was the official publication of the Virginia Education Association, Inc., headquartered in Richmond, Virginia. The organization was called the Educational Association of Virginia between 1863 and 1882, then the First Virginia Teachers Reading Association until 1888, then the Virginia Educational Association between 1891 and 1894, the Virginia Teachers League between 1898 and 1924. In 1925, its name became the Virginia Education Association. Before 1870 and the establishment of the public school system, members were private schoolteachers. Public schoolteachers and administrators became actively involved soon thereafter.

[2] Edwin A. Alderman, "The Present State of Higher Education in Virginia," an address delivered before the Virginia Education Conference, Norfolk, Virginia, November 25, 1925, RG 10/1/1.711 Box 4

[3] *University of Virginia Record—Extension Series, Conference of District J,* 390, 372.

[4] Manahan, memo to faculty, December 1935, RG 2/1/2 491 Box 10

[5] RG 10/1/6.85 Box 1

[6] Faculty minutes, September 6, 1966, RG 10/7/1.851 Box 2

[7] Faculty minutes, September 21, 1971, RG 10/7/1.851 Box 2

[8] Athena Angelus, personal correspondence, 2002; *The Virginia Journal of Education,* May 1966, 25. Angelus received another honor when she was elected the first female president of the School of Education's student group.

CHAPTER 5

Raising Confidence and Enhancing Visibility: Lindley J. Stiles, 1949–1955

[1] Stiles to Virginius Dabney, September 16, 1953, RG 2/1/2.631 Box 15; Stiles, interview, February 2001

[2] "Proposed Qualifications for the Dean of the Department of Education," RG 2/1/2.561 Box 7

[3] Stiles, interview, 2001

[4] See, for instance, the work of Arthur Bestor.

[5] Faculty meetings were held infrequently during Manahan's last ten years as dean, a source of concern for education faculty members.

[6] Faculty minutes, October 24, 1949, RG 10/7/1.851 Box 1

[7] Stiles to Darden, "Plans for the future of the Department of Education," November 16, 1949. The M.A. and Ph.D. degrees were still awarded through the College of Arts and Sciences, a practice that continued through June 1996 when the Education School began awarding all education degrees. RG 2/1/2.561 Box 7

[8] RG 10/1/6.851 Box 1

[9] Ivey Lewis to Darden, December 20, 1951, RG 10/7/1.851 Box 1

[10] RG 10/7/1.851 Box 1. The announcement specifies requirements for enrollment and degrees, adding that "with respect to the amount and quality of work required and to their professional reputableness, graduate and graduate-professional degrees in education, at both the master's and doctoral levels, are comparable."

[11] Darden to Stiles, February 13, 1950, RG 2/1/2.562 Box 11

[12] Darden to Stiles, February 20, 1950, RG 2/1/2.562 Box 11

[13] *College Topics,* November 1, 1950

[14] Stiles to Darden, November 14, 1950, RG 2/1/2.562 Box 11

[15] Annual Report 1950, 3, RG 10/1/6.851 Box 1

[16] W. E. Rosenstegel and Lee G. Garber to Robert Fisk, April 15, 1951, *Cooperative Project in Education Administration,* Teachers College, Columbia University, RG 2/1/2.581 Box 12

[17] Darden to Stiles, October 17, 1951, RG 2/1/2.581 Box 12

[18] Annual Report, December 14, 1954, 4, RG 10/1/6.851 Box 2

[19] March 4, 1950, RG 2/1/2.562 Box 11

[20] Stiles, interview, March 2001: "We got away from the old idea that graduate study in education was quoting from an old musty textbook. . . . We said research we're going to do is live research with *real* problems."

[21] Cherry to Shannon, memo, November 21, 1962, Of changing admission requirements, Cherry wrote, "Our experience indicates that we can make better selections after the student has been in college two years." RG 2/1/2.661 Box 10

[22] The faculty was now meeting at least twice monthly to consider changes and recommendations for future growth.

[23] October 20, 1950. This summary includes the analysis of admission policies, the increase of students majoring in elementary and secondary education, the fact that men outnumber women, and the fact that graduate enrollment in residence was almost double that of the fall of 1949. Darden wrote on October 24, commending Stiles for his work, especially for the "increased emphasis being placed upon the selection of able students." He also cautioned Stiles to maintain the "greatest vigilance in selecting teachers to carry on the extension work," since "the capacity of these individuals determines the worth of the whole undertaking." RG 2/1/2.562 Box 11

[24] Annual Report, January 18, 1950, RG 10/1/6.851 Box 1

[25] "A Proposed Organization of a State-Wide Program of Graduate Work in Education," August 17, 1950, RG 2/1/2.562 Box 11

[26] *College Topics,* November 4, 1950. Stiles addressed more than thirty-five school groups in 1950 alone, an indication of his intent to link the Department of Education with the schools of the state.

[27] Stiles, *Cowboy in the Classroom,* 65–67

[28] July 27, 1950, RG 2/1/2.562 Box 28. The attorney general of Virginia ruled that Negro students should be admitted to white institutions when comparable degree programs were not offered in Virginia State College. Stiles clarified this ruling's pertinence to Negroes applying for the master's degree program, saying that since VSC offered this degree, "we are not free under this ruling to admit Negro students to the University" (Stiles to Mrs. C. L. Pinkney, Natchez, Tennessee, March 27, 1953, RG 2/1/2.631 Box 15).

[29] Stiles to Darden, September 26, 1950. Explaining Ridley's application, Stiles notes that Ridley "desires no publicity regarding his application to our doctoral program" and "does not intend to carry the matter through legal means. He is hopeful he may be admitted as are other doctoral students." Ridley had begun doctoral work at the University of Minnesota. He had passed his preliminary exam for a Ph.D. but was financially unable to continue studying there while still teaching at Virginia Union. RG 2/1/2.562 Box 11

[30] V. Dabney, 380. The Atlanta branch of the NAACP sent President Darden a telegram commending his action in November. RG 2/1/2.562 Box 28

[31] Stiles to Darden, November 16, 1951, personal correspondence and copy of testimony. RG 2/1/2.581 Box 12

[32] Stiles to Dean David Breneman, January 14, 1998, personal correspondence

[33] Stiles, interview, March 2001

[34] Stiles, *Cowboy in the Classroom,* 77

[35] Annual Report 1952, RG 10/1/6.851 Box 1. Stiles reported that the Division of Educational Research would coordinate the research efforts of faculty and graduate students, would "initiate special research projects aimed at the discovery of new knowledge in the field of education," and would give "special attention will be given to the field of human learning." He further noted that the division "is planned to accord persistent and searching study to a few primary areas of knowledge which are fundamental to the entire process of education."

[36] Faculty minutes, September 11, 1957, RG 10/7/1.851 Box 1

[37] "Report of the Division of Educational Research: Calendar Year 1954," RG 10/1/6.851 Box 2

[38] Stiles to Darden, September 16, 1953, RG 2/1/2.631 Box 15

[39] Faculty minutes, January 7, 1954, RG 10/7/1.851 Box 1

[40] *Curry School of Education Newsletter,* Spring 1991, 4; Bernard Busse, "Music Education in the School of Education 1960," RG 10/1/6.851 Box 2

[41] Jerry Moore, interview, October 2004

[42] Annual Report 1952, RG 10/1/6.851 Box 1

[43] *Curry School of Education Newsletter,* December 1, 1953, 5, RG 2/1/2.632 Box 9

[44] V. Dabney, 330

[45] Office of Institutional Assessment and Studies

[46] Annual Report 1954, 5, RG 10/1/6.851 Box 2

[47] V. Dabney, 330. Dabney says of Shea that he had great "behind-the-scenes influence over many aspects of the institution's life. In fact it would probably be fair to say that for a few decades nobody in the institution except the president was as quietly potent as he."

[48] Stiles to Virginius Dabney, September 16, 1953, RG 2/1/2.631 Box 15

[49] *Cavalier Daily,* March 2, 1955, 2

[50] *Cavalier Daily,* March 15, 1955, 2. The next day, an education school student replied to Hawthorn's column with strong refutations, calling for the *Cavalier Daily* to eliminate such judgmental pieces and objecting to the fact that students had to pay compulsory fees to support the newspaper.

[51] Stiles, unpublished manuscript, n.d.

[52] Annual Report 1952, 15. In the 1954 annual report, Stiles described the schoolwide self-evaluation process that began in the Fall of 1953: "No other School within the University, and very likely no other School of Education in any university, can claim such growth during these years. The School of Education, once the smallest division of the University in terms of enrollment, now ranks third with respect to resident enrollment and second only to the College of Arts and Sciences when enrollments in Graduate Extension courses are included. During the Summer Session the School of Education with almost 50% of the total student population, ranks first as compared to other schools of the University with respect to enrollment." RG 10/1/6.851 Box 1

[53] Joseph N. Payne (Ph.D. 1955), personal correspondence, January 5, 2005

[54] Stiles, interview, March 2001; Stiles, *Cowboy in the Classroom.* As Virginius Dabney, historian of the University of Virginia, observed in 1981, Stiles's leadership did much to restore credibility to the education school, and although he was "tactless" at times, antagonizing some administrators and professors in other departments with his efforts, his record was constructive" (V. Dabney, 357–359).

Speech and Hearing

[1] Ralph Stoudt, interview, June 2004. Stoudt provided a vivid description of those who traveled the state and provided feedback for children and their families. After surveying populations, the teams would go to school boards and recommend children identified as having special needs. Another description of these trips is provided by Professor Ralph Bralley, the first doctoral candidate in the program: "One time we tested the hearing of all the school children in Roanoke in two and a half days. . . . We went throughout the state promoting speech and hearing rehabilitation, pointing out the need for public schools to have these services. We also generated local enthusiasm for speech and hearing centers, and we assisted in getting clinics started in Danville, Virginia Beach, Petersburg, Blacksburg, and Northern Virginia."

[2] Sublette, "Hearing Things and Talking Back," 1992

[3] Stoudt, interview, June 2004; faculty minutes, October 6, 1960, RG 10/7/1.851 Box 1

[4] *Curry School of Education Newsletter,* May 10, 1967, RG 2/1/2.79 Box 15

[5] September 5, 1967, RG 2/1/2.741 Box 18

[6] Carol Dudding, personal communication, January 2005

The Bureau of Educational Research

[1] Much of the following is based on Edith Mosher, "Brief History of the Bureau of Educational Research" (1971), an unpublished document written at the request of Dean Cyphert. RG 10/1/1.861 Box 13

[2] Frank Banghart, 1958 Annual Report Division of Educational Research, 3

[3] Cherry to Shannon, October 3, 1961: "The report received much favorable attention." RG 2/1/2.651 Box 13

[4] Banghart to Shannon, September 9, 1960, RG 2/1/2.641 Box 10. Banghart writes about attending a conference on "auto-instructional methods," saying that "New developments in educational theory and practice will help teachers 'zero in' more precisely on what needs to be learned" and that "new programming techniques permit education to control much more precisely the behavioral patterns which the educator wished to elicit."

[5] Mosher, "Brief History"

[6] Shannon to Senator FitzGerald Bemiss, October 12, 1961, RG 2/1/2.651 Box 15

[7] Cherry to Shannon, September 25, 1964, RG 2/1/2.681 Box 12. Also "Review of Research and Public Service Centers, University of Virginia," unpublished document ca. 1990, RG 3/1/2.991 Box 13

[8] Representative of activities in the late 1970s and early 1980s, the bureau engaged in forty-two projects with state, regional, and local agencies in Virginia, provided student practicum experiences, and generated funds to support forty-two graduate students in 1980–1981. Richard M. Brandt. "School of Education Highlights: Selected Activities," unpublished document, 1982

[9] For example, between 1986 and 1988 the bureau completed forty-nine client-oriented projects for a total of twenty-one clients in public and private organizations "Review of Research and Public Service Centers" [1990], unpublished document, RG 3/1/2.991 Box 13

CHAPTER 6

The Challenges of Growth and Expansion: Ralph W. Cherry, 1956–1968

[1] Ralph W. Cherry, "The Curry Memorial School of Education: A Dean's Eye View," *Education Review,* vol. 1, no. 1, 1963

[2] Ward to Darden, December 19, 1955, RG 10/1/6.851 Box 2

[3] On April 8, 1956, an article in the *Richmond Times-Dispatch* quoted Ward negatively about the future of working in public education in Virginia (Darden to Stiles [now in Wisconsin], April 9, 1956). Stiles wrote to Darden in connection with the article, saying he had just visited Ward, who had not expressed any animosity toward the University and felt that this was a misrepresentation of what was in fact going on. "It is my belief that the announcement of an appointment of a Dean will go far to settle things down," wrote Stiles (April 12, 1956). "All institutions seem to go through a period of uneasiness during the time that a deanship is open. When the selection is made, typically, they settle down to work." RG 2/1/2.634 Box 9

[4] Moran, interview with Ralph Cherry, 1976

[5] RG 10/7/1.851 Box 1. On March 1, 1956, Darden wrote Stiles to ask his opinion of this selection; Stiles responded, saying that Cherry was "well regarded in educational circles and would bring to the University of Virginia a fine professional and personal reputation." RG 2/1/2.654 Box 9

[6] On May 1, 1956, the *Curry School of Education Newsletter* reported that Cherry was the first choice of all groups, hence the "only person to whom the position was offered" (1).

[7] James Bash, interview, March 4, 2001. In Virginius Dabney's words, "It was the opinion of influential members of the Arts and Sciences faculty that Dean Cherry raised the stature of the School of Education markedly within the university" (359).

[8] Moran, interview with Ralph Cherry, 1976

[9] Herbst, 174–184. Lawrence Cremin (1954) and Arthur Powell (1980), among others, point out that these developments were related to concerns with developing a legitimate basis of pedagogical knowledge, leading to a rise in educational research, a separate field from training students to be teachers.

[10] William Johnson in Warren, ed., 239

[11] Koerner, 50–61. Koerner concluded his study of teaching by saying, "By now it must be clear that the education of American teachers is trapped in a series of circular problems that makes reforms extremely difficult. A weak faculty operates a weak program that attracts weak students" (242).

[12] Clifford and Guthrie, 177–182; also see Conant. The programs received additional impetus from the Ford Foundation's Fund for the Advancement of Education. Beginning in 1950 and continuing through the 1960s, the Ford Foundation invested $70 million in innovations in teacher education. In addition to funding graduate students, the foundation launched "Breakthrough Programs" beginning in 1958, designed to involve academic faculty in teacher preparation. Conant described a need for increased academic training and for a stronger liberal arts program for each college or university to "develop in detail whatever program of teacher education it considers most desirable," and also argued that competition between institutions preparing teachers was one way of invigorating programs.

[13] Faculty minutes, March 19, 1959, RG 10/7/L851 Box 1

[14] Office of Institutional Assessment and Studies

[15] This was a critical step in continuing the teacher education program. The most influential national accrediting board for teacher education, NCATE was founded in 1954. As of 1960, when Curry was accredited, 141 institutions in addition to the original institutions transferred from AACTE had been accredited; U.Va. was the only Virginia institution to be newly accredited, since the other state institutions of teacher education (Longwood College, Madison College, Radford College, the Women's Division of VPI, and Virginia State College) were all accredited under earlier standards (*NCATE: Seventh Annual List, Effective July 1, 1960–June 30, 1961,* RG 2/1/2.2651 Box 12).

[16] "Report on Teacher Education," RG 2/1/2.641 Box 10

[17] May 27, 1964. The report also expressed interest in the MAT program and developments in the internship program for pre-service students' student teaching placements (RG 2/1/2.671 Box 12).

[18] Hall to Newcomb, May 11, 1939: "All teachers need first to acquire mastery of the liberal arts and sciences, and secondly, to be well-trained in the techniques and procedures for the impartation of knowledge to the individuals to be taught. Since handicapped children are in greater need of assistance and guidance than other children, it would appear that some recognition of this need would be appropriate in terms of courses in education of teachers along these lines" (RG 2/1/2.491 Box 7).

[19] Kauffman, 7–8. Professional organizations concerned with care of exceptional children were founded in the 1920s; between 1901 and 1950, special education became an identifiable part of public education.

[20] The education of handicapped children was of special interest to Stiles and his wife, as one of their children had rheumatic fever when she was five and required the services of a visiting teacher. So impressed were Stiles and his wife with the quality of the teacher's work that he began lobbying for government funding to work with children with special needs. Stiles published a book of poems, *Moods and Moments,* in 1955, the royalties from which were to be used for scholarships at the University of Virginia for teachers preparing to work with handicapped children.

[21] "Special Education: University of Virginia" (May 1957), and "Tentative Special Education Proposal" (1955), RG 7337 Box 1

[22] Ibid., 4. The report further explains that "these areas of Exceptionality have been chosen because of the great need for teachers in these areas in Virginia and because of the immediately available and potential facilities on or near the University grounds."

[23] Faculty minutes, June 8, 1957, RG 10/7/1.851 Box 1

[24] Faculty minutes, January 9, 1957, RG 10/7/1.851 Box 1. This policy was in effect only through 1962, when the faculty moved to return to a policy of admitting all students after two years of college work.

[25] Darden to Cherry et al., June 24, 1957, RG 2/1/2.635 Box 8

[26] As part of the University-wide evaluation of professional schools, grade distribution for the fall semester of 1959–1960 was reported. In the education school, grades were fairly evenly distributed between A's (31%), B's (35%), and C's (23%), with the rest D's or F's (11%); in the engineering school, grades recorded were 13% A's, 24% B's, 28% C's, and the remaining (37%) D's or lower; the architecture school's grades were 18% A's, 25% B's, 39% C's, and 16% D's or lower ("Distribution of Grades, First Semester 1959–1960," May 27, 1960). RG 2/1/2.641 Box 10

[27] Faculty minutes, September 26, 1957, RG 10/7/1.851 Box 1

[28] Annual Report 1957, Cherry to Darden, January 28, 1958, RG 10/1/6.851

[29] Members of Phi Delta Kappa to Darden, March 17, 1957, RG 2/1/2.635 Box 11

[30] Faculty minutes, April 29, 1958, RG 10/7/1.851

[31] Cherry to Darden, October 17, 1958. As he enumerates programmatic changes underway in all of the School of Education's programs, Cherry also reiterates the need for clearer coordination with the College of Arts and Sciences: "It is increasingly clear that an effective program of teacher education can be developed only through the cooperative planning and effort of the College and School of Education faculties" (RG 2/1/2.635 Box 12).

[32] Moran, interview with Ralph Cherry, 1976

[33] Memorial for Ralph Cherry [1978], unpublished document, private files of Richard Brandt

[34] Cherry to Shannon, November 21, 1962, RG 2/1/2.661 Box 10; Cherry, memo to Shannon, December 8, 1962, re: school's action to limit application for admission to those who have completed two years of college work, a decision to take place as of 1964. This memo cites the possibility of discontinuing the undergraduate program for pre-service students in a few years' time, reflecting national trends. RG 2/1/2.681 Box 1

[35] Many Curry faculty members contributed articles related to their areas of specialization, with topics including program evaluation, instructional practices, and curriculum development, among others.

[36] RG 10/6/1.791 Box 2. The origins of the humanities emphasis in secondary education were related to the work of Mortimer Adler, who, among other things, fostered the development of the Great Books Movement at the University of Chicago in 1943.

[37] O. Allan Gianniny to Dr. Woodrow Wilkerson, Superintendent of Public Instruction, January 4, 1972, RG 10/6/1.791 Box 7

[38] Memorandum to the Dean of the School of Education [1971], unpublished document, RG 10/6/1.791 Box 1 Folder 12

[39] "Humanities Education in Virginia: A Newsletter Published by the Humanities Development Panel, Old Dominion Foundation Fellowship Program, and the University of Virginia," vol. 2, no. 1 (Fall 1970), 1, RG 10/6/1.791 Box 7

[40] September 5, 1967, RG 2/1/2.741 Box 18

[41] Project Criteria: School of Education Building, October 1, 1966, RG 2/1/2.701 Box 15

[42] Shannon to FitzPatrick, February 2, 1967, RG 2/1/2.701 Box 15

[43] University of Virginia School of Education, "Education Day Remarks of Frank Hereford, President of the University of Virginia" (1976), pamphlet, 17

[44] Caudill, Rowlett and Scott to Shannon, September 12, 1968, RG 2/1/2.721

[45] "The Kresge Center for Educational Experimentation," June 1972, 1–2, RG 2/1/2.742 Box 17. Referring to the lengthy time taken with the design process, University President Hereford said of the new building in 1976, "I think that the trips back and forth to the Art Commission and the fine work the architects did was certainly evident in the fine building we have today."

[46] Cherry to Shannon, September 12, 1968, RG 2/1/2.721 Box 24

[47] In 1976, reflecting back over his years as dean, Cherry felt especially that student issues were taking more of his time than he wanted, hampering his efforts to guide the school productively—reflecting national student unrest on campuses in the late 1960s (Moran, interview with Ralph Cherry, 1976).

[48] Moran, interview with Ralph Cherry, 1976

[49] V. Dabney, 359

Counselor Education

[1] RG 2/1/2.821 Box 7

Special Education

[1] John F. Mesinger, correspondence, November 2002

[2] "UVA Awarded $132,750 to train 19 teachers," *Charlottesville Daily Progress,* July 24, 1964

[3] *Curry School of Education Newsletter,* December 1, 1964, RG 2/1/2.681 Box 12

[4] Annual Report 1967, RG 10/1/6.851 Box 2

[5] Mesinger, correspondence, January 2005

[6] Cherry to Shannon (asking permission to apply for the grant), June 28, 1966, RG 2/1/2.691 Box 12

[7] October 23, 1977, RG 10/1/1.861 Box 12. The institute was housed in Peyton House on Rugby Road, sharing space with other Curry programs including those in multicultural education.

[8] Mesinger, correspondence, January 2005. Writing of the students' participation in the program, Mesinger said, "Most reported they hated my guts during the first few weeks living with disturbed children full time. At the end of the 9 weeks it was a love affair with the kids and appreciation for the program."

[9] RG 2/1/2.901 Box 17

[10] Ward served as an advisor as the Commonwealth of Virginia planned a governor's school for the gifted in 1971. See meeting notes, October 18, 1972, RG 10/5/1.791 Box 7.

[11] Carolyn M. Callahan, memo, August 22, 2005

The Consultative Resource Center on School Desegregation

[1] Greg L. Michel of the University of Texas at San Antonio provided much of the information on the "Deseg Center" and its history, arising out of his work as a President's Postdoctoral Fellow at the University of Virginia's Carter G. Woodson Institute in 1999–2000.

[2] "School Desegregation Resource Center Established," *Curry School of Education Newsletter,* May 1967, 2

[3] Michel, "Fellowship Report," 2000

[4] *Curry School of Education Newsletter,* Fall, 1993, 3. When Johnson retired in 1979, University President Hereford wrote him, saying, "The history of the University will record you as the first black faculty member at the University, and as a substantial contributor to many aspects of both secondary and higher education" (RG 2/1/2.811 Box 4).

[5] "UVa Unit Plans Name Change," *Charlottesville Daily Progress,* July 14, 1972, RG 2/1/2.761 Box 13

[6] Michel, 3
[7] James Bash and Howard Allen, interview, 2002.
[8] Hylton, "A Historical Review" (1973), summarizes the activities of the Deseg Center between 1967 and 1972, including workshops, institutes, and seminars offered, together with a listing of the number of program attendees.
[9] John Mesinger describes the way a typical workshop ran: During a three-week workshop in Front Royal, he worked with children in the morning, and then their teachers in the afternoon in an effort to improve teaching practices (Mesinger, memo, 2005).
[10] *The CRC Bulletin,* June 1974, RG 2/1/2.761 Box 13. The CRC personnel made personal contact with "almost all" of the 134 district superintendents during the workshops on school law and the implications of implementing the Civil Rights Act of 1971.
[11] Richards, Johnson, and Bash, 25–26
[12] Michel, "Fellowship Report." Michel argues that that the CRC's history had been a "forgotten part" of University history and, as such, its absence from the University of Virginia's civil rights narrative "reflects the deep ambivalence which, at the time, many within the university community had about school desegregation, in general, and the center, in particular."
[13] Sondra Stallard, presently dean of the School of Continuing and Professional Studies, is one of many faculty members who urged me to be sure to include the story of the activities of the CRC in this history. Some of her earliest associations with the University were traveling the state as part of the Center's programs. "The stories I could tell . . . ," adds John Mesinger.

CHAPTER 7

A Vision for the Role of Educational Research: Frederick R. Cyphert, 1968–1974

[1] August 10, 1970, "Clarifying Goals and Functions of the School of Education," RG 2/1/2.741 Box 15
[2] Frederick R. Cyphert, interview, March 1997
[3] Lagemann, 218–222
[4] Cyphert, interview, March 1996. In retrospect, Cyphert felt that this study and the resulting clarification of the school's direction and goals were among the most significant achievements of his deanship.
[5] Cyphert and Grant, "The Delphi Technique," 417–425.
[6] Cyphert, interview, 1996: "I rounded up two or three faculty members [regularly] and drove to Washington to HEW and would take them around [to meet people] . . . I probably made twenty trips like that"—and, he said, it helped develop connections between the school and government agencies.
[7] Hereford to Cyphert, memo, December 19, 1969, RG 2/1/2.781 Box 13
[8] Cyphert, interview, 1996: "They seemed reasonably satisfied. Then I pushed and said there was a word I was looking for and I said how many of you use this and they all denied it: the word was 'excited.' About four or five years later I did the same thing and the word 'exciting' came up frequently."
[9] RG 10/1/6.851 Box 2
[10] "Report of NCATE Team Visit to the University of Virginia, March 8–11, 1970," 78–79, RG 2/1/2.731 Box 16
[11] A 1945 coordinate agreement with Mary Washington College facilitated women's transferring to the University of Virginia.
[12] V. Dabney, 490–491
[13] "Report of the Woody Committee on Co-Education," 32–33, RG 2/1/2.721 Box 19
[14] Faculty minutes, May 22, 1970, RG 10/7/1.851 Box 2; *Curry School of Education Newsletter,* April 1970, RG 2/1/2.731 Box 16
[15] Faculty minutes, November 21, 1972, RG 10/7/1.851 Box 2
[16] Faculty minutes, June 1, 1971, RG 10/7/1.851 Box 2
[17] Faculty minutes, July 19, 1971, RG 10/7/1.851 Box 2
[18] "Mid-Atlantic Center for Community Education School of Education," memo to University of Virginia, February 21, 1975, RG 2/1/2.773 Box 10
[19] Michael Kaplan, ed., *Public Schools: Use Them Don't Waste Them,* published by the Mid-Atlantic Center for Community Education and based on Sylvia Porter, "Your Money's Worth," a newspaper column widely read and considered influential in the popular press of the early 1970s.
[20] *Newsletter of the Mid-Atlantic Center for Community Education,* vol. 1, no. 2 (May 1973), RG 2/1/2.751 Box 17
[21] Cyphert to Francis Berkley, October 14, 1967, RG 2/1/2.721 Box 24
[22] "New Ed School Building Shows Structural Flaws," *Cavalier Daily,* September 11, 1974
[23] Cyphert to Maphis, January 1974, RG2/1/2.761 Box 15
[24] Ruffner, *Second Annual Report, Superintendent of Public Instruction,* Part II, 63–64
[25] Richard M. Brandt, "Notes on William Henry Ruffner on the Occasion of the Dedication, in His Name, of the Building of the School of Education at the University of Virginia" (April 23, 1976).
[26] Faculty minutes, September 18, 1973, bound volume
[27] Cyphert, "Report on Data from Sponsored Programs," to David Shannon, August 13, 1973, RG 2/1/2.761 Box 15
[28] RG 3/1/2.802
[29] "Future of the School of Education," February 26, 1974, unpublished document
[30] Cyphert, interview, 1996
[31] Edgar Shannon, Remarks, May 10, 1974, RG 2/1/2.761 Box 15

The Center for the Study of Higher Education

[1] Much of the following is based on the record compiled by Jennings Wagoner in *Celebration of Twenty Years: A Twenty Year Retrospective 1969–1989* (Center for the Study of Higher Education, University of Virginia Department of Educational Leadership and Policy Studies, 1989).
[2] Ibid. The Center originated in a "dark and damp corner in the basement of aging Peabody Hall" and moved to a "rudely converted 'office space' in a classroom on the first floor of Peabody Hall during its second year. With only a pegboard separating them, faculty members Chronister and Kellams shared space with graduate students, a fledgling library, and a pot of coffee, not an ideal setting in which to advise students and conduct sensitive conversations."
[3] Center for the Study of Higher Education, *Handbook,* 2004.

CHAPTER 8

Creating a Base for Private Financial Support of Education: Richard M. Brandt 1974–1984

[1] Richard M. Brandt, "Initial Perspectives of a New Dean," September 17, 1974, RG 3/1/2.802 Box 3
[2] Brandt, *Public Education Under Scrutiny,* University Press of America, 1981
[3] Discussions related to promotion and tenure had begun under Cyphert's deanship. Since he had hired large numbers of faculty, many more than normal were becoming eligible for advancement.
[4] Brandt, "Initial Perspectives." A study of grading patterns at the University in 1973 showed that education students received the highest grades offered in the University; a June 1973 analysis of doctoral graduates revealed some overall decrease in the total number of hours taken by these students.
[5] RG 10/1/1.861 Box 6. Before this, Curry alumni gifts came through the University-wide development offices.
[6] *Curry School of Education Newsletter,* Spring 2001, 7–10.
[7] Certificate of Incorporation, The University of Virginia School of Education Foundation, Inc., Program for Education Day 1978, from the papers of Richard M. Brandt
[8] *Curry School of Education Newsletter,* 1976, 1, RG 2/1/2.781 Box 12
[9] Faculty minutes, February 10, 1976, bound volume
[10] Bird to Brandt, memo, August 6, 1979, RG 10/1/1.861 Box 11
[11] Michael McMahon to Brandt, May 13, 1976: "Obviously, correcting present imbalance is no small task . . . the recruitment of Black faculty members must assume the highest priority," RG 10/1/1.861 Box 11
[12] http://www.edchange.org/multicultural/
[13] Faculty minutes, October 17, 1977, RG 10/1/1.861 Box 23
[14] Pate to Chronister, April 28, 1976; James Kauffman to Brandt, September 22, 1976, RG 10/1/1.861 Box 6. Office of Institutional Assessment and Studies
[15] RG 3/1/2.802 Box 3
[16] Minutes of Teacher Education Committee, April 2, 1975, RG 2/1/2.773 Box 7
[17] *Phi Delta Kappan,* October 1980. One of many critics focusing on this issue, Smith asserted that the currently entrenched courses—and faculty—in educational pedagogy would never change unless placed under duress.
[18] December 4, 1980; December 15, 1980
[19] Brandt to Gordon Davies, State Council of Higher Education, July 11, 1979, RG 10/1/1.861 Box 5
[20] "Report of the Visiting Committee, March 20–22, 1980": "Unless the University can describe and defend the elements of its preeminence, professional schools such as Education, Commerce, or Engineering cannot clearly understand their own special roles vis-à-vis professional schools in other institutions in Virginia." RG 3/1/2.821 Box 16
[21] Eight faculty retreats were held, each organized by separate steering committees and attended by between twenty and forty people each; 90% of the faculty participated. Brandt felt the retreats were very productive in identifying areas for faculty to make changes; he also felt there were issues of "territorial competition" between departments and programs and a sense of "disillusionment over the state of education and fear that the School of Education is deteriorating" among the faculty. Brandt said he did not share these feelings. He recognized that education "is under attack as it has been before; but out of such stress and turmoil lie the greatest opportunities for major changes and improvements" ("Retreat Activity: A New Venture," 4/17/79, notes for faculty meeting, RG 10/1/1.861 Box 5).
[22] University of Virginia Retreat Summary, July 18, 1979, RG 10/1/1.861 Box 5
[23] Report of the Advisory Committee on Teacher Education, April 11 and April 24, 1984, RG 3/1/2.882. Robert Pate chaired this committee and was praised by Provost Floyd, who called the report a "remarkable job." "You have all carried out a job of immense importance to the University with great integrity, devotion and responsibility. . . . I reiterate my warmest thanks to all of you for carrying out a most difficult job done under the very heaviest of pressures." Report of the Study Committee on Teacher Preparation in the Arts and Sciences, December 20, 1983, RG 2/1/2.861 Box 11
[24] Teacher education was again noted: "Despite the presentation of the plan as the School direction for Teacher Education it was never implemented. The implementation seems to have stalled due to resistance of some faculty and lack of administrative resolve" (RG 3/1/2.882).
[25] "Improving the Quality of Public Education," program, July 17–20, 1982, RG 2/1/2.851 Box 7
[26] Thomas Toch, "Ed. Schools Coping Poorly With Fiscal Trouble, Study Says," October 13, 1982. This study was commissioned by the land grant deans and based on responses from 119 members of the land grant deans' association and on a number of interviews with deans.

The report began, "Teacher training programs are suffering serious widespread fiscal difficulties that could very well result in the elimination of education programs in some universities, and in general the leaders of these programs have done little to assess the effects of their financial problems or to find ways of lessening their impact." RG 3/1/2.871 Box 20

27 Faculty minutes, March 23, 1983, RG 3/1/2.871 Box 20

28 "Academic Plan of the School of Education," March 31, 1983, RG 2/1/2.861 Box 11

29 "University will look to boost Education School," *University Journal*, November 21, 1983

30 *Curry School of Education Newsletter,* Spring 1984

31 Brandt, Statement to the Faculty, April 1984, unpublished document

32 Ibid.

Clinical Psychology

1 Christopher Reiss and Professor Ronald Reeve provided information on the origins of the Clinical Psychology program.

2 Brandt to Shannon, memo, September 6, 1972, RG 2/1/2.751 Box 17

3 *Curry School of Education Newsletter,* Fall 1995, 5

4 Memo, December 10, 1982, RG 2/1/2.851 Box 7

5 "Curry Addresses Violence in Our Schools," *Curry School of Education Newsletter,* Spring 1997; http://youthviolence.edschool.virginia.edu/. Findings from Cornell and Sheras's research have led to developing teaching strategies related to conflict resolution, now incorporated into several courses taught in the Curry School.

The Curry School Foundation

1 Richard M. Brandt, personal correspondence, January 1996

2 *Funding a Changing Mission for the Curry Memorial School of Education* was the first publication to illustrate the ways in which fundraising efforts related to school initiatives.

3 *Curry School of Education Newsletter,* Spring 2001

4 Jay Jackson, memo, March 2005

CHAPTER 9

The Five-Year Teacher Education Program: James M. Cooper, 1984–1994

1 "Curry School of Education Mission Statement," June 1, 1992

2 The Holmes Group issued a report in 1986 calling for reform in teacher education and recommending that future teachers major in the liberal arts as undergraduates then pursue graduate degrees in education. The unique feature of the Curry School program was its design as an integrated program: Students were to take academic courses along with education courses, receiving a master of teaching degree and a bachelor of arts degree at the end of five years.

3 James M. Cooper, personal communication, February 2005

4 James M. Cooper, remarks during faculty retreat, September 6, 1984

5 Cooper to Floyd, January 15, 1985: "In seeking a unique identity for the School, the faculty and I find the use of the word 'Memorial' overly cumbersome and lengthy. It is also the only named school at the University that incorporates the word 'Memorial' in its identification," RG 2/1/2.871 Box 8

6 All teacher education courses fell under the Department of Curriculum, Instruction and Special Education. Educational Studies included Educational Psychology, Social Foundation of Education, Research and Evaluation, and Instructional Technology. Education Leadership included Administration and Supervision and Higher Education. Human Services included Communication Disorders, Counselor Education, Health and Physical Education, and the Institute of Clinical Psychology.

7 Glen Bull, interview, November 2003

8 A faculty member in the College of Arts and Sciences explained in 1989 that there was little opposition to the program because it represented a philosophy of educating students in the subject area they would be teaching: "Since the primary purpose of the program was to make the students more knowledgeable about the subjects they were going to teach, it gives them an indispensable education . . . They have the best of both worlds. It used to be a little bit of education and not enough content . . . The price tag of five years is worth it because the students get two degrees."

9 The M.T. degree was created to reflect the integrated path to the master's degree. The degree was formally approved by the University's Board of Visitors on January 5, 1988. RG 2/1/2.901 Box 17

10 "Teacher Education Program" (1985), 2. Citing the influence of the AACTE report *Extended Programs for Teacher Education* (1983) and B. Othaniel Smith's *A Design for a School of Pedagogy* (1980), creators of the program stated: "Several features of the new program design are radical departures from the current program. The proposed program is founded upon a set of beliefs regarding characteristics of effective teacher education programs and the requirements necessary to implement these characteristics."

11 "I've been compared to the Maytag repairman who sits by the phone waiting for it to ring," Cooper has said. "It almost never did" *(University of Virginia Alumni News,* March 2005).

12 "Self-Study, Commonwealth Center for the Education of Teachers," 1993. Among the Center's accomplishments were the conferences involving 180 participants from the state and beyond; support of more than sixty papers presented at professional meetings; and the publication of forty-one professional journal articles, nine book chapters, and one book. Additionally, the Center regularly distributed a newsletter to more than 4,000 readers nationally and internationally.

13 *Curry School of Education Newsletter,* Spring 1990

14 Cooper to O'Neil, January 11, 1990, RG 2/1/2.921 Box 14

15 Canady and Rettig, 1996

16 RG 2/1/2.962 Box 21

Technology in Education

1 John Bunch, interview, November 2003

2 Glen Bull, interview, November 2003; *Curry School of Education Newsletter,* Spring 1988, 1

3 *Curry School of Education Newsletter,* Spring 1988

4 The project, "Teaching Teachers to Use Technology: What Works and Why," is funded by the Center for the Study of Learning Instruction and Teacher Development at the University of Illinois at Chicago.

5 *Curry School of Education Newsletter,* Spring 2002, 3. Drucker notes, "What Curry has over almost any other school of education is a history of supporting the technology needs of the faculty."

6 http://curry.edschool.virginia.edu/go/frog/Frog2/

CHAPTER 10

Spires of Excellence: David W. Breneman, 1995–

1 "The Dean's Pronouncements," December 2000, unpublished document

2 Thomas Jackson, Vice President and Provost, to the Curry School of Education faculty, September 27, 1993, unpublished memorandum

3 *Curry School of Education Newsletter,* Spring 1996, 4

4 Ibid., Fall 1996, 4

5 "The Dean's Pronouncements"

6 Dean's office, December 2004

7 *Curry School of Education Newsletter,* Spring 2002, 8

8 Dean's office, December 2004

9 *Curry School of Education Newsletter,* Spring 2004, 2

At-Risk Programs

1 *Curry School of Education Newsletter,* Fall 2002, 4

2 Robert Pianta, interview, December 2004

Foundation for a New Building

1 *Curry School of Education Newsletter,* Fall 2004, 3

2 *Inside UVA,* October 1, 2004

AFTERWORD

The Curry School in the Twenty-first Century

1 December 18, 2001. Stiles says he "concocted" this story when he was dean and told it to many groups around the state to highlight the importance of strengthening the Curry School. "When President Darden hired me, [it was part of his intention to make the University] of and for Virginians. . . . It was [Darden's] belief that the School of Education had to take leadership to reach out to the people of the State through its public school system" *(Cowboy in the Classroom,* chapter 8).

2 *University of Virginia Record—The Curry Memorial Department of Education,* 1919–20, 2–3

Index

NOTE: page numbers in *italics* indicate photographs.

The Curry School of Education at the University of Virginia, 1905–2005
by Eleanor Vernon Wilson

Executive Editor	Jay Jackson
Managing Editor	Susan Tyler Hitchcock
Art Director	Diane Nelson
Photo Editors	N. Wayne Siler, Jeanne Nicholson Siler
Copy Editor	Gail Hyder Wiley
Proofreader	Suzanne Z. Slezak
Indexer	Deborah Patton

Published by the Curry School of Education Foundation
Printed by The Stinehour Press, Lunenburg, Vermont

Wilson, Eleanor Vernon, 1940–
The Curry School of Education at the University of Virginia, 1905–2005: preparing men and women for leadership in scientific educational work / Eleanor Vernon Wilson.
p. cm.
Includes bibliographical references (p. 136) and index.
ISBN 0-9776312-0-6
1. Curry School of Education—History. I. Curry School of Education. II. Title.
LB1972.C48W55 2006
370.71'109755481—dc22
2006040182

Curry School of Education Foundation
University of Virginia
405 Emmet Street South, PO Box 400276
475 Ruffner Hall
Charlottesville, 22904-4276

ILLUSTRATION CREDITS

Albemarle Charlottesville Historical Society: 6, 17, 62
Albert and Shirley Small Special Collections Library, University of Virginia: x, 7, 8(top), 8(bottom), 9, 10, 12, 13, 14, 15, 19(top), 20, 23, 24, 26(both), 27, 29, 32, 36(both), 40, 44, 46, 47, 51, 55, 59, 61(both), 65, 70(both), 73, 78, 79, 80, 82, 83, 84, 85, 87, 88, 90, 91, 92, 93, 94, 95, 96(both), 97, 101, 102, 116, 118, 125, 132
Center for Nursing Historical Inquiry, School of Nursing, University of Virginia: 34, 35
The Chain, Lane High School (Charlottesville) yearbook, courtesy of the Albemarle Charlottesville Historical Society: vi, ix, 42, 53, 57, 68
Corks & Curls, University of Virginia yearbook: 31, 56, 67, 103
Courtesy of Athena Angelus: 64
Courtesy of the Central Rappahannock Heritage Center, Fredericksburg, Virginia: 52
Courtesy of Charlottesville City Schools: 62, 66
Courtesy of Elizabeth Burnley Smith: 37, 60(both)
Courtesy of Venable School: 33, 89
Courtesy of Ralph Rush: 75
Courtesy of Robin Lee: 54
Curry School of Education Foundation i, ii, iv, vii, 72(both), 108, 109, 112, 113, 114, 119, 120, 121, 122, 123, 124, 126(both), 127(both), 128, 130, 133
Holsinger Collection, Small Special Collections Library, University of Virginia: 11, 16(bottom), 18, 19(top), 22, 28, 30
Jackson-Davis Collection, Small Special Collections Library, University of Virginia: 39
Photo by Ian Bradshaw: v
Photo by Nic Siler: 48
Photo by Lynn Bell, Center for Technology and Teacher Education: 117
Special Collections, Vanderbilt University: 16(top)
Suffolk Public Library, Hamblin Studio Photograph Collection at the Library of Virginia. Reproduced with permission of the City of Suffolk, Virginia: 76
University News Office, University of Virginia: 41
University of Virginia Record: 75, 81, 86, 104, 105(both), 107, 110, 115